Critical Muslim 26

Gastronomy

Critical Muslim is published quarterly by C. Hurst & Co. (Publishers) Ltd. on behalf of and in conjunction with Critical Muslim Ltd. and the Muslim Institute, London. *Critical Muslim* acknowledges the support of the Aziz Foundation, London.

All correspondence to Muslim Institute, CAN Mezzanine, 49-51 East Road, London N1 6AH, United Kingdom

e-mail for editorial: editorial@criticalmuslim.com

The editors do not necessarily agree with the opinions expressed by the contributors. We reserve the right to make such editorial changes as may be necessary to make submissions to *Critical Muslim* suitable for publication.

C. Hurst & Co (Publishers) Ltd.,41 Great Russell Street, London WC1B 3PL

ISBN: 978-1-84904-972-6 ISSN: 2048-8475

To subscribe or place an order by credit/debit card or cheque (pounds sterling only) please contact Kathleen May at the Hurst address above or e-mail kathleen@hurstpub.co.uk

Tel: 020 7255 2201

A one year subscription, inclusive of postage (four issues), costs £50 (UK), £65 (Europe) and £75 (rest of the world).

The right of Ziauddin Sardar and the Contributors to be identified as the authors of this publication is asserted by them in accordance with the Copyright, Designs and Patents Act, 1988.

A Cataloguing-in-Publication data record for this book is available from the British Library

Critical Muslim

Subscribe to Critical Muslim

Now in its seventh year in print, Hurst is pleased to announce that *Critical Muslim* is also available online. Users can access the site for just £3.30 per month – or for those with a print subscription it is included as part of the package. In return, you'll get access to everything in the series (including our entire archive), and a clean, accessible reading experience for desktop computers and handheld devices — entirely free of advertising.

Full subscription

The print edition of *Critical Muslim* is published quarterly in January, April, July and October. As a subscriber to the print edition, you'll receive new issues directly to your door, as well as full access to our digital archive.

United Kingdom £50/year
Europe £65/year
Rest of the World £75/year

Digital Only

Immediate online access to *Critical Muslim*

Browse the full *Critical Muslim* archive

Cancel any time

£3.30 per month

www.criticalmuslim.io

CONTENTS

GASTRONOMY

ARTS AND LETTERS

REVIEWS

ET CETERA

VALUES

INTRODUCTION: POSTNORMAL FARE

Merryl Wyn Davies

Nothing is more telling of the times in which we live than our relationship to food. People will always need to eat but the mechanics of how this most basic necessity is serviced nowadays plays a significant role in hurtling humanity to the edge of the abyss. The foodie culture of our globalised world is distinguished by the complexity, chaos and contradictions it generates. Bon appetit, my friends! Welcome to postnormal gastronomy.

Foodie culture comprises a great deal more than what we eat. It is the *accessorie* of refined living. Foodie culture is not one option. It is a plethora of choices available in multiple versions to suit a diversity of styles and budgets. It is the commodified *accessorie* that betokens a lifestyle, a set of attitudes, ideas and preferences. And like all accessories it is a fashion choice, which can be both pick and mix and mix and match. Fashion is simultaneously art, passing phase, fad and fancy, and of course moveable feast. Fashion is a concept, a total look, a personal style. The *accessorie* of your choice entails a host of further supporting accoutrements. When it comes to food one does not choose mere ingredients but a whole paraphernalia of condiments and equipment dictated by how the ingredients are to be prepared, cooked and served. Foodie culture is consumer culture writ large and all pervasive.

The range of foodie choices runs from prehistoric eating to foraging from hedgerows and seashore to alchemical refashioning of food by wizardly mechanical means. All the way to Michelin-rated restaurants around the world where one can wait months for a seat at a table to sample eighteen-course tasting menus where ingredients from the humblest to most exotic are luxuriously transformed into fantastically presented morsels with inordinate attention to minute detail, sophistication and gargantuan cost. In between these options it is possible to eat one's way through the entire history and geography of the globe via restaurants, takeaways or recreated at home. Each choice comes with the supporting appropriately styled gadgetry, cutlery, crockery and beverage. In the world of gastronomy cost betokens taste, not necessarily of the food consumed but most definitely of the paying customer, the consumer. The complexity of the supply chain that makes this cornucopia of choice available at a supermarket or restaurant near you is riddled with contradictions. As more and more people attain the ability to make foodie choices the sustainability of the world's food supply and the natural balance of food ecology becomes more and more chaotic. Before long we will be staring into an abyss and our food choices rendered in constraint to nature's man-made ailments. The food we will be eating tomorrow is uncertain but fear not, our list of foods we will be eating in the future promises tasty premonitions involving locusts and algae.

Foodie culture is the construct of affluence, the essence of abundance. It is not eating to live but living to eat in style – a lifestyle of all-enveloping commodification. Feasting has always been part of human culture. Born and brought up in Azerbaijan, Gunel Isakova links to her Caucasian roots through the traditional food made by her grandmother for the family; comfort food that reminds her of chilly winters in the mountains of Dagestan. The presentation of festival foods in Dagestan and throughout the world mark high days and holidays of religious and social significance for different cultures; occasional times of indulgence were not uncommonly preceded by fasting to underline the importance and exceptional nature of excess. Feasting has always been the presentation of power: where people sat at the table, when and what they ate indicated status. In other social arrangements power had a redistributive function. An obligation of the powerful made manifest through making food available for all with regular communal dining – when the powerful ate, everyone could join the sitting. Alternatively, eating together or feeding all who came expressed common bonds of fellowship communion and belonging as well as charity. Foodie culture is something quite different. It is perennial, everyday abundance for the masses, at a variety of price points made possible by industrialised production supply chains and delivery. It is marketable feasting conveniently available for ready money – or alternative means of payment. Festival foods are no longer occasional and seasonal but on the shelves year round. Actual festivals are marked by increased food consumption and the search for ever more luxurious and exotic dainties to titillate the palate and confirm that the good times are truly here. Feasting has become entertaining which is not so much a show of power as a way of showing off, which masquerades as sharing with family, friends and neighbours.

The very naming of foodies is the mark of this new global dispensation. The foodie is one who delights in not only the taste of finely prepared indigenous food but glories in the variety and diversity of food cultures it is possible to sample. The foodie wants to ingest the ambience and culture of food in ways only attainable thanks to globalisation. What shall we eat today is a complex question with multiple answers. Should it be French, Italian, Spanish, Mediterranean, Greek, Moroccan, Turkish, Middle Eastern, Indian, Chinese, Mexican, Thai, Korean, Malay, Japanese or fusion, a mingling of styles, ingredients and techniques?

The foodie gurus have much to say about lifestyle, what food is for as an *accessorie* of lifestyle as well as an ethos directly related to the kind of food we buy and eat. Let us begin with the ingredients, a very fine place to start. The foodie gurus are unanimous in the quest for authentic fresh and first rate fare. Never a blemish, bump or bulge mars the photogenic excellence of the ingredients they slice and dice. The produce must conform to the exacting expectations of the foodie consumer who finds his or her self so far removed from the un-airbrushed process of food production. Ugly Food, as Misha Monaghan laments in her review of the book with exactly that same title, is a thoroughly Western vision. Having been brought up eating haggis bonbons and cow brains courtesy of her respective Scottish and Indian heritage, this is a sheltering she cannot quite reconcile. Even when the foodie goes shopping to high end artisanal shops and markets where they engage the proprietor in earnest conversation about the provenance of the food being sold, aesthetics remain paramount. Nevertheless, the superior quality of their ingredients is the hallmark of how to achieve the true foodie experience. The ingredients betoken the seriousness of one's determination to be a genuine foodie acolyte and this choice has consequences. The artisanal food shops where the gurus sample and taste before they buy are not available to the masses who aspire to acolyte status. The pressure is on the purveyors of mass consumption, the supermarket chains, to respond. The result is a beauty contest for vegetables and meats – if it doesn't look good it will not sell. The pressure falls most heavily on producers, the farmers, who end up ditching perfectly edible tomatoes, potatoes or whatever, before they can even enter the supply chain. Size, colour and form all matter in the aesthetic of foodie culture.

The artisanal craze goes much further. The gurus regularly venture from their picture perfect homes where they manipulate picture perfect ingredients. When this is not an excursion into their manicured gardens to harvest the freshest of fresh seasonal ingredients it is more extensive travel to search out small scale producers who lavish personal care on their products. Be that animal, vegetable or mineral. The dream of self-sufficiency, even in the case of window box herb-growing, is a lovely idea of immense impracticality. Aspirational the audience may be but the mechanics – city dwelling, modern homes, plot sizes and the innumerable demands of quality living – just do not compute. The gurus always assuage audience anxiety with the familiar formula that such items or passable substitutes are easily available at your local supermarket. Even the populist moral philosophers of our age are allowed their little white lies. It all depends on where one lives and true foodie credentials will be assessed by how far one is prepared to travel to buy the must-have product. On the other hand, creating demand is precisely why the foodie gurus exist and supermarket supply chains have felt the pressure. In Britain, for example, there was the memorable goose fat Christmas when one television cook insisted the sure-fire way to the perfect roast potato in a nation of roast potato fanatics was to cook them in goose fat. What stocks existed (highly limited) were quickly exhausted leading to panic, complaint and sullen discontent the length and breadth of the country. In consequence goose fat has now become a staple and is included in the mechanics of producing and advertising frozen roast potatoes.

While the adult population is being seduced by the diversity of foodie culture, that culture's sustainability must be questioned. The question revolves around a gaping generational contradiction, or is it just a time lag conundrum? In Britain it is not uncommon to find children traumatised by broccoli or unhinged by cabbage. It is normal for restaurants to provide children's menus, separate and different orders of foodie treats for tiny tots while the horror stories of the child that simply screams at the mere presence of an unfamiliar food, we need not be blunt and name it vegetable, are commonplace gruesome details of the rite of passage awaiting all young parents. Choice is the watchword and choice must be extended and indulged to empower even the most perverse mini emperor. The child-friendly choice centres around the burger, sausage, fish finger, fries and baked beans end of the spectrum and barely if at all touching the fresh vegetable end of said spectrum. The entire production chain of manufacturing, marketing, advertising is dedicated to the idea that children are a distinct order of homo sapiens requiring a particular food culture including snacks such as crisps, popcorn thickly coated with sweetening agents, chocolates and candies, all manner of biscuits and cakes and anything else that can be laden with sugar. Starch and sugar, the premium food groups of immaturity, are of course prime suspects in the obesity epidemic afflicting the world. Is this the whole story when it comes to fast food? Hussein Kesvani argues there is another narrative. He describes the way in which halal fried chicken shops have created spaces where young, impoverished and marginalised members of society can find a 'home'. Halal fried chicken shops are as much a feature of the High Street as that ultimate sign of gentrification – the coffee shop. Tahir Abbas has found his own 'home' in the world of coffee, his travels so closely informed and enriched by memories of encounters with beans from around the world.

It is interesting to note that it is with conscientising the taste buds of children that one comes to a great bifurcation of culture. The divide is between the Anglo-American influenced and the continental, or should we say the French in particular, although it would be churlish not to point out that both are united by their love of coffee. Notwithstanding, childish food obstinacy is not unknown in continental Europe, it is however ignored to eradication no matter how much fuss and racket the child initially offers. Soon enough, well behaved little gourmands without a murmur are munching smaller portions of what the adults are eating (minus the caffeine and alcohol of course). When this became a topic of op-ed debate it seemed the French way was considered almost tantamount to child abuse among British commentators. We can presume that French observers would find incomprehensible the actions of organised mothers who banded together to throw bags of chips over the school railings to save their children from the nutritional healthy menu of entirely unfamiliar foods newly introduced for school dinners. The subversive menus were an attempt to counter the rise of obesity. To the mothers and their precious charges, choice of the unfamiliar was positive lack of real choice to eat only what they wanted – the things they were used to eating, even if the chip butties were diabetes-inducing or incipient heart attacks. In this vein, Kesvani illustrates that the halal fried chicken shop is also an emblem of choice. Amongst loud disdain for the cholesterol-infusing, life-shortening, cheap and cheerless, definitely non-organic offerings, these outlets represent a symbiosis between chicken shops and youth sub-cultures that are already considered to be deeply problematised, according to societal norms. Just as Vicky Bishop describes in her Last Word on the Halal Snack Pack, for Kesvani and the mothers of youngsters deprived of their beloved chips, foodie culture becomes symbolic of communities, cohesion, geopolitics, alienation and empowerment. Foodie culture is politicised.

The British, for all the embrace of foodie culture evident on every chicken shop-filled High Street and shopping outlet, are nevertheless also infamous for knowing what they like, and liking only what they know, as northern mothers and generations of British tourists to the Spanish Costas prove. This contradiction leads us into some of the unexplored depths of foodie philosophy. Much to Jeremy Henzell-Thomas' rancour, celebrity chefs have expanded their horizons from the kitchen to the world. The new genre, no bar to commodification whatsoever, is the foodie travelogue. Instead of touring around their native heath for the finest and freshest, the gurus take off to uncover the secrets of another food culture. The Mediterranean, where so many Europeans take their holidays or choose to retire in search of the good life, unsurprisingly is the most familiar and well-worn path. The audience can realistically aspire to finding the artisanal preservers of timeless tradition, the bursting markets of freshness where only locally-made produce is to be had and sitting down to eat in the ravishing locations frequented by the celebrity chef tour guide. The travelogues also venture much further afield – India, Thailand, China – places on the long haul tourist routes. It is a basic premise of these tours that food is culture, rooted in tradition and the age old relationship to the land from which it hails. It is the uniqueness of the relationship ingredients and the recipes that the celebrity chef is searching for and about which they seek to entertainingly educate their audience. Much that stands as tradition is the legacy of poverty, a peasant existence making the most of what is available. Thus the mantra, for example, that Mediterranean cooking is simplicity and locally sourced produce. Boyd Tonkin's interview with Claudia Roden reveals that, apart from this, food has been greatly influenced by history, the history of encounters between different cultures that have occurred in a particular region. 'In Roden's cooking, and her writing, three layers of remembrance seamlessly interact,' he writes. 'Her recipes, and the deep background she invests in them, allow personal, family and cultural memories to converge. With those memories come the emotions that particular foods carry in their rituals and their tastes, often over frontiers of time and place.' In this way our would-be foodie philosophers, a pale imitation of the likes of Roden, miss the most profound implications of how diet operates with their soundbites and platitudes.

Our stomachs appear to be the most multicultural organs of the human person. Our stomachs embrace opportunity and can readily adapt to new tastes and flavours as Yasmin Alibhai-Brown movingly explores in her food memories of a twice removed migrant. Even the recalcitrant northern mothers more than likely enjoy the occasional curry or Chinese takeaway, it has become part of the British way. True chicken tikka masala, a bland concoction with a creamy 'tomato-ish' sauce, has become the nation's favourite dish while having only the most tangential relationship to 'Indian' cuisine. The recipe was invented purely for the British palate with no interest in authenticity, but a yen for minimally spicy taste. The importance is less in the nature of the actual recipe than the speed of the transformation of the British diet. It is argued that the first tandoori restaurant opened in Britain in the mid-1960s and was located in Charlotte Street, a renowned multicultural eating venue in London. In which case I ate there very soon after its opening. A small enclave of anthropologists located at nearby University College among whom I counted myself, were dedicated participant observers frequently to be found among the diners experiencing the newness of tandoori chicken. The timeline from that to tikka masala becoming a commonplace favourite is little more than a decade. British stomachs have adapted and integrated far quicker than a true accommodation between the bringers of this taste sensation and the rest of the population just as Australian stomachs have welcomed the Halal Snack Pack into their culinary routine. Racism, prejudice and discrimination do not vanish as 'Indian' restaurants proliferate and 'curry' products become normal items on supermarket shelves. The foodie influence is a record of encounter, not a guide to the nature and content of that encounter.

Take another example with considerable contemporary relevance. The American diet, especially in the western states has been massively influenced by Mexican cooking. Chilli, burrito and taco are such staples that they have become fast food chains across the nation. The food supply chain that stocks American supermarkets with its vast array of produce would be neither so abundant nor cheap were it not for Mexican migrant labour. Of course in the western states of the United States the Mexicans were residents before the territory became American. Today the American President fulminates about Mexican illegal immigration and demands a wall to keep Mexicans out and looks forward to deporting as many Mexicans as possible. And all the while the general populace keeps on ingesting Mexican foods with thankless relish.

The Mexican case brings us to the other profoundly important but undervalued reality of human history. The face of the planet has been regularly reconstructed by the transplantation of plants and animals to service human dietary needs, tastes and fashions. No region has contributed more with less recognition than Mexico itself. Think of Italian cuisine without tomatoes, or indeed virtually any style of cooking sans the aptly styled love apple. Think of Thai cuisine without chillies, little if anything comes to mind. Both tomatoes and chillies were unknown in either locale before Cortes landed in Mexico. Potatoes can be added to the tally along with squash, avocado, maize – one wonders what anyone ate before the horticultural genius of the Americas became known to the wider world. Though I have to ask if it was entirely necessary to transport manioc/cassava. In fact it was to provide a cheap source of uninspiring calories that could be grown easily, especially by those pressed into service to grow more valuable cash crops or those forcibly settled to an agrarian life. Having spent some time living off manioc porridge I can report it smells like damp hay, tastes of nothing, but any leftovers are indispensable as glutinous glue. Can be used to secure a car windscreen is hardly a foodie recommendation – but should you need the recipe manioc is just the thing.

The transportation of crops and animals is a complex story of food for the haves and food for the have-nots. The mutiny on the good ship Bounty occurred on a voyage designed to transport breadfruit plants to the West Indies as a food crop for the slaves. The Moors brought oranges to Spain and Spain took them to Florida. The Amazon rainforest is cleared to make way for grazing cattle to supply the burger bars of the world. It is not always the refined foodie tastes that lead to scouring the globe for the suitable crop. The complex shuffling of species has not resolved the enduring contradiction of dietary inequity. Recurrent technological improvements since the dawn of human history keep on increasing the total amount of food produced yet human society has signally failed to ensure it can be distributed sufficiently equitably to avoid endemic hardship, hunger and periodic famine. As studies have demonstrated down the ages it's not the food supply, stupid, nor is it simply a matter of population numbers – the Malthusian arithmetic of more people meaning not enough food was simply wrong. The great famines of history were disasters of poverty not collapse of food supply. People do not starve to death because they are too many. The rich always eat, it is the poor who starve because they cannot sustain the increased costs of acquiring food which is readily available even in times of crop failure. Ireland continued to export food at the height of the potato famine because the rich were never dependent on potatoes for their principal diet. The same is true for India in the serial cereal famines before the Green Revolution increased crop yields.

The hungry poor are always with us. The postnormal contradiction is where they are located and how they relate to the abundance that has become the norm for increasing numbers of people around the globe. It is not just food supply which has grown – so has wealth. The grotesqueness of islands of wealth floating on seas of poverty is now chaotically endemic in developed and developing nations. Increasing insecurity of the middle classes in rich nations has produced the unedifying statistics for the rise of child poverty. Food banks, which should be termed vicarious charity, have become the familiar last resort of the working poor in the richest nations. In the richest country on earth, the USA, it is reported that one in six Americans struggle to get enough to eat. In 2013 the USDA reported that

14.3 per cent of American households did not have sufficient food. The farrago of so-called global economic crisis, the collapse of the banks, provided the unedifying spectacle of the richest fat cats being secured from harm while the generality of the population made up the losses and suffered the consequences of austerity, which ate into living standards. The only moral hazard left is not having enough money to be worth protecting from economic failure. The food poor can watch the television cooking shows, press up against the screen and imagine. But they are mere onlookers unable to participate in foodie culture. Wealth has been created by agricultural revolutions that have made abundance possible. Yet in the most advanced countries the poor still survive on bad food mass-produced cheaply, making use of the entrails of the food production system.

Agribusiness on an industrial scale is the source of contemporary abundance. Large scale operation allows for complex mechanisation. It requires huge inputs of capital and the opening of agricultural land for the convenience of machinery. Cereal crops no longer nestle within hedgerows that provide habitat for insects, birds and animals that can give prudential service by containing or controlling pests. Cropping is now done in vast open areas of monocultures. The scale and scope of this system is most conducive to mechanisation but much more vulnerable to pests and far more likely to degrade the fertility of the soil. It therefore requires large inputs of fertilisers and pesticides. The chemical run-off of unnatural substances pollutes water courses and can kill off freshwater fish, wildlife and plants before it ends up in the oceans. There it accumulates, threatening similar toxic consequences for marine life. To circumvent the fertiliser pesticide conundrum botanical science is at pains to develop new strains of crops genetically attuned to the environments in which they are located and resistant to pest and blights. Advanced seed technology is highly productive but costly. The complex requirements of growing food at competitive prices squeezes out small farms making the system more dependent on large scale integrated mega producers who can keep up the supply of cheap food to manufacturers and supermarkets. Crop revolutions increase the total supply of food, concentrate the ownership of land in fewer wealthier hands, increase the number of landless labourers who lead more precarious insecure lives dependent on the vagaries of the market for their food. Both Timothy Bartel and Imran Kausar write about the food production process from the perspective of a family who run the UK's first organic halal farm, to the doctor-turned-entrepreneur who founded the Haloodies range of halal food products. For both, the ritualistic approach to the term 'halal' that has seen it reduced to an insular debate over stunned versus un-stunned slaughter, proved extremely unsatisfactory. Motivated by a desire to raise standards in the farming and food production process, they set out to explore and embrace the holistic concept that is halal and infuse the Islamic values of sustainability, animal welfare, respect for the environment, health and safety and honesty into every step from the creation of an animal's life to its consumption.

Their dedication to such lofty principles stands out because what prevails is a great imbalance between those who savour delicacies and those who can barely afford a meagre sustenance, which is only one element of the chaos that is now inherent in the food industry. Increasing pressures come from the rising numbers to have clawed their way out of poverty and suddenly can afford the delights of meat with every meal and a goodly addition of fruit and veg as well. All those extra crops and animals demand more land and especially water. And don't forget the flowers to decorate the table, they occupy land and drink in enormous quantities of water as well. Water security is the great growing threat to food security worldwide. More marginal land has been brought into basic food cultivation. Marginal land was once the standby reserve, the prudential possibilities for times of difficulty. The prudential systems of subsistence agriculture and peasant agriculture have been overtaken by the imperatives of profit and need. There are few prudential systems that can stand against rising global temperatures and over-utilisation of water resources. Irrigation has been part of agricultural technology for millennia but the relocation of crops to new environments that demand intensive irrigation while the growth of population means increased demands for water is an unstable chaotic conjunction. Rivers that cross national boundaries are potential flashpoints for conflict over water. Water scarcity is the new reality. An insecurity heightened when one's neighbour has the ability to literally turn off the taps and stop the rivers flowing. It is not the advance of desertification alone the world must worry about but the control and management of the water itself. Some years ago I boarded a crowded flight between Malaysia and Indonesia and could not understand why so many passengers insisted on taking huge plastic jerry cans of water with them. It was not post-hajj, it could not be Zamzam water from Mecca. Answer: a drought on Java, the equatorial rains no longer regularly deluge the land. Migrant workers always bring home presents when they visit, this time the best gift was water!

The business model that underpins foodie culture is not just about the relocation of crops, it is also the transportation of produce. To support the increased demand for exotic, as in not locally available foods, your meals may well earn more air miles than the average citizen can muster in a lifetime of foreign holidays. To feast like a citizen of the world, to explore the delights of some far flung cuisine more pollution must be created. As more and more producers become involved in the long supply chains of a globalised food market with the power to demand standards and set prices, complexity breeds chaos and incipient instability as part and parcel of profitability. It is not the artisanal produce beloved of the celebrity chefs that flies around the world but ever great integration of corporate systems in which the producers have less and less bargaining power.

The greatest contradiction of all is that as foodie culture spreads, as abundance is attainable by more and more of the haves, there is an ever great accumulation of waste. According to the UN Food and Agriculture Organisation roughly one third of the food produced in the world for human consumption gets lost or wasted every year. That is approximately 1.3 billion tons of food, equivalent to more than half of the world's annual cereal crop. Meanwhile 795 million people around the world were suffering chronic undernourishment in 2014–2016. Consumers in rich countries waste almost as much as the entire net food production of sub-Saharan Africa.

Waste is part of the system. Much of it is a deliberate choice fostered by the marketing system and the ethos of foodie culture. There is waste implicit in the beauty contest on supermarket shelves. Some fruit and veg are just too ugly and ill-formed to be set before the delicate sensibilities of shoppers schooled in the idea of freshest and finest. What does not conform to stipulated supermarket standards is consigned to the bins. One third of produce is lost before it ever enters the supply chain. Then there is the great sell-by date debacle. I swear the only time to buy melon or passion fruit or varied other scrumptious items from supermarkets is well after their sell-by date. Acquire them only from the reduced to clear shelf before the supermarket gets around to putting it in the bin. Sell-by dates are manufacturers' estimates of peak freshness, not deadlines for safe consumption. Then there are the contents of the burgeoning fridges of the world where good food goes to die before we, the finickity consumer, administer the smell test and close examination under strong lighting and consign it to the bins. For many consumers this is not waste, once past its sell-by date or having sat too long in the fridge it is considered spoiled and no longer food. Supermarkets do not help selling two-for-one offers, which only sound like a bargain – that second bag of spinach will go off before you find the opportunity to cook it, ditto the second bag of prepared salad leaves. Under no circumstances remove the wrapping from the airfreighted chilled broccoli and think it is possible to use some now and use the rest for another meal. By the time you return it will be yellowed and honking, fit only for the bin.

The figures for food waste are in typical contradictory fashion remarkably equitable. Responsibility is shared in roughly equal thirds by producers, supply chain and retail and household consumers. It takes some 28 per cent of the world's agricultural area to produce the food that will never been eaten. And remembering the coming water crisis the total volume of water lost or wasted each year has been estimated as equivalent to the annual flow of the Volga river or three times the volume of Lake Geneva. While fruit and veg are the most likely candidates to be wasted a similar fate awaits 20 per cent of meat and dairy products and 35 per cent of fish. So when you are contemplating what kind of foodie culture you fancy tonight spare a thought for the complexity, chaos and contradictions that go into every food culture around the world today. As you plan your feast add a few prudential ideas such as composting your left overs or recycling as much food waste as possible along with all the packaging. Foodie culture has released demons rather than found the multicultural rapprochement of a globalised world where we can all share each other's traditions and tastes. Don't tell Jeremy Henzell-Thomas but I cannot deny that I enjoy picking up ideas from television chefs. However, at the end of it all I hear a small voice in my head. My grandmother, just like Gunel Isakova's grandmother in the Caucasus, always said and still repeats in my consciousness: 'anyone can cook with the best ingredients. It takes a real cook to make a good meal with whatever you can afford.' My grandmother knew whereof she spoke having lived through the Depression and wartime rationing. Isakova's grandmother found that all she needed was flour, water and some oil, to feed her family through the winter, my own grandmother always cooked from fresh. She could make anything including a non-alcoholic drink known as small beer (probably because it did have a tendency to be combustible or should I say positively explosive) to the most delicious peppermint sweets such as no shop ever stocked. Her repertoire was extensive and delicious but confined by the paucity of ingredients available in the local shops. I am sure it is a testament to her tutelage that my stomach ends up being a peasant in every culture though I have never lacked for sampling the finer refined luxury goodies. The trouble with abundant luxury is all the hidden costs and down the line troubles it breeds by just doing its thing. When I reflect on the commercialised foodie culture and all it brings in its wake I am minded of the lines from a Dorothy Parker poem: 'With this the tale and sum of it/ What earthly good can come of it.'

When it comes to gastronautic activity I have been fortunate. I have dined finely, by which I mean I have had my share of fine dining experiences. Posh restaurants, Michelin-starred eating and I have not been strangers. What is more I rank my stomach as a citizen of the world: I have noshed my way through a plethora of cuisines with relish. And when I cook – did I mention I love to cook? – I have pleasure in bringing the gastronomic traditions of the world to my table and transport myself to the tables of those with whom I have dined, just as Sami Zubaidi's personal account transports us to the kitchen of the 1940s Jewish Baghdad household he grew up in. And yet…

Every time I contemplate food there reverberates within me the voice of she who articulates the rules of the universe. My grandmother was a small, gentle, quiet and apparently undemonstrative lady. One should not be fooled by appearance, however. My Nan, as we called her, laid down the law definitively and indelibly - as she decreed so it must be and still is all these years later. Now my Nan was a superb cook and I learnt at her direction the processes and procedures and basic recipes of how to cook. And my Nan always said 'you can call yourself a real cook when you can make something from what is readily available'.

TWICE REMOVED MIGRANT

Yasmin Alibhai-Brown

In January 2018, I went back to Kampala, the capital of Uganda, my birthplace. We Ugandan Asians were exiled from the country in 1972. I settled in London, vibrant, exciting, ever-changing. In time that past faded like newsprint on old papers. Decades later, I was back in the land that made and nourished me. The visit was emotional and, at first, disorientating. The country is still lush, green and gorgeous; Ugandans are still calm, stoic, full of laughter and generous. In some parts the city hadn't changed at all. But the centre was overcome by too many cars, too much noise, vainglorious tall edifices – hotels for the very rich, casinos, big businesses.

My young driver, John B and I had been educated at the same, excellent primary school. It was demolished, the land sold to developers. A desolate structure stands there, incomplete after ten years. John raged, I cried a little. Outside this eyesore, on the pavement, sat a man selling cut mangoes sprinkled with chilli powder and salt. John and I relished them as our eyes watered. Those old days came alive. As Proust wrote in 'Swann's Way', the first volume of *The Remembrance of Things Past*: 'When nothing subsists of an old past, after the death of people, after destruction of things, alone, frailer, but more enduring, more immaterial, more persistent, more faithful, smell and taste remain for a long time, like souls remembering, watching, waiting and hoping for their moment, amid the ruins of all the rest.'

At times I felt like an interloper and at others, like a long lost wanderer coming home. I found the tiny flat where I spent my early years. This is where my mother used to cook food for weddings, engagements and birthdays. Funerals too. In that sooty, airless kitchen she produced vats of what East African Shia Muslims call '*akni*' – a subtly spiced rice and meat dish, piquant goat meat, coconut chicken, aubergine and potato dry curry. It was all done on coal-fuelled or Primus stoves. Her devoted assistant was Japani, a black Ugandan. They sang Hindi film songs while they worked.

His favourite was an anticolonial ditty, 'Mera Joota Hai Japani', from the 1955 film, *Shree 420*. He decided to change his name from 'John' to Japani. When I was little, I used to run down to the big food bazaar near our flat. One of the sellers would drag me back home and deliver me to my frantic mum. They called me '*toto potea*', lost child, in Swahili. In the market this time I was that *toto potea* again, touching mangoes, jackfruits and pineapples, blocking my ears as they beheaded the chickens. Congolese music was playing. I started to dance. People joined in. A blissful moment of belonging.

In my sunny, hi-tech kitchen in my London flat, one small cupboard keeps cooking paraphernalia I brought over from Kampala in 1972. Why I transported old pots and pans to England I cannot explain. During cleaning fits, I chuck them into a box to be dumped and they return back to the house, just in time.

There is a wooden contraption used to grate hairy, brown shelled coconuts. The device has not been used on these shores and is mummified with paper and layers of oil to keep it from cracking and rusting. Two slabs of wood are cleverly put together to make a folding stool. A flat, oval, rusting, metal blade sticks out in front, like the head of a tortoise. The coconut was broken, its sweet, cloudy juice drained into a glass which always went to the favourite child in the extended family, always a boy, always overweight and a bloody nuisance. Then the kitchen servants sat astride the grater, as if on a saddle except it was so low their knees come up almost to the shoulders. With both hands they rolled the half sphere over the blade with a zigzag edge. Sometimes, they slashed their hands and harsh employers abused them for what they thought was native idiocy. Or for contaminating the white flesh with their inferior blood. Boiling water was added to the grated coconut and the mixture was then poured into a straw basket shaped like a long sausage to be squeezed. Imagine the agony. The burning, pitchy hands added a sweetness you can never reproduce. Now smart machines do the job but never as well. And tinned coconut milk tastes insipid.

Then there is a formica *chapatti patlo*, a round block with small legs, previously made of grainy wood to roll out various Indian breads. The new model (1970) was made by Mr Desai, a compulsive moderniser who went from house to house in a tweedy, dank-smelling suit to demonstrate the easy-clean properties of this very latest 'British' material. My mother bought an FP, as they were known, then had to pay for it in pitifully small weekly sums. I use it often. One day in 1988, it helped me capture the heart of my Englishman, four months after my Ugandan Asian husband flew the nest, took his best clothes and irreplaceable, lived recollections of the old land and England as it was when we came.

A brass device came too. Shaped like a mug, it has a circulating handle at the top and plates you insert and secure at the bottom. One plate has holes the size of match-heads, another has tinier perforations, another a star. The 'mug' was stuffed with a spicy, thick gram flour mix then held over boiling vats of oil, the handle turned by a fearless hand. Thin or thick threads, looking like wet noodles fell in and were flash fried.

Some eccentric items I carried over were made by a crooning artisan who called himself Mr Harry Belafonte the Third. The singer has left his song in his handiwork. My rimmed, aluminium bowl shaped like a scarecrow's hat capers merrily when you put it on a flat surface and a huge *karai* – an Indian wok – bops on the cooker as the heat warms it. On the coldest days of winter, torpidity appears to enter these metals, the rocking slows down.

Abdullah, a fat and agile man who could bend right down and walk on fours made the colander I brought over, with a handle nearly a foot long. It was noisily hammered out on the street one afternoon. My mum had sent me and my cousin, Alnoor, with exact, memorised instructions for the dexterous metal beater. This was in 1958. We were eight years old. Abdullah was what we rudely called a '*chotara*' – a black/brown mix, the son of an old Asian trader and his teenage African servant girl who warmed and received his body before a proper wife, Suraya, arrived from India. She immediately sacked the willing maid, a mother by then of three coffee coloured babies. Suraya, whose belly looked perpetually pregnant, remained barren and turned sullen. Abdullah boasted his father was a fabulously wealthy sugar cane plantation owner who *would* claim his street son. One day. 'Man need son. He will call me for sure.' Abdullah's clothes were frayed, his eyes droopy and drippy.

He wrapped his creations in newspapers and we knew my mother would find fault with them and send them back at least twice. My own transported relics were also wrapped in newspapers. Over the years I had to throw out the old papers as they disintegrated – copies of the *Uganda Argus*. The papers carried many accounts of petty criminals beaten or burnt to death by crowds of excited men, women and laughing children. In the grainy photos taken after the kill, some of the proud slayers had their feet on the pulped prey, just like the white bwana hunters with their trophy lion and leopard scalps.

I remember ululations rising up, the calls of a gathering crowd as a thief was spotted grabbing fruit or bread from some vendor. The mob included honest folk and sprightly felons hoping it would never be their turn. The petrified quarry was almost always strangely silent and curled up small. They kicked him softly, burned his arms with matches, pushed in his face and eyes. Then a gang of big men finished him off. The pack of the poor and disenfranchised briefly exerted power as cruel custodians of virtue. Sometimes the thieves would run into our building. Jena sheltered some of them, gave them sugary tea to stop them shaking.

Other newspaper pictures were of the latest high cost government folly, posed tableaux of staged political rallies and ministerial weddings, (adolescent brides smiling nervously in white, nylon gowns). On every page were adverts – Royal Baking Powder, Kenya Gold butter, Bird's Custard and Instant Whip, Coca Cola, Kraft cheese, fancy kitchens and GEC ovens. Only snobbish, rich Asians bought these made-in-England goods. We had better stuff to eat.

Some of the deceased men and women I knew as a child come back to jostle for space in my head, calling from the other side. Particular foods remind me of each individual. During the forty days of mourning after they were sent off to their graves by the chanting congregation, their favourite dishes were brought to the mosque by relatives. Love and memory, cooked and blessed. When my mother died in the spring of 2006, aged 85, I made the cakes and curries she loved but refused in her last years as she sought an end to life. After prayers, the sacred victuals are bought for a nominal sum by the poor, lonely, ill and hard pressed whose pleasure upon eating will be transported to the tongues of the departed as they enter the forgiving gates of paradise, so we believe.

After the funeral prayers for Jena, an old auntie from Mombasa shuffled up and gave me some ubani. 'Here, take, you liked it so much when you were small, always chewing, even in mosque. Took them from my purse, you naughty girl.' I stared at the amber nuggets – edible gum resin – and wondered what they were. That naughty girl in mosque exists in the memories of others, gone from mine.

I see my Maami in my sleep, my mother's brother's wife, eating her coriander omelette every morning with two thick slices of white toast. Her life had been hard as a widow with many wayward children. At night after dinner, she sucked on wedges of sharp, acidic oranges to break open the clogged arteries, she said. Her heart gave up anyway and she lies cold and alone in a cemetery in New York where her youngest son had moved on to after many years in Britain.

I dream of Roshan Aunty, a family friend. She had the grace of a gazelle. Her husband, Nazar, adorned her long neck with many strings of creamy Japanese pearls. She made dainty, crisp samosas the size of large Toblerones, eaten in one bite. Wearing her pearls and a pink, quilted housecoat, Roshan hummed as she rolled out the samosa pastry. My generation buys ready-made frozen piles from expert pensioners who supplement their incomes selling foods that take time and patience. That skill will pass into the void within a few years and we will make do with factory produced, spring roll pastry. One of my biggest regrets is that I never learnt to make those perfect little samosas.

The dough is simple enough – hot water, salt and white flour kneaded well. Eight pieces are broken off and rolled to the size and shape of saucers. They are layered, one upon another, with flour and oil smeared between each. Then the rolling begins again, gentle, coaxing. The pastry is slapped on to a hot *tawa*, iron flat pan, and turned over again and again by hand. Like firewalkers, experts are immune to the scorching heat. They peel off layers of pastry as it blisters. These are cut into thin strips and folded like posh napkins, stuffed with spicy mince or vegetables, and finally sealed tight to be fried in a vast bubbling wok of oil, big enough to bath a new born.

My once cherished ex-mother-in-law made excellent samosas too and nobody ever made mince kebabs like Kulsum, my cousin's wife, and my mother's coconut dhal is famous in the Diaspora from Vancouver to Cape Town. I can smell out food cooked by East African Asians, in kitchens, on clothes and breaths, on buses and tubes.

In 1978, on bus number 207 going to Shepherd's Bush, my mother was told to get off by a conductor because she was smelling like a 'curry pot'.

She replied (without budging) in halting English: 'Sir not to mind. You must come and taste it one day, my curry. You people love it, isn't it?' She *was* stinking, having gone out in the same cardi she wore when cooking. I have that cooking cardigan still. Still unwashed. When I miss her I smell her and food still in the acrylic fibres. These days, the odours are less strong. Soon they will be gone too.

To my son and daughter, I am from a sad place in Africa where there are big beasts, safari jeeps, spectacular views, but too much butchery and poverty for their refined western sensibilities. They feel detached from my complicated upbringing and when I insist on reminding them of it they switch off or rebuke me sharply. I speak four non-European languages and tried to pass them on with no success. They, true born Brits, never could be bothered to learn my sweet mother tongue, Kutchi, spoken in parts of India and Sindh in Pakistan. In her last years when Jena found it harder to communicate in English, my children never got to know what she said and how she really felt. Perhaps they are apprehensive that to accept their multipart, cluttered heritage is to thin down their entitlement to be truly, purely, deeply British.

They are gluttons for East African Asian foods though. Favourites are fried mogo (cassava) and kuku paka, a coconut chicken dish originally from Zanzibar. When my daughter was a toddler, I fed her what I had been fed as a child – 'red rice', boiled basmati mixed with tomato puree, garlic and butter which she loves to this day and my adult son makes his own version of chilli and sour cream to eat with what we call fish cutlets – the old English fishcake recipe only 'repaired and much better' as my mother used to put it. Mashed potatoes and steamed fish are pummelled together with salt, turmeric, lime juice, chopped green chillies, coriander and dill. Then they are shaped into patties, dipped in beaten egg, then breadcrumbs and shallow fried. We colonised the British palate while they took everything else.

While my son and daughter eat, I reminisce, more haltingly these days, link the dishes to times and places repeatedly, so when I am gone, my voice will echo in their heads to remind them who they really are, that they didn't arrive on ground zero the day they were born.

Although there are times of immense dislocation and sadness, I now understand our nomadic history has made us into enthusiastic, incorrigible cosmopolitans, winners in a globalised world. Our food bears testimony to this dynamic existence – creative, sometimes impertinent and playful blends of Indian, Pakistani, Arab, African, Chinese and English, now Italian and American foods too, forever in a flux.

Living in the UK, our food is constantly updated, adapted, altered, recast, much is borrowed. Other British Asians are becoming similarly dynamic, but we were the first to embrace the ceaseless movement of modernity. (There was no choice.) Our place is in the here and now, which too will change. Inevitably.

Food is intrinsically connected to economics, politics, communication, knowledge, marriages, trade and the movements of peoples. Once upon a time in Britain, East African Asian food expressed both desperate nostalgia and hardship. Happiness then was eating a mango (two if you earned more than barely enough working in factories, hospitals, or for British Rail) or adding an aubergine to spicy potato and making dhal less watery. I can make ten different potato dishes – all invented when I was a poor postgraduate at Oxford.

Then came the small savings which built up to bigger piles. East African Asian corner shops became sustainable; more imports were flown over faster. As families began to have small money surpluses, they dressed in best and ventured out together to cafes selling Indian snacks. Food in the home grew varied and more luxuries were added. Our ancestors in East Africa went through this same cycle from deprivation to abundance. You never forget back then.

Most of us consider it immoral to spend huge amounts of money on food and we pride ourselves on being able to turn wilted vegetables and the cheapest cuts of meat into delightful dishes. We are canny and know where to get vine tomatoes for 12 pence per half kilo, six bunches of fresh, aromatic coriander for a pound, boxes of Alphonso mangoes for a fiver, inexpensive sacks of rice, dhals, chapatti flours, gram flour, rice flour and fresh pickles made by local women. As we become time poor we take short cuts – ready ground spices and pastes, frozen parathas, yam, bhindis and karela (bitter gourd), crushed garlic and ginger and green chillies.

I used to make bhindi (okra) from scratch. It took nearly an hour to wipe and cook. Now I use frozen bhindi to make a favourite dish, dry cooked bhindi with scrambled eggs in fifteen minutes, a dish I served the doyen

Madhur Jaffrey. Being able to make favourite dishes fast and with less hassle. What could be better for an enthusiastic cook?

I got the answer when back in Uganda, as I ate plantain and groundnut sauce, barbequed chicken and corn. We gained much after our forced migration. But lost that deep connection with really fresh, from-the-market, good food. Nothing here will ever taste the same again.

WILLOWBROOK FARM: FARMING AS IF CREATION MATTERED

T.W. Bartel

I

'Forasmuch as it hath pleased Almighty God of his great mercy to take unto himself the soul of our dear sister here departed, we therefore commit her body to the ground; earth to earth, ashes to ashes, dust to dust; in sure and certain hope of the Resurrection to eternal life'. Prompted by these words of the Prayer Book service of Christian burial, and feeling desolate and forsaken, I poured the cremated remains of the mortal body of my wife, Jennifer Swift, into the earth, in the Fellows' Garden of Magdalen College Oxford, on the banks of the river Cherwell. Yes, I committed those remains to the ground in the blessed hope of the Resurrection, a hope from which Jennifer never wavered. But she had departed this life suddenly, leaving no time for farewells, at the age of fifty-four. It was a staggering loss, and not only for me: after her death the deputy editor of one national newspaper who published her freelance journalism told me she was irreplaceable, and an editor of another told me that she wished all their journalists were as brilliant as her. Not least, though, Jennifer was saddened by the walls of hostility that seemingly divide Christians and Muslims, and she did her utmost to break them down, earning not merely the respect of Muslims but their admiration: in an obituary in one of these newspapers, her closest Muslim friend testified that her devotion to God had 'carved her name in me'.

Five-and-a-half years later, in February 2015, one of my email newsletters carried an appeal for volunteers to plant one hundred organic fruit and nut trees, all of them heritage varieties, the following Sunday at Willowbrook Farm, eight miles north-west of Jennifer's burial site, also on the banks of the Cherwell. Life had been a brutal ordeal since Jennifer's death; in particular, it was dispiritingly short of meaningful long-term projects. Despite that, I had kept alive an interest in sustainable farming and horticulture, managing to find opportunities, however brief, to work for myself, or to volunteer for others, on allotments, commercial vegetable plots, orchards, ornamental gardens, organic farms, and woodlands. One of those opportunities, as it happened, was as part of a team supervising several dozen volunteers planting eighty organic fruit and nut trees on a farm. So even if nothing further were to come of this day on Willowbrook Farm, I had nothing to lose: instead of having to endure another lonely Sunday, I could at least use my expertise to help others as well as myself, and possibly enjoy a bit of companionship. So immediately I clicked on the link to the full text of the appeal on the farm's website.

I halted, abruptly, after reading the first sentence: The Prophet (pbuh) said 'If the Day of Judgment comes while you are planting a new tree, carry on and plant it.' So was Willowbrook owned by a Muslim family? I checked the home page of the website: indeed it was. While Jennifer was alive, I had shared and supported her affection for Islam; but since her death my contacts with Muslims, and my study of Islam, had languished. And I realised that I owed it to Jennifer to revive these. Perhaps my involvement with Willowbrook might amount to more than merely yet another one-off spell of organic horticulture.

And so it proved. The plan for the day was ambitious. One hundred bare-rooted trees, most of them more than six feet long from roots to crown, had to be properly planted and staked, and protected with tree guards, before darkness closed in; and 150 metres of fencing had to be put up, including the fence posts, to keep out the sheep. After about an hour, by the family's own admission, it was clear that things were not running like clockwork. While all of the planting holes had already been dug, many of them had since filled with water; the compost for the holes had to be mixed with glutinous Oxfordshire clay, which could scarcely be sliced, let alone broken up; few of the forty volunteers had ever planted a tree, and many of them had not arrived; and as it was lambing season on the farm, throughout the day one or more members of the family would have to head off to a remote field to tend to ewes who were giving birth, or who were having trouble feeding their newborns. So I was invited to join the supervisory team of family and long-term volunteers. We beat the darkness in the end, with time enough for lunch.

I returned the following Sunday for more volunteering, and have returned almost every Sunday since then, and, for the past two years, on Wednesdays as well.

II

Why have I kept coming back to volunteer at Willowbrook? Ultimately, the answer to that question is inseparably linked to three others which need answering first: how was Willowbrook started?; what is its guiding ethos?; and how is that ethos realised in practice?

Like many others, Lutfi and Ruby Radwan, the founders of Willowbrook Farm, left behind a comfortable, secure life when they went into organic agriculture. By the late 1990s, Lutfi had a lecturing post in the School of Geography at Oxford University, in addition to a steady stream of work as a rural development consultant and researcher, and Ruby had a reliable income as a tutor at an A-level college. But Lutfi had become thoroughly disenchanted with so-called 'development': 'I realised,' he says, 'that projects in developing countries often just make things worse: they increase inequalities and speed up the process of environmental degradation.' He had also become cynical of higher education: 'it trains students,' he adds, 'to dodge the deeper and more fundamental questions'. Moreover, both Lutfi and Ruby were deeply dissatisfied with the quality of 'halal' meat available, so much so that they considered doing without meat altogether. 'It's not just that the ritual requirements of mentioning God's name aren't observed very well in the modern halal food industry,' Lutfi explains to me; 'Muslims need to be aware that every aspect of factory farming and mass slaughter, not only the awful treatment of animals, is incompatible with the requirements of halal. Most meat sold as halal in the UK isn't halal in any meaningful sense; they're just going through the motions.'

Lutfi and Ruby were aware, naturally, that they were in no position to make a huge impact on these global problems, but they kept looking for ways to make a small but vital difference. Around the year 2000 they decided they should raise and grow their own food. 'Of course we wanted to guarantee ourselves a supply of genuinely halal meat,' Ruby says, 'but we also wanted a better quality of family life – more control over our circumstances, more time together, the real opportunity to work together as a family unit, living closer to the land and more connected to God's Creation.'

So in 2002, when their four children were between two and twelve years old, they bought a caravan and a forty-five-acre plot of land at the edge of the hamlet of Hampton Gay in Oxfordshire, in the Cherwell Environmentally Sensitive Area. 'In a way, God chose it for us,' said Ruby. 'We were looking for land close to home because we couldn't afford to quit our jobs yet. We found a farm we liked but we lost it to another buyer, and then right afterwards a farmer gave us first option on a smaller plot which he owned.' They bought the land and shortly thereafter, they quit their jobs and sold their house.

For the first three years their new life was difficult in every way for the whole family – it was an unrelenting strain on their finances, their physical strength, their morale. 'We had no inkling of what we had got ourselves into,' Ruby recalls. 'There were many times when we wanted to turn back – but we'd sold everything we had so there was no turning back. And we had no idea when things would get better – or if they would.' Lutfi adds: 'Our survival as a farm was on a knife edge.' After they sold the house, all six of the family moved to a campsite, then to a rented flat in Oxford, before moving onto their land and squeezing into two caravans.

Gradually, however, their perseverance was rewarded. At first they produced only organic eggs, selling to a large supermarket distributor; then they were fortunate enough to land a contract to supply Co-op supermarkets directly with their eggs; then they branched out to selling eggs in Oxford to cafés, restaurants and colleges. In 2004, they became the first organic halal meat producers in the UK. 'We started out by selling organic lamb just to friends and family,' Ruby explains, 'but the reputation of the farm spread and demand picked up, so we decided to enlarge our range by adding poultry production. At that point our customer base was still pretty small, but it grew steadily through farmgate sales and through the local farmers' markets.' (The Radwans themselves have played a major role in the development of these markets. A couple of years after the first farmers' market was established in Oxford, at Wolvercote, by a friend and local organic farmer, Ruby took over as chair, an office she held for many years. Both Ruby and Lutfi also served on the founding committee of the East Oxford Farmers' and Community Market.) 'Progress was slow,' Ruby continues, 'because we relied entirely on word of mouth and support from our loyal customers. And all of the profits had to be reinvested in the farm.'

But as time passed, their burdens eased. Already by the time their fifth child was born, three years after they had bought the farm, they had managed to construct two farm buildings themselves and had established themselves in a simple self-build timber cabin. 'It was only fifty square metres for a family of seven,' Ruby says, 'but it seemed like luxury after the caravan.' With the farm on a more stable footing, they gained planning permission for a permanent home. Construction began in 2011 and four years later, they moved into the first building that could house all of them comfortably – a substantial, elegant thatched dwelling in a traditional English farmhouse style, also built themselves.

Sixteen years since inception, the farm has reached a state of equilibrium. Poultry production takes up about 15 acres, while much of the remaining 30 acres is grazed by a flock of sheep guarded by their capable alpaca shepherds. 'Nature sets limits to the growth of sustainable farms,' says Lutfi, 'so as a commercial enterprise our farm will always be small scale and vulnerable to market forces. But we were fully aware of this when we set up the business.'

III

I ask Lutfi and Ruby to elaborate on a point they made earlier, and that they emphasise frequently in public – that the principles and practices of organic farming are easily reconciled with the principles of Islam. Or, as Ruby expresses it in a television interview: 'The Qur'an is essentially an organic guidebook.'

Ruby replies: 'Islam is a holistic religion, and halal is an all-encompassing concept: halal is what does least harm to the Earth and to society. So to produce halal food, you have to take a holistic approach to every element of food production, not just the moment of slaughter or even animal welfare. You have to take responsibility for what you're doing to the natural environment, and to the relations with each other that the economic system engenders. The Qur'an says we should be a community that calls for what is good, urges what is right, and forbids what is wrong – these are the ones who will prosper.'

'Look at it this way,' says Lutfi. 'The concept of "organic" farming, like "halal" food, is often defined far too narrowly. Organic farming is much more than just refusing to use certain products, like GM feed, or hormones and antibiotics. And it's much more than just what you need to get organic certification. We'd actually prefer a term that's gaining a lot of currency now as the best word for sustainable farming: agroecology. Farming based on agroecology goes beyond traditional ecology, which studies only the relations of natural organisms to each other and to their physical environment. It also looks closely at the social and economic aspects of farming, because farming is sustainable only if our socioeconomic system is sustainable. So the essential performance criteria for agroecology overlap quite a lot with the Islamic ideal of a healthy society overall – access to adequate food for everyone in the world; local, egalitarian control over the food supply; full employment in satisfying jobs; the long-term viability and fairness of the whole economic system, including the financial sector; community spirit; and so on. You can sum it all up as social justice, moderation and peace, which is what the Qur'an commands us to promote as stewards of Creation.'

It is evident enough that the Radwans go to great lengths to satisfy the physical criteria of agroecology. Numbers of livestock are kept down to naturally sustainable levels, with ample access to fresh pasture. The sheep are protected from the deadly flystrike disease by finding the maggots individually and killing them by hand, rather than gang-spraying the flock with an aggressive insecticide three or four times a year. Struggling newborn lambs are typically bottle-fed, and sometimes, when in critical condition, cared for in the sitting room of the family home, at least at crucial periods. The table birds – the poultry raised for eating – are traditional, slower-growing breeds. With the completion of the compost toilets on the eco-campsite last year, all of the animal and human excreta produced on the farm can now be recycled – the latter either by the compost toilets or the biodisc sewage treatment system installed for the main farm buildings. Much of the electricity needed (around 30 per cent) is obtained from solar panels or wind power, and a wood-fired boiler, fuelled by sustainable forestry, supplies all of the farm's space heating and hot water. The family home itself could be taken as an iconic symbol of ethically responsible farming and rural living. The walls are cob, a traditional mixture of natural clay, sand and straw that is a highly efficient insulator, and the rest of the insulation is provided by wool from the farm's own lambs.

What of the social dimensions of agroecology? One of them, most obviously, is charitable action, and the Radwans have for many years donated eggs, meat and other produce to the Oxford homeless shelter, encouraging their customers to donate as well to the shelter whenever they place an order.

But the Radwans' efforts to foster a more humane, compassionate society range well beyond charitable giving, and consume much of their time and attention. Some of their energy goes into getting the word out, on their website and social media outlets and in their increasingly frequent interviews in the media. However, says Lutfi, 'Important as it is to inform the public about the dire state of halal meat production, it's even more important to get people to see what real halal farming looks like, and to get them involved on the land.' So Willowbrook hosts a wide range of events and activities to this end. On Sundays from March through October, Ramadan excepted, the farm is open to the public for an organised visit, which offers a guided educational tour of the entire farm, hands-on interaction with the animals, and seasonal workshops and demonstrations, from sheep-shearing and wool-spinning to cob workshops and harvest-time activities. The farm can also arrange day-long educational visits for schools, university students, and others who want to study ethical farming in more depth. There is an opportunity almost every Sunday to get involved in the land especially closely, as a farm labourer – joining the family in their work on the farm as a volunteer. In addition, almost all of these events offer, quite literally, a taste of organic agriculture, as the Radwans provide a lunch which features produce from the farm.

As one might expect, the great majority of participants are Muslim, and their needs are catered for not just with halal produce, but also space for salah. However, a significant proportion of non-Muslims also attend. Both Lutfi and Ruby feel that this places a great responsibility on them to tackle the misconceptions that both Muslims and non-Muslims harbour toward the concept of halal. 'For many Muslims,' Ruby notes, 'the concept has been reduced to an often meaningless ritual, and for many non-Muslims the media stereotypes have had a strong and negative influence.' Lutfi adds, 'We feel it is our duty to present the concepts of khalifa [stewardship] and halal in a holistic and practical manner as part of a living tradition.'

IV

Why, then, have I kept coming back to Willowbrook? Or rather, why come back to this question? It might well seem perverse, if not narcissistic, to focus on autobiography rather than the basic mission of the farm, and how it is realised in practice. I believe, however, that exploring my most basic reasons for volunteering at Willowbrook will also lead us directly to the very foundations of halal farming – to a deep, unified, holistic justification for agroecological farming within a Muslim framework, a synthesis which subsumes and binds together the principal concepts in Islam relevant to agriculture, such as halal, tayeeb (pure, wholesome), khalifa, and amanah (trustworthiness). I can sketch only the barest outline of such a synthesis in this article, but I trust that it could be developed and defended in much greater detail. Furthermore, I submit, my synthesis will serve equally well for at least the greater part of a foundational justification for agroecological farming in Christian theology.

So to answer my question: I keep coming back to Willowbrook because in labouring there as a Christian believer, I am following in the footsteps of the prophets, proclaiming their message to the world. And so, as Muslims, are the Radwans. This mission – this vocation – that I share with them is at the heart of both Christianity and Islam: it sums up what it means for Christians and Muslims to do the will of God, to honour His name. In the words of the New Testament, the Radwans and I work together as 'partners in a heavenly calling'. And what calling could be more fulfilling, more glorious than that?

Of course the popular mind tends to reduce prophecy to denunciation, and that does not loom large in the Radwans' work – though as we have seen, neither is it wholly absent, nor should we expect it to be. After all, the first statement in the Qur'an of the command to eat of what is halal and tayeeb is immediately followed by another: 'Do not follow in the footsteps of Satan' (2:168). And the production, distribution and consumption of food these days, it must be said, follows in the footsteps of Satan: it exacerbates air pollution, water pollution, the build-up of waste, deforestation, depletion of topsoil, depletion of fish stocks, loss of biodiversity, drought and other water shortages, epidemics both animal and human, famine, climate change, and social degradation – rural depopulation, the spread of urban slums, unemployment, suicide, civil unrest, international warfare, and much else. Not only are the worst of these effects borne by the world's poorest; those with the greatest power to alleviate their misery use that power to aggravate it.

The Radwans are under no illusions about the severity of the crisis in modern agriculture. Lutfi observes that, 'As the Qur'an reminds us, "Pollution (corruption) has appeared in the land and the sea on account of what the hands of men have wrought, that He may make them taste a part of that which they have done, so that they may return"' (30:41). As I work alongside them, it is plain to me that, in the arresting words of Pope Francis, they 'dare to turn what is happening to the world into [their] own personal suffering', that they regard the suffering of God's Creation from our maltreatment with as much concern as the suffering of their own souls and bodies.

But of course, denunciation is far from the only function of prophecy in Christianity and Islam. For both these religions are, in essence, religions of hope, and of supreme hope: the paramount desire of the true prophet for humankind is God's desire, not just that a tiny remnant will escape the wrath to come, but that the whole world – indeed the whole of Creation – should be saved.

How, though, can prophecy inspire and sustain that hope? As a first step, by recognising that one of the most formidable barriers to the enlightened oversight of Creation is that the dominant attitude toward agriculture holds not just our intellect, but also our imagination, in a powerful grip. It has taken hold of *every* constituent of the human psyche that is susceptible to persuasion, rational or otherwise – including the unconscious ones. We need look no further than advertising. Obviously, it peddles perverted attitudes toward food by vividly associating unsustainable habits of eating with a glamorous lifestyle – a self-indulgent life of competitive, insatiable overconsumption. One of these unsustainable habits, as the Radwans are happy to acknowledge, is the overconsumption of meat: one of their many responses to the complaint that their meat is so expensive is that it isn't all that costly if you only eat as much as is good for you. (They don't fear a loss of income from reduced meat consumption, reasoning that this would go hand in hand with greater demand for sustainably produced meat like theirs.) But more remarkably, and more insidiously, advertising strengthens the hold of industrial food production on our imagination by so often insinuating that food is, not an essential ingredient of the glamorous life, but an impediment to it – or indeed, to any form of worthwhile existence. How else to explain the success of marketing campaigns that harp on about the low price of a food product, or how rapidly it can be prepared, as if these factors were all-important? They are all-important only if meals are, at best, a necessary evil, mere refuelling, no more significant than elimination.

While this first step remains within the realm of denunciation, it leads us to a crucial insight that takes us beyond it. Our contemptuous, ruinous behaviour toward Creation is glamorised by a vision of the good life that is calculated, by its clever use of vivid, forceful imagery, to manipulate our imaginative outlook on the world. We need to purge our imagination of that vision, of course – and that is one of the functions of prophecy. But we must also refurbish our imagination with an alternative, positive vision of human fulfilment that will motivate us to strive for a world in which farming is conducted as if Creation mattered – an even more important function of prophecy.

An utterly indispensable element of any such vision is the love of created beauty, the counterforce to the love of glamour, its parody and counterfeit. Surprising as it may appear, there is no contradiction in the notion of sustainable farming that is purely functional – farming for which beauty is of no value except as a means, for example to producing enough food to satisfy the nutritional requirements of the world indefinitely. But that is not an option in the Abrahamic religions. God is not just the maker of beauty, He is its exemplar: in so far as Creation is beautiful, it participates in, and reflects and expresses, His infinite beauty. Moreover, it follows from the fundamental Islamic doctrine of tawheed – and it is also fundamental to the concept of God in mainstream Christianity – that God is a perfect unity: He is not a motley jumble of properties, but the exemplar of all perfections. Thus, in so far as Creation is beautiful, it also participates in, and reflects, other attributes of divine glory, such as His infinite power, wisdom, majesty and love. Hence, we are obliged as stewards of God's Creation both to preserve and enhance the beauty of the created order we have been given in trust, not just for other ends, or just for our own delight, but to give acceptable worship to God by gratefully manifesting His glory in the world. In Islamic terms, halal farming, at its most basic level, is tawheed farming – and, it can be said, so is farming that measures up to Christian morality.

And the preservation and enhancement of the beauty of Creation and of the public appreciation of that beauty, apart from its utility to any of the commercial enterprises, is a major priority on Willowbrook Farm. For the sake of the local wildlife, the Radwans have planted several thousand trees round the farm, have dredged out a derelict pond and created a new one, and, with the aid of an ecumenical group of Jewish, Christian and Muslim volunteers, have planted over a hundred metres of hedgerow with nine different native species. They maintain a permanent menagerie of animals – from guinea fowl to pygmy goats – in an attractive wooded enclosure, and encourage visitors to interact with and handle them. They keep a little flock of Ouessant sheep – reputedly the world's smallest breed – and Ruby uses their wool in the spinning workshops on visitor days. They have greatly improved a monocultural conifer wood inherited from the previous owner by transforming most of it into a sizeable children's play area with exquisite wooden installations, including a tree house with an old piano sounding board on one wall that can be strummed, wafting through the woodland the captivating sounds of the Aeolian harp. Perhaps the most conspicuous sign of Willowbrook's commitment to beauty, however, is the annual two-day arts and music festival they host on their farm every summer. It has a great deal to offer the spectator, with a musical programme that features artists such as Dawud Wharnsby, the Pearls of Islam, Faraz and the Sophistas, and world musicians, including a classical Chinese lute player and a Mongolian throat-singer who undoubtedly stole the show the year he performed. But it also strongly encourages visitors to participate in the creation of art, with workshops in disciplines such as song-writing (taught by Dawud Wharnsby), choral singing, watercolour painting, African drumming, poetry reading, and stop-motion animation.

And – last but certainly not least – there is a workshop in tajweed (proper recitation of the Qur'an) led by a trained reciter. The Radwans make great effort to convey all of these beauties of the farm and its activities, and many more, to a broad public through their social media.

But the visions in Christianity and Islam of the life worth living are not limited to the present age. They encompass the age to come, the Hereafter, the state of everlasting blessedness following upon the Resurrection. So our stewardship of Creation not only requires us, as a duty and a joy, to manifest the glory of God in the world, but also demands, as a duty and a joy, to manifest the glory of Paradise in the world as well. And responsible farming is a particularly fitting way of doing so, for the vision of Paradise in both the Christian and Muslim Scriptures is full of imagery drawn from human cultivation. Paradise, of course, is portrayed in the Qur'an as gardens, adorned with fruit-laden trees, fountains and lush meadows. In the New Testament, life in Heaven is represented as a wedding feast; and the central rite of Christianity, the Eucharist, in which the two agricultural products of bread and wine are consumed, is a symbolic anticipation of the heavenly banquet. Nor, in orthodox Christianity and Islam, is this imagery merely a crude metaphor for a blissful disembodied existence: however different the resurrection life may be, it will be life in a body, with bodily pleasures and bodily delights, not an escape from the prison-house of the soul.

I have completed my account of the prophetic vision of human fulfilment that informs my work, and that of the Radwans, on Willowbrook Farm. Yet I cannot rest content with that. So far this account may have succeeded in refurbishing the intellect, offering it, in discursive form, a satisfying alternative to the malignant vision of the life of glamour. But what about refurbishing the imagination? What can be done about that?

For that, I am going back to Willowbrook Farm. I invite my readers to follow me there.

V

I arrive at the farm again, on an overcast, tranquil morning in early December, not long after sunrise – in my experience, an atmosphere that favours meditation. I walk out to the orchard where I had helped supervise the volunteer planting nearly three years ago, and stop in front of a Black Mulberry tree.

The Radwans have recouped the cost of all the trees in this orchard through a sponsorship scheme – each tree has been paid for by an individual or family in return for a share of the eventual harvest. Two months after my first visit to the Farm, I learned that one tree was still unsponsored – a Black Mulberry. I paid the sponsorship fee, and dedicated the Mulberry as a memorial to Jennifer.

The tree is not ravishing in its beauty: it is leafless and spindly. I can reach the top by stretching my hand above my head. The main stem is no more than an inch thick, even at ground level. There is only one lateral branch, thinner than my little finger. Few of the side shoots on either lateral or main stem are longer than my hand. And nowhere is its canopy as broad as a metre.

But I am not seeking purely aesthetic delights this morning. I am seeking certain signs – signs for those who reflect.

I recall the verse in Sura al-Rum: '[God] brings forth the living from the dead, and brings forth the dead from the living, and He revives the earth after its death. Even so shall you be brought forth' (30:19).

Yes, to the casual eye my spindly little Mulberry tree looks dead. But scrape off only the top layer of bark, and the layer underneath is a vibrant, living green. If all goes well, my tree will someday grow at least six metres high, and could yield twenty kilos or more of fruit per season.

How often it seems that the forces arrayed against sustainable farming are invincible. How often it seems that Death is invincible.

But how promising was the future of Christianity in the first century, with its small, dispersed groups of believers, taking on the might of the Roman Empire unarmed?

And how bright were the prospects of the few dozen persecuted followers of the Prophet who escaped to Abyssinia?

I think of my bereavement, the loss of a wife who was truly a garment for me, and a burning and a shining lamp to the world. That loss still casts a dark shadow over my life, still sadly blunts my capacity to feel joy of all kinds, especially the joy of consolation. Even in prayer and meditation, I rarely feel the sweetness of divine consolation; I usually feel that I am drinking from a dry well. Yet, as twenty centuries of Christian spirituality teach us, that is no mark of one's worthiness in the sight of God: many of our greatest saints spent years in spiritual aridity; some were even assailed by doubts over life after death. What matters is whether the virtues are still alive and flourishing in the soul: justice, wisdom, courage, moderation; faith, hope, love.

I think of the verses in Sura al-Baqarah: 'give good news to those who persevere – those who say, when afflicted with a calamity, "We belong to God and to Him we shall return. These will be given blessings and mercy from their Lord"' (2:155–156).

And I think of the saying of Jesus in the Gospels, after he has foretold to his disciples that one calamity after another will afflict his Church and the world: 'the one who endures to the end will be saved.'

Ultimately, joy is a gift – like everything else that is good in Creation, a gift from God. By all means, keep your heart prepared for joy and savour it to the fullest when it is bestowed upon you; but remember where it comes from, and how little it depends on mere human effort. Just hold fast to the promise to God's faithful that in the life to come, as the Bible proclaims, 'God will wipe away every tear from their eyes'.

I notice a stick nearby, and am reminded how the Negus of Abyssinia responded after one of the Muslim refugees had instructed him as to what Muslims believe of Jesus: he took up a piece of wood and said, 'Jesus the Son of Mary does not exceed what you have said by the length of this stick.'

What if Christians and Muslims – we who profess belief in the resurrection of the body and the life everlasting – behaved as those who truly believe and trust in these? For example – what if together we practised and promoted agriculture as if Creation mattered? Might not humankind turn from its wicked ways, and live?

CELEBRITY CHEFS

Jeremy Henzell-Thomas

Paul Bocuse, the most celebrated French chef of the postwar era, died in January 2018 at the age of 91. Cheered on by Henri Gault and Christian Millau, the publishers of the influential Gault-Millau Guide, he had been a leading figure in the pioneering culinary movement known as nouvelle cuisine, a modernised version of classic French cooking devoted to fresh ingredients, lighter sauces, sleek aesthetics, creative flavour combinations and constant innovation. A conspicuous presence in the news media and on television, he exploited his cuisine, image and celebrity status, as well as his savvy business acumen, in building a globe-spanning gastronomic empire and in so doing he became a role model for contemporary chef-entrepreneurs like Jacques Pépin. In 2011, Bocuse was named 'chef of the century' by the Culinary Institute of America. Pépin commented, 'Now the chefs are stars and it's because of Paul Bocuse. We are indebted to him for them.' As the *Japan Times* put it, he 'raised the profile of top chefs from invisible kitchen artists to international celebrities'. It's a measure of his own profile that around 1,500 chefs from around the world, clad in their working whites, gathered in Lyon at the St Jean Cathedral for his funeral on 26 January.

Now, I have no wish to cast a churlish shadow over the funeral of this revered paragon of culinary arts (and may God rest his soul and lead him to a place of sublime nourishment) but there is a valid need to examine the wider culture that has given rise to the phenomenon of the celebrity chef. The famous British soldier, military strategist, adventurer and scholar, Lieutenant-General Sir John Bagot Glubb (1897–1986), also known as Glubb Pasha, famous for the twenty-six years he spent organising and commanding the Jordan Arab Legion, which became Jordan's army, pulls no punches in his book, *The Fate of Empires and Search for Survival*, even though this was written forty years ago before the advent of the fêted chefs whose presence dominates such a broad spectrum of our media. Here, he expounded a system in which empires go through distinct stages, starting with the Age of Pioneers and the Age of Conquest, evolving through the Age of Commerce, the Age of Intellect and the Age of Affluence, and terminating in the Age of Decadence. This terminal stage is, according to Bagot, marked not only by a lowering of moral standards within society, but also by 'a show of wealth and conspicuous consumption lifestyles' of which the 'glorification of celebrities' is a prime feature. Glubb is even more specific in noting that celebrity chefs were one of the most visible symbols of obscene over-consumption in the decadent twilight of the Roman empire.

A striking aspect of the cultural elevation of the celebrity chef has been the use of inflated (and some would say hyperbolic and pretentious) superlatives to describe them, their techniques, and their output, with such eulogies often couched in spiritual-sounding language that seems at odds with the focus on carnal appetite, no matter how 'sophisticated', aesthetically pleasing or high-sounding the cuisine designed to feed it. Bocuse, often referred to as the 'Pope of French cuisine', and himself a follower of Fernand Point, the 'spiritual father' of nouvelle cuisine, declared that there could be no room for 'guesswork' in his style of cooking which demands that 'one must be immutable, unattackable, monumental'.

Given the 'sinful' status of gluttony in religious traditions (one of the seven deadly sins or cardinal vices in Christianity, along with pride, lust, envy, sloth, greed, and wrath) there is an obvious tension between this 'spiritualisation' of gastronomy (and its associated chef-worship) and its antithesis in the well-attested frugality associated with the Prophet Muhammad, even though since his time Muslim societies have of course become noted for the great variety and delectability of their gastronomic traditions. According to Tirmidhi and Ibn Majah, the Prophet is reported to have said, 'Nothing is worse than a person who fills his stomach. It should be enough for the son of Adam to have a few bites to satisfy his hunger.' Another saying attributed to him by Ibn Abbas in Sahih Bukhari goes like this: 'He is not a believer who eats to his fill but his neighbour goes without food.'

The Prophet's principles have obvious implications in today's world, most urgently for the alleviation of widespread famine. In February 2017 the Secretary General of the United Nations expressed alarm that in northern Nigeria, Somalia, Yemen, and South Sudan 20 million people were 'on the brink of famine in a world of plenty', including 1.4 million children at imminent risk of death. In October 2017, the Disasters Emergency Committee charity reported that of the half a million Rohingya refugees that had poured into Bangladesh, approximately 145,000 were children under the age of five at risk of malnutrition. Two months later, a UNICEF analysis revealed that nearly a quarter of all the Rohingya refugee children in the Bangladeshi camps aged between six months and five years were malnourished. Worse, it found around 7.5 per cent of all children – around 17,000 youngsters – affected by severe acute malnutrition. Children make up around 40 per cent of the refugee influx, and are particularly vulnerable to starvation's effects.

Charitable principles also sharpen our awareness of the hunger faced by the homeless and by many struggling families even in the richest countries in the world, where the growing wealth and income gap has produced shocking inequalities that leave many dependent on food stamps or the food bank. It is surely scandalous that data released by the United States Department of Agriculture, on 5 January 2018, revealed that 45.6 million Americans received benefits under the Supplemental Nutrition Assistance Program (SNAP), commonly referred to as food stamps. This is equivalent to the population of a country as large as Spain.

In the same way, an investigation in April 2017 by the Trussell Trust's Foodbank Network, an anti-poverty charity that runs more than 420 food banks across the UK, found a sharp increase in the number of people using food banks – a stark indication that food poverty was continuing to rise across the country.

The charity provided 1,182,954 three-day emergency food supplies to people in crisis between April 2016 and March 2017, compared with 1,109,309 the previous year. Of these, 436,000 went to children. Five years ago, Will Self had already highlighted the incongruity of the British 'obsession with food' in view of the large number of charity food banks in British towns which showed that hunger was a deep-rooted social issue that should not be ignored. Claiming that Britain in 2012 was the 'most food-obsessed nation in Europe – if not the world', he urged people to undergo a 'major lifestyle change in the year to come' and to pay 'a bit less attention to what's on the end of our forks, and a bit more to what's at the end of our roads.' In a BBC blog entitled 'A Point of View: The British Vomitorium', he wrote: 'It is arguably gastronomy that has replaced social democracy as the prevailing credo of our era. But whereas in the case of the National Health Service and state education it was politicians, social activists and campaigners who forged the new consensus, the vanguard of this chomping revolution was constituted by restaurateurs, television producers and celebrity chefs.'

As well as the obligation to feed the needy and destitute, the Prophet also emphasised the importance of the social dimension of sharing food with family, relatives and friends. There is convergence here with the principles of Jeong Kwan, the celebrated Zen Buddhist Korean nun who prepares vegan meals for her community (and the occasional visitor) at Baekyangsa Temple, which is located 169 miles south of Seoul. In an instalment of David Gelb's Netflix documentary series, *Chef's Table*, Jeong Kwan explains how she approaches food and cooking: 'With food we can share and communicate our emotions. It's that mindset of sharing that is really what you're eating.'

There has, however, been much lamentation over the decline of sharing in the 'death of the family dinner' in Britain. An article in the *Daily Mail* of five years ago reported that 46 per cent of families no longer shared an evening meal together every day, and it is very likely that the percentage is now significantly higher. Reasons for this disconnection included work patterns (56 per cent), eating in front of the TV or computer (49 per cent), eating in separate rooms (32 per cent), not believing it was important to eat together (30 per cent) and not getting on with other family members (9 per cent). Yet, 'research paper after research paper show that families that eat together are more stable – the family that eats together stays together.' Psychologists also argue that a main family meal cultivates social skills, good manners and conversational abilities. According to a number of reports issued by the National Center on Addiction and Substance Abuse at Columbia University (CASA), children who eat at least five times a week with their family are also at lower risk of developing poor eating habits, weight problems or alcohol and substance dependencies, and tend to perform better academically than their peers who frequently eat alone or away from home.

The emphasis on moderation, frugality, dignity, charity, and sharing, lies at the heart of Islamic spirituality, which also encompasses those principles of *adab* such as refined manners and human decency that are conspicuously lacking in the kitchens of those chefs who gain celebrity status partly through exploiting what Tim Garman has described as 'Obsessive Chef's Disorder' (OCD). The kitchen banishments and screaming fits showcased in the reality TV show 'Hell's Kitchen', hosted by foul-mouthed chef Gordon Ramsay, are par for the course. Garman includes in the OCD Hall of Fame 'London's Marco Pierre White, the knife-wielding, customer-threatening chef who taught Gordon Ramsay how to be an asshole.' It is typical of celebrity culture that low character and bad behaviour often earn the biggest and most profitable circulation.

Quite apart from the worship of traits of bad character, one can only wonder at what the Prophet would have made of the excessive allure of some of Paul Bocuse's signature dishes that 'not only pleased the palate' but also 'seduced the eye and piqued the imagination'. These included truffle soup V.G.E., a heady mixture of truffles and foie gras in chicken broth, baked in a single-serving bowl covered in puff pastry. First served at a dinner at the Élysée Palace in 1975, the soup was named for the French president Valéry Giscard d'Estaing, who had just awarded Bocuse the French Légion d'Honneur. Other famous Bocuse dishes included sea bass stuffed with lobster mousse and encased in pastry scales and fins, and a truffled Bresse chicken poached inside a pig's bladder. By the same token, frugality and simplicity do not stand out as the hallmarks of the revival of fine Ottoman imperial cuisine in the 400 dishes on the menu of Asitane Restaurant in Istanbul. Gerdaniyye, for example, is a lamb chuck slowly braised with aromatic vegetables and herbs blended with lamb brains and served with a sour black plum extract. Two dishes from 1539 also stand out: Stuffed Quince is baked quince stuffed with a blend of minced lamb and beef, rice, aromatic herbs, pine nuts, currants and flavoured with grape molasses; Goose Kebab is a slowly roasted Çankiri goose served on a bed of almond pilaf in crunchy Turkish 'Yufka'. Rated one of the ten best restaurants in Turkey, Asitane reclaims the refined culinary tradition of the imperial courts and the metropolitan elites in Istanbul, bringing together elements of regional cuisines from across the empires, notably the tastes of the Middle East, the Balkans, the Caucasus and central Anatolia. The traditions of Ottoman cuisine continue not only in Turkish cuisine and in the Middle East, but also in the cuisines of Albania, Algeria, Serbia, Bulgaria, Azerbaijan, Iran, Armenia, Ukraine, Cyprus, Romania, Georgia and the Sephardic communities.

But to return to France, the cradle of 'haute cuisine' and celebrity chefs. Jean Anthelme Brillat-Savarin (1755-1826) is sometimes called the 'father of gastronomy' because of his early and influential characterisation of cooking and eating as science in *Physiologie du Goût* (*The Physiology of Taste*). Mary Fitzgerald describes how much of Brillat-Savarin's wisdom has become idiomatic: he was, for example, 'the first to coin the phrase: "You are what you eat"— item four in a long list of Aphorisms of the Professor intended as a lasting foundation for the science of gastronomy.' His handbook is 'an intimate account of a man's passionate relationship with food', full of flamboyant recipes, and summed up perhaps by his hyperbolic pronouncement that the discovery of a new dish does wonders to enhance human happiness, while a dinner which ends without cheese is like a beautiful woman with only one eye.

In his famous essay on this 'father of gastronomy', semiotician Roland Barthes goes so far as to describe gastronomy as a perversion, the indulgence of a pointless desire. We might well concur that this judgement aptly reflects the modern obsession with gastronomic perfectionism. Jonathan Eburne, in describing what he calls 'cooking beyond the pleasure principle', or the 'chef drive', relates how the face of gastronomy changed on 24 February 2003, when 'after the lunch service at his famous Côte d'Or restaurant in Saulieu, three-star chef Bernard Loiseau returned to his bedroom and shot himself in the mouth.' Eburne comments that 'in the aftermath of Loiseau's suicide, fellow chefs, food critics and freelance writers alike have speculated on the causes for this violent self-erasure.' Was it, he asks, 'the threat of losing a Michelin star, and the rating reduction from 19 to 17 in the Gault Millau guide, that provoked this act?'

To put into immediate context the gastronomic pinnacle represented by three Michelin stars, the most recent Michelin Guide names five restaurants in Great Britain and Ireland as achieving a three-star rating, the latest of which is a sushi restaurant, the Araki, off Regent Street in London.

This has nine seats, every one of which is 'at the chef's table' according to the restaurant's website, and charges £300 a head for its set menu. The high-end fashionable trend of eating 'at the chef's table' is also evident in the chef David Bouley's new restaurant in New York, a restaurant without waiters. Here, you enter a whitewashed space, a long narrow kitchen lined with counters, hobs and ovens, with chefs chopping and stirring at workstations. You sit here on stools at the workstations where the chefs are preparing your eleven-course $225 meal.

If it wasn't the catastrophic threat of losing a Michelin star that drove Loiseau to suicide, was it perhaps (as Eburne suggests) 'the fragile ego of a man consumed by the caprices of haute cuisine?' Whatever the cause, 'the event marked a major shift in gastronomic discourse. Whereas the historical canon of food writing is overwhelmingly attuned to the pleasures of the table, more recent popular literature has begun to account for the compulsions of the kitchen.'

And the corresponding compulsion of viewers, observers and consumers in the current fascination for the cultism surrounding celebrity chefs and foodie venues is only too evident in the observation of media psychologist, Emma Kenny, that with eighteen days' worth of cookery shows available on our screens each week, 'as a nation, we are fixated with any activity related to food culture.' A striking illustration of the false reality that can arise from such fixations is provided by the recent case (April 2017) of a man who tricked TripAdvisor, the largest travel site in the world, into listing his shed as London's No. 1-rated trendy restaurant (The Shed at Dulwich) after a plethora of fake reviews describing it as a small, appointment-only destination for foodies. People around the world called the owner begging to book a reservation and even tried to blackmail him to get tables, even though the fancied restaurant does not of course exist. Its website claimed not to have a 'traditional menu' composed of 'meals' but rather of 'moods'. You choose a mood 'which fits your day' and the chef interprets it. Examples of 'moods' the restaurant claimed to have served in the past include 'Lust', served up as 'rabbit kidneys on toast seasoned with saffron and an oyster bisque' and 'a side of pomegranate soufflé'. The mood of Contemplation was realised as a 'deconstructed Aberdeen stew' served with 'warm beef tea', and the mood of Comfort by a 'Yorkshire blue Macaroni Cheese seasoned with bacon shavings and served in a 600TC [thread count] Egyptian cotton bowl'. The extent of the illusion created by these mouth-watering descriptions is amplified by photos on the website, one of which depicts a tempting 'foodie-style' dish which is actually made with bleach tablets and shaving cream.

The kudos afforded to the fragile egos of narcissists in gaining a place at a venue like The Shed is doubtless matched by the sense of vanity achieved by those who are given better seats in restaurants because they are judged to be 'attractive diners'. Researchers for Channel 4's documentary series, 'Tricks of the Restaurant Trade', reported in the *Daily Telegraph* in January 2016, found restaurants purposely seat people they deem attractive at their best tables, while regular customers, or those who were considered to be less attractive, are given tables near the kitchen or toilets or are told there are no tables available at all.

According to TV chef Simon Rimmer, this method is common practice in the catering industry: 'Every restaurant has a golden table where they sit the best looking customers. A restaurant's clientele give off a certain message about the place. Good looking customers attract more people and make you more cash, so you sit them where they can be seen.' As part of the Channel 4 investigation, models posing as customers were sent into three top London restaurants and were given 'golden tables' in all three. Actor Adam Pearson, whose neurofibromatosis has left his face covered in tumours, followed the models into one of the restaurants, but he and his friends were hidden away or refused tables.

A survey conducted by Lurpak and reported in the *Daily Telegraph* in September 2016 found that Britons now spend more than five hours a week consuming 'food media', but only four hours actually cooking. The average adult spends more time watching, scrolling and reading about food on social media than they do cooking their daily meals. Amongst those surveyed, this amounted to 44 minutes on Facebook, 20 minutes on Twitter, 19 minutes on Instagram and Pinterest and 34 minutes on YouTube. It's estimated that Britons also spend 58 minutes every week reading food websites and blogs, and 15 minutes snapchatting about food. One in five also admitted to making a dish at home just to take a photograph and share it on social media sites like Instagram.

More than half of the 2,000 people surveyed admitted they would rather watch a meal being cooked on TV, or look at photos online, than cook. In fact, despite our love of cooking shows and magazines, over a fifth of people have never cooked an evening meal from scratch. The study found the average adult spends one hour and 37 minutes a week watching food-related shows, of which the 'The Great British Bake Off', 'Masterchef' and 'Come Dine with Me' are the most popular.

In 'The Cult of the Celebrity Chef Goes Global', Lisa Abend quotes best-selling food author Michael Pollan's observation that the 'dramatic decline in home cooking' has coincided with 'the age of the TV chef'. Pollan, named by *Time* magazine in 2010 as one of this year's 100 most influential people in the world, had argued that 'by making food a spectacle, shows like "Iron Chef" and "The F Word" have reinforced the message that cooking is best left to the professionals. By turning chefs into entertainers, we have widened the breach between ourselves and the once ordinary task of cooking.' Michelin-starred chef Michel Roux Jr has hit out at shows such as 'MasterChef' and 'The Great British Bake Off' for 'putting chefs on a pedestal'. And yet, as Abend, points out, 'our alienation from food and its preparation is matched only by our obsession with it.' Droves of ordinary folk now 'blog about every course of every restaurant meal they eat' and 'the camera-happy movement has gotten so bad that Grant Achatz, the famously avant-garde chef of Chicago's Alinea, recently chastised diners who take photos – and video – of the food he serves.' Such trends, says Abend, 'are fed by chefs' newfound prominence' and 'in a world in which what and how we eat have become fetishised, celebrity chefs are finding new ways to harness their star power.'

Alexander Sehmer refers to a study carried out at Oxford University and published in the journal *Brain and Cognition* in 2015 which found that 'those of us currently living in the Western world are watching more cookery shows on TV than ever before', and 'the practice of glamorising food by posting pictures of mouth-watering meals on Instagram or other social media sites may well be playing havoc with people's waistlines.' Even amid Britain's obesity crisis, we are 'bombarded with gastroporn' via social media, books on food, advertising and cookery shows, and 'it feels as though we are being exposed to ever more appetising (and typically high calorie) images of food' everyday. On Pinterest, one of the top 10 largest social network services with millions of visitors every week, the food boards are the most popular boards, and the extensive galleries of dishes on the website foodporndaily.com enable one to stare at food all day if one so wishes.

There is much in all of this that we might find strangely dysfunctional, not least what it tells us about the alienation from authentic personal experience and the sensory deprivation so evident in the penchant for mediating (and impoverishing) three-dimensional, multi-sensory experience through the fixation on flat screens. This comes through in the current obsession with taking photographs of everything. Interviewed by Joe Pinsker in his article 'Why Are Millennials So Obsessed With Food?' in *The Atlantic* in 2015, Eve Turow relates how when she was in college she was content subsisting on 'gelatinous brown rice, pre-cooked mushy pinto beans, [and] blocks of bouncy tofu', but if she were in college now, she says, 'she'd be taking rice-bowl inspiration from Pinterest and making good use of the nearby farmer's market and the greenhouse attached to the science library.' Her book *A Taste of Generation Yum: How the Millennial Generation's Love for Organic Fare, Celebrity Chefs, and Microbrews Will Make or Break the Future of Food* includes interviews with a variety of millennials (broadly defined as those who reached adulthood around the turn of the twenty-first century) as well as food luminaries – including Anthony Bourdain, Michael Pollan, Mark Bittman, Marion Nestle and more – helping her try to figure out why food came to be something she and her generation obsesses over.

Turow explains that there are roughly 80 million millennials in America. According to research by the advertising agency network BBDO, half of them identify as 'foodies'. 'They buy organic groceries, fawn over Chemex coffee, Instagram images of pork belly and spend their recession-dented incomes on high-end meals out. Young adults with degrees from prestigious universities apply their learnings to harvests instead of hedge funds. Never before has a young generation paid this much attention to food.' She characterises the quintessential millennial experience this way: 'You got into a top tier high school, you hustled through college – you've done everything society told you – and you're not rewarded. You're told, "You will be jobless." And yet, these same people, are, as one New York magazine headline noted, spending 25 per cent of their pay packets on pickled lamb's tongues.'

As Pinsker comments, 'Turow's theory is that in a digital-first era, many people latch onto food as something that engages all of the senses and brings people together in physical space.' She is convinced that 'it comes down to technology, for a few reasons. One, is sensory deprivation. We have formed into a society that's so accustomed to sitting in front of a screen and typing, for the vast majority of the day. And the truth of the matter is that it's not exciting all of our senses. Through interviews over and over again, I kept hearing that people want something that's tangible, that they can see and feel and smell and taste. At the same time, it's also making us more isolated. We're craving community.'

There are of course many reasons, from the relatively understandable to the bizarre, underlying the 'foodie' craze, including genuine environmental concerns, the problem of sensory deprivation associated with overuse of digital devices, and other psychological factors that could be usefully brought to light, but I would like to conclude by placing the related cult of the celebrity chef in the wider context of the rampant celebrity culture and the promotion of 'Idols' in popular TV programmes that for many historians, social commentators and cultural critics mark the terminal decline of civilisation. John Bagot Glubb's judgement that the 'glorification of celebrities' is a prime feature of the Age of Decadence is echoed with considerable power in the words of critics such as Chris Hedges, a columnist for the progressive news and commentary website *Truthdig*, who lamented in 2009 in his essay 'Addicted to Nonsense' that 'we are enraptured by the revels of a dying civilisation.' As he says, 'celebrity worship has banished the real from public discourse.' This 'frenzy' and 'devotion' is 'all part of the yearning to see ourselves in those we worship...We are waiting for our cue to walk on stage and be admired and envied, to become known and celebrated. Nothing else in life counts...We build pages on social networking sites devoted to presenting our image to the world. We seek to control how others think of us. We define our worth solely by our visibility.' And, of course, that image so obsessively fabricated and transmitted is more often than not a decidedly false and idealised image.

Here, the principles of Islam have much to offer in guiding us to 'the real'. In Islamic eschatology, the one-eyed 'Dajjal', equivalent to the Antichrist or the Armilus in Christian and Jewish eschatology respectively, is anticipated to appear in the 'end times' as the 'deceiver' or 'impostor', pretending to be the Messiah. According to E.W. Lane's Arabic-English Lexicon, one of the vivid concrete senses of the Arabic root of the word 'Dajjal' is to 'spread tar on a mangy camel', to cover over what is defective to make it more saleable, to impart false glitter to what is corrupt, to give the appearance of total veracity to what is entirely fabricated. And the capacity to do this is being amplified exponentially in the digital world, as Daniel Finkelstein pointed out in an article in *The Times*: 'Soon,' he wrote, 'it will be possible to create almost flawless films of apparently real and recognisable people engaged in activities that are entirely made up.' The Prophet himself prayed that he might be protected from the 'hidden shirk' by which we unconsciously worship something other than God, and was well aware that the desire for approbation loomed large as one of those false idols.

We can of course strive to see through bogus realities, whether in the world or within ourselves, without subscribing to the doctrinal position that we have actually reached the 'end times' even if we may interpret such falsity as evidence of the Age of Decadence that befalls a civilisation in decline. To that end, the words of Chris Hedges strike home with considerable power:

> The illusionists who shape our culture, and who profit from our incredulity, hold up the gilded cult of Us. Popular expressions of religious belief, personal empowerment, corporatism, political participation and self-definition argue that all of us are special, entitled and unique. All of us, by tapping into our inner reserves of personal will and undiscovered talent, by visualising what we want, can achieve, and deserve to achieve, happiness, fame and success. This relentless message cuts across ideological lines. This mantra has seeped into every aspect of our lives. We are all entitled to everything. And because of this self-absorption, and deep self-delusion, we have become a country of child-like adults who speak and think in the inane gibberish of popular culture.

Again, 'the chatter that passes for news, the gossip that is peddled by the windbags on the airwaves, the noise that drowns out rational discourse, and the timidity and cowardice of what is left of the newspaper industry reflect our flight into collective insanity. We stand on the cusp of one of the most seismic and disturbing dislocations in human history, one that is radically reconfiguring our economy as it is the environment, and our obsessions revolve around the trivial and the absurd.' Rowan Williams said as much when he described our 'broken society' as one of 'dysfunctionality, triviality and desolation.'

I have given ample space here to Hedges' forensic analysis of contemporary 'dislocation' not because I am a killjoy, a sternly Puritan ascetic addicted to gruel, a bleak pessimist issuing a gloomy Jeremiad about the imminent collapse of society, or a doctrinaire 'Traditionalist' thumping on about the irredeemable 'crisis of modernity', but because it is surely incumbent on us to champion with honesty and rigour the critical discernment, ethical values and spiritual insights that represent, in Arnold Toynbee's terms, a creative response to the challenges posed by a civilisation in crisis. Toynbee considered that a civilisation could be saved from decline by the provision of a new transformative spiritual insight which he called the principle of 'Transcendence', espoused and transmitted by a 'creative minority'. We might want to add that the arrest of decline might also be facilitated by the renewal of existing traditions and their recontextualisation in the light of contemporary conditions, and this applies as much to decline within religious communities as it does to secular modernity. A forensic analysis and critique of celebrity culture can be seen as a test case of how the challenges posed by a civilisation in decline might be met, for that 'collective insanity' and 'disturbing dislocation' encompass so many of the vices that emerge from the loss of any vision of transcendence or model of exemplary human conduct – the vices of self-absorption, narcissism, sense of entitlement, and, perhaps most damaging of all, the deeply unconscious projection of the higher potential of our own souls onto the worship of all manner of trivial, illusory and defective idols and the false reality this engenders.

WINE IN SUFI POETRY

Charles Upton

The symbolism of wine in the spiritual life has a long and distinguished history. The use of bread and wine as 'species' for the Christian Holy Eucharist harks back to the 'sacrament' of Melchizedec, the 'shaykh' of the prophet Abraham; they may be taken, among other things, as emblems of the union of Truth and Life, of Knowledge and Love, or of the states of Sobriety and Intoxication described by the Sufis. And Anacreon, the great celebrator of wine among the Greeks, though his poetry was unabashedly pagan and earthy, yet provided symbols and metaphors that in other hands were capable of the greatest sublimation:

> Bring me the winebowl, come my boy
> To drink in one long swallow back
> Ten cups of water, five of wine,
> And do me proud before its god....

> Eros the blacksmith
> Hammers me again,
> Striking while I'm hot
> And thrusts me sizzling
> In the ice-cold stream.

Who can fail to recognise, in these verses dedicated to Dionysus, the wine-god, and Eros, the god of love, backward echoes of the poetry of the Persian Sufis, with their celebration of the Saki, the Cupbearer, and their passionate exaltation and lament at the states of Expansion (*bast*) and Contraction (*qabd*) sent by God the Beloved, Giver of *al-Jamal*, Beauty, and *al-Jalal*, Rigor and Majesty? From Zeus' cupbearer Ganymede, to Christ, bearer of the cup that was later to become the Holy Grail—and the Catholic or Orthodox priest who stands in for him at Mass or Divine Liturgy—to the representation, in the tradition of *Tasawwuf*, of the Sufi shaykh—or else of Allah Himself—as the Saki, wine and the wine-steward have long been associated, in one way or another, with the merciful Grace and devastating Beauty of the Divinity.

According to some scholars, the first poet of the Sufi tradition to use wine as a symbol of spiritual intoxication was the early woman Sufi Rabi'a al-Adawiyya. Here is my 'transcreation' of one of her poems:

> Cup, Wine, and Friend make three
> And I, thirsty with love, am Four....
> The Cupbearer hands to each, one after another,
> The cup of unending joy:
> If I look, it's Him I am looking for;
> And if I arrive, then He is my eyes.

> Don't blame me if I am in love with His beauty,
> Because, by God, my ears cannot hear your slander.
> Again and again, passion and the bitterness of attachment
> Have turned my eyes into rivers.

> My tears don't stop falling;
> Nor am I allowed to stay with Him;
> Nor can my burning eyes ever let me sleep.

Rabi'a, like most of the early Sufis, was a *zahid*, an ascetic; no-one could accuse her of addiction to earthly wine. And though Christians do not prohibit wine-drinking, much the same can be said of her Christian predecessor, St. Gregory Nazianzen, who used the symbol of wine in a way very similar to hers in his own poems. Nor is the use of wine as a metaphor for spiritual exaltation in any way un-Islamic, as witness the following verses from the Qur'an:

> A similitude of the Garden which those who keep their duty (to Allah)
> are promised: Therein are rivers of water unpolluted, and rivers of milk
> whereof the flavour changeth not, and rivers of wine delicious to the
> drinkers, and rivers of clear-run honey....[47:15]

> A cup from a gushing spring is brought round for them,

White, delicious to the drinkers,
Wherein there is no headache nor are they made mad thereby. [37:45-47]

Their raiment will be fine green silk and gold embroidery. Bracelets of
silver will they wear. Their Lord will slake their thirst with a pure drink.
[76:21]

They are given to drink of a pure wine, sealed,
Whose seal is musk—for this let (all) those strive who strive for bliss—
And mixed with water of Tasnim,
A spring whence those brought near (to Allah) drink. [83:25-28]

Some consider the various spiritual states experienced in prayer to be
foretastes of Paradise. The Sufis, however—while in no way denying the
reality of the afterlife—are more likely to take the Qur'anic references to
Paradise as metaphors for spiritual realities that can be actualised in this
very life.

It should come as no surprise that the finest poems of wine in the
spiritual sense, of ecstasy and intoxication, were composed in the Persian
tongue. Jalaluddin Rumi, the pre-eminent Sufi poet and one of the greatest
spiritual poets of all time, often employs wine as a metaphor. For example,
in one of his Quatrains (in my own transcreation of the translations of
Gamard and Farhadi), he writes:

Because of You I beheld the jar of Love, bubbling and fermenting;
Because of You I attained to my true substance—*wine!*
But no! *You* are the wine; I am only the water.
When we are blended together, You alone appear; I am nowhere to be seen.

But the greatest poet of wine and spiritual drunkenness in the Persian
tongue was, of course, Hafez; in the opinion of Javad Nurbakhsh, past Pir
of the Nimatullahi Sufi Order (which originated in Iran), 'Rumi was a Sufi
who was also a poet; Hafez was a poet who was also a Sufi.' We can be
confident that Rabi'a, an Arab Sufi living in Basra, Iraq, in the early years of
Islam, was not an alcoholic, and that her references to wine were thus
symbolic of divine realities. The same can be said of Rumi. In the case of
Hafez, however—a poet, and a Persian at that—we can't be quite so sure

that his references to wine, which were clearly drawn from the Sufi symbolic lexicon and thus primarily refer to things of the Spirit, owe nothing to a personal experience of the wine of the grape in his earlier years. Like Khayyam, Hafez affects an antinomianism in the manner common to many Persian Sufis, who often called themselves 'rakes, drunkards, libertines' in response to the accusations of the exoterics, as if to say: 'You call us drunkards, but we are even worse drunkards than you imagine: we are drunk on Allah!'

Likewise the Quakers, Shakers and Methodists of the western world adopted the insulting epithets of their detractors as badges of distinction. Wine-drinking is universally recognised as a sin in Islam, yet in the Persia of Hafez' day it was probably not an unfamiliar sin; in any case it can be stated with certainty that, in normative Sufism—excluding such heterodox groups as the Bektashi dervishes, among whom wine-drinking is practiced—wine never refers to the literal wine of the grape, but always to the wine of the Spirit, and the poetry of Hafez is certainly considered canonical among orthodox Sufis. The following are my 'transcreations' of nine *ghazals* (lyric poems) of Hafez, from the translation of H. Wilberforce Clarke:

Ghazal 1

Saki! Pass the pitcher.
Love seemed easy at first
But now, the bitter edge.

Because of the dizzying scent the breeze brushed loose
Just before dawn from that lock of hair
That twisted, musky curl
What blood shook the hearts of my friends!

Dye your prayer-rug with wine
If the Zoroastrian master commands it:
The one who has made the journey
Knows the route, and the milestones,
And the etiquette of the road.
At the kilometre of the Beloved

What joy I knew, and what relief
When the death-bell briefly spoke, and told me:
Pack your bags!

This dark night, this fear of the wave
And the terrible whirlpool—
How can those who left their burdens on the shore,
The ones who travel light—
How can they know our state?

My life's-work brought public shame
Because I followed my dream;
How can the mystery of love still remain a secret
When it's debated in public assemblies?

Hafez! If you crave His presence
Then be present for *Him;*
When you visit your Beloved, leave the world behind:
Let it slip from your grasp.

Ghazal 4

Come here, Sufi:
Because the mirror of the cup is bright
You can see the ruby light of the wine.

No-one hunts the Anka, so dismantle your trap;
Nothing remains in the hand of the snare
But the wind. Let your struggle live
In the pleasure of the moment, and remember:
When the well ran dry
Adam himself let go of the Garden and the house of
safety.

At the banquet of time, have one for host, one for the road

And then go: perpetual union, here
Is not in the cards.

O heart! The strength of youth has gone
Before you could pick even one rose from the garden of
life.
Hedonists, libertines,
Drunk as the Mystery that lies hidden in the veil,
For the elevated, self-denying ones
Your state is not becoming.

But as for us, hanging on your doorsill
We're yours to command.
Look again on your slave, Sir; take pity on him!

The day this heart placed its reins
In the hand of Your love,
I gave up the desire for an easy life.

I am the disciple of Jamshid's cup: I am Hafez.
Breeze, take a greeting from this nameless slave
To the Shaykh of Jam.

Ghazal 5

Saki. One more drink if you please.
Throw your dust on the head
Of time's anguish.

Place the winecup in my hand
So I can strip this patched shirt of midnight blue
From my breast.

The wise call us notorious—
What do we want with their good opinion?

Bring wine! How long, tossed
In the wind of pride? How much dust on the head
Of useless desire?

When I sighed, the smoke of my blazing heart
Incinerated all the punks.

In high society, or in the gutter with the lowlife:
Not one friend of the secret
Of my ravaged heart.

Yet my heart is glad with a Comforter
Who once, from my heart, took comfort.

Whoever has seen the Silver Cypress
Will never set eyes on the cypress in the field again.

Patience in adversity, both day and night, Hafez,
May bring you in the end to your desire.

Ghazal 6

For God's sake, pious ones!
My heart has flown from my hand—
Holy ones, for God's sake!
The pain of this mystery is begging to be revealed.

We are the ones whose boat is stranded.
Rise, wind! Then maybe once again
We'll behold the face of the Beloved.

The planets distribute their magic and sorcery
For no more than ten days;
Consider our friendship, O Friend, as your plunder.

Last night in the assembly of Rose and Wine
The bulbul sang deliciously:
Steward! Bring wine! Drunken ones—come to life!

The winecup is the mirror of Alexander:
Gaze into it and see the sorry state
Of the empire of Darius.

Generous One: In gratitude for your own safety
Maybe some day you'll inquire as to the welfare
Of this starving wretch
Of a dervish.

The comfort of the two worlds
Is in the meaning of these two words:
Kindness to friends; courtesy to enemies.

They refused to admit us
To the street of good reputation;
If you disagree with their decision,
Then change our fate.

This bitter wine, the one the Sufi called 'mother of
iniquities'
Is sweeter and more pleasant to us
Than the kisses of virgins.

When times are hard, go after pleasure;
See just how drunk you can get.
This potion of Existence makes a beggar rich as Karun.

But don't be arrogant, or the anger of the Heart-Ravisher
In whose hand even flint turns to wax
Will burn you out like a candle.
These lovely ones, whispering and giggling in the Persian
tongue

Are the givers of life. Wine-steward,
Take news of this to the old men of Fars;

If the minstrel calls on the companions
Of this Persian lyric to dance,
It will attract those old men.

Hafez didn't put on this patched and wine-stained robe
all by himself;
O shaykh whose robe is clean,
Forgive our hopeless ways.

Ghazal 7

The splendour of youth has returned to the garden;
The good news of the rose has reached the bulbul;
His song is sweet.

Breeze, if you come again to the young men seated in
the meadow,
Bring this prayer to the cypress, the rose and the sweet
basil.

If the young Zoroastrian wine-seller reveals his glory
openly,
I'll turn my eye-lash into a dust-broom
And sweep the dust at the
Door of his tavern.

When you draw the veil of black ambergris
Over the face of the Moon,
Don't drive me crazy; my head is spinning already.

The crowd jeers at us for drinking the dregs;
Am I afraid of them?

They will ruin their faith in the end.

Be the friend of the men of God, and remember:
There was a handful of dust in Noah's Ark
That wasn't interested in buying up the whole flood
For one drop of water.

Tell him whose last bed
Is two handfuls of earth: What interest do you still have
In building towers that reach to heaven?

Clear out of this house, whose roof is the sky,
And don't ask for bread:
The dark cup, in the end, always kills the guest.

That Moon of Canaan, that Throne of Egypt is yours:
It's time to tell your prison-house good-bye!

What plot do you keep in the tip of your curl
That makes you let down, once more, the flood
Of that perfumed hair?
If your head keeps spinning in the circle of what *might* be,
You will never begin to know the mysteries
Of what *must* be.

The kingdom of liberty, and somewhere within it, a little
corner of contentment
Is a prize the Sultan himself can't take with the sword.

Drink wine, Hafez, and practice dissipation. Be happy.
But don't, in your happiness— like some others have—
Turn the Holy Qur'an
Into your snare of deceit.

Ghazal 8

If that Turk of Shiraz takes my heart,
I'll give Bokhara and Samarkand both for the mole on
her cheek.

Steward! Bring out what's left of the wine.
In Paradise you will have neither the grassy bank of the
Ruknabad
Nor the rose in the garden of Musalla.

These sweet, teasing workers, the torment of the city
Steal patience from the heart, just like the Turks
Lift tribute from the tray.

What does the Beloved's beauty
Need with our own flawed beauty?
Loveliness Itself requires neither makeup, nor rouge,
Nor painted mole, nor penciled eyebrow.

When I saw that every day Joseph became more beautiful,
I knew that love for him would bring out Zulaikha
From behind the curtain of virginity.

Sing the story of troubadour and wine,
Forget trying to catch the mystery of time.
No-one has ever solved it, with all the skill at their
command;
And you will fail too.

You insulted me, and I was happy;
Now that you've taken to flattering me,
May God Almighty forgive you.
Bitter words are more appropriate
Coming from that red, succulent, sugar-greedy lip.

You strung pearls on the thread of the night when you
sang that lyric;
Maybe, if Hafez sings sweetly enough,
The thread will break— scatter the constellation
Of the Pleiades.

Ghazal 10

Our Pir abandoned the mosque last night
And headed for the tavern instead!
Now what should his poor disciples do?
How can we face toward the Kaaba
When our Teacher can't face in any direction at all
Except toward the Winemaster?
I suppose we'll have to take up residence
In the Tavern of the Fire-worshipper;
That must have been our destiny
Since before the beginning of time.

Locked in that lock,
In the hangman's noose of that dark hair,
His heart is happy.
(The wise would lose their minds
If wisdom only knew.)

One day, my heart
Caught the bird of peace in its snare—
Then, you let down your hair.
Unaware of the trembling of my hand,
I let the bird go.

When I saw the beauty of your face
Suddenly I understood the meaning of a verse of the
Qur'an
That had long eluded me:

Ever since that night, grace and beauty
Have been the whole of my exegesis.

What has one night
Of sighs raining like fire—
What has the fire of the heart
Burning in the blackness of one night ever accomplished
Against the stone of your heart?

When the wind ruffled the mass of your hair,
The world before me turned black.
Passion for that hair of yours (to speak of anything further
would dishonour me)
Shot my sigh like an arrow
Across the border of the sky.
Have mercy on your soul, Hafez. Keep silent.
Avoid the arrow of your friends.
Since our Pir has turned into a drunkard,
I'll sleep every night in the doorway of his tavern—
Like Hafez.

Ghazal 17

The morning blossoms, and immediately the cloud conceals it
under her veil.
The cup of the morning, my friends! The morning cup!

The face of the tulip is withered
In the grip of the frost—wine, my friends! Bring wine!

From the meadow the breeze of Paradise is blowing,
So drink pure wine—without pause, without end.

The rose has set her emerald throne in the centre of the
meadow—

Bring wine red as ruby, wine red as fire!

The tavern door, again they've closed it—
Open it for us, you Opener of Doors!
It's amazing how quickly they rush to close it,
And always at a time like this!

Your ruby lip holds the rights of salt
Against those whose wounded hearts
Are roasted on a spit;

Let the ascetic drink wine like the reveller;
Let the wise fear God.

If your quest is for the water of life
Then drink sweet wine to the sound of the harp;

If you boldly seek for life like Alexander,
Then take as your trophy
The crimson lip of the Beloved.

To the memory of the Saki, formed like the youths of
Paradise
Drink pure wine in the season of the rose.

Don't grieve, Hafez; your fortune has been told:
Some day the Beloved will lift for you
The corner of the veil.

Ghazal 18

The morning of good fortune has come!
Where is the bowl, beaten and burnished like the sun?
Bring the cup quickly, for opportunity knocks.

In this house without strife, the Cupbearer is my friend
And subtle wisdom flows
From the minstrel's lips.

It is the season of youth, the hour of ease;
From hand to hand, the cup goes round.

This cup of gold was mixed with the ruby elixir
Only to expand the heart, to adorn it with the jewel
Of beauty and of gladness.

The drunken ones are dancing, the Beloved and his
minstrel are waving their arms
In time to the music;
The Saki has stolen sleep from every eye.

This house of safety, this secret cell, this hidden chamber
of pleasure
Where best friends meet—
Whoever has found his way into our company
Has found the locked and guarded house
Where a hundred doors stand open.

Thinking to add even further grace to the essence of wine
The subtle breeze, Nature's coutourier
Placed rose-water in the leaf of the rose.

When I knew that the Full Moon had paid with his soul for
those pearls of Hafez,
In that very moment, the sharp twang of the lute
Touched the ear of Zuhra!

Javad Nurbakhsh's fifteen-volume encyclopaedia *Sufi Symbolism* has over
sixty references relating to wine. Each one of these has a specific symbolic
meaning, most often referring to a known and defined *hal* or spiritual state.
I have not been able to find an English transliteration of Hafez' *Divan*, and the

rules for transliterating Persian into English are not standardised in any case, so it may be that not all the following attributions strictly apply to the specific terms that appear in Wilberforce Clarke's translations or my 'transcreations'. Nonetheless, in surveying them, we can begin to get an idea of the vast compendium of traditional symbology that Hafez drew upon.

According to *Sufi Symbolism*, *ruby wine* 'is said to symbolise tidings of the Beloved and the pleasurable savour of love'. *Pure wine* 'refers to pure, unadulterated pleasure which distances the Sufi from his egoistic identity.' *Bitter wine* 'is said to denote an overpowering love which divests the Sufi of the fictional character of his being.' The *dreg-drinker* 'is said to represent a perfect Sufi who is too preoccupied with God's love to attend to his personal suffering, enduring to live in complete deprivation.' *Morning wine* traditionally symbolises 'conversation (*mohadatha*)....which refers to God's discourse through formal means in the visible world, the particular instance of which was His address to Moses through the burning bush.' Continue on and you come across *Musky wine,* which 'is said to symbolise a theophany of the Divine Actions'. At times we read of the *pitcher* (*sabu*) who traditionally represents 'certain formal limitations, particularly those pertaining to identification with oneself', while the *beaker* (*piyala*) 'symbolises various individual determinations of Being (*ta'ayyonat-e hasti*), each of which acts as a mirror of God.' The *Saki* 'symbolises the Absolute Beloved as well as the master of the Spiritual Path'; and the *wine seller* has the same meaning. The *wine cup* 'is said to symbolise the heart of the Sufi' while the *wine glass* represents 'the gnostic's heart and the go-between (*wasetah*) between the lover and the Beloved'. When we read of the *tavern* we are understanding it 'symbolises the heart of the perfect Sufi, the master who has realised union with God, and the house of the Sufi master (*khaneqah*)'. The *harp* 'is said to symbolise the perfection of amorous yearning and spiritual savor, which is manifested to the wayfarer in the phase of his innermost consciousness'. The *lute* represents 'universal love and the fullness of yearning and passionate love which is experienced in the phase of the spirit.' The *minstrel* 'is said to represent the 'raiser of consciousness'.' whereas *singer* (*moghanni*)—exemplified by Zuhra—'is said to symbolise the harbinger of graces.' Many more images, such as *Zoroastrian* and *the wine-cup as divinatory mirror* have similarly specific meanings.

So we can see here that the true meaning of wine and its accoutrements in Sufi poetry can only be truly understood according to the science of the *ahwal*, the spiritual states, in particular the state of Intoxication. Spiritual Intoxication is the merging of subject and object so that the experiencer is no longer distinguished from his or her experience; consequently the world as a separate reality disappears. In the state of Intoxication, the overwhelming rapture of Allah's Presence paralyses both thought and will. Thought cannot encompass Him, nor can the will will anything unless He wills it first. The ability to fulfill one's duties, worldly or religious, is swept away, proving that even the most impeccable faithfulness to legal and moral standards cannot command Allah's Mercy nor avert His Justice, and that when religion becomes defined and conditioned by the World, the *Dunya*, when the pursuit of and identification with religion constitutes membership in the *Dunya*, the only ones who truly remain faithful to Allah are those who are drunk and ruined. Intoxication is the *malamati* way, the Path of Blame, the road to liberation from the false shame of the World, from the chains of hypocrisy and the prison of social pride.

Intoxication is the obliteration of all claims to separate existence in the Presence of God. The state of Intoxication dissolves the knots and crystallisations of the affections that are produced by the heedlessness and fixed ideas of the impure intellect and the impulses and refusals of the impure will. In the state of Drunkenness the affections are overwhelmed with the rapture of Divine Love, and both the will and the intellect helplessly submit to this Love. Through this submission to rapturous Love the will moves beyond the station of raw will-power—which cannot be maintained for any length of time and can be destructive if it becomes an obsession—and gains the power to *love what it intends,* and intend it more forcefully, thus producing constancy in both interpersonal relations and spiritual practice. And the intellect, through its own submission to this rapturous Love, gains the power to come into true intimacy with the Object of its knowledge, and so learns to *love what it knows*, and through this love to know It more deeply. Intoxication dissolves the deficient, excessive and imbalanced connections between thought, feeling and will; consequently the use of music and poetry in Sufism is not some kind of sentimentality or spiritual self-indulgence (though it can certainly degenerate into these) but rather a *science of Intoxication* to be employed only at the appropriate time and for the appropriate purposes—a method for dissolving, by the power of Allah, the knots and crystallisations of the feeling-substance (its *egos*, its *idols*) so that the energy of liberated emotion can give substance and depth to the intellect to *know* Allah, and also feed and strengthen the will to *obey* Allah. Intoxication qualifies the Heart with the virtues of sincerity, Divine eros (*ishq*), renunciation of the world, humility, and trust in God.

The metaphysical principle behind the state of Intoxication is a reflection, in the spiritual Heart, of the reality that God is Love; it is an expression of Allah in His Name *Al-Fattah*, the Opener, *Al-Karim*, the Generous, and *Al-Wadud*, the Loving-kind. Love is the source of insight, but Love in Intoxication transcends insight, and bewilders it. Love is the source of loyalty, but Intoxicated Love—the Rapturous Love known as *Ishq*—by the profusion of its Generosity, swallows up loyalty, providing it with no fixed object to which it might remain loyal. Intoxication is a Divine infusion that arrives from beyond human feeling—and since it transcends feeling, it has the power to suffuse feeling, to transform it from this or that emotion, directed to this or that object, into *pure* feeling, feeling which is its own object. Intoxication is Love without a Lover, Love in which there is nothing but the Beloved—a state in which Love for the Beloved is not directed *to* the Beloved, but *is* the Beloved.

Every spiritual state is based on, and demands, a particular mode of *taslim* or submission to God. The practice of taslim in the state of Intoxication is to renounce all attempts to decide for yourself what to do next—even in terms of trying to show Allah how much you love Him—but to place yourself instead, with absolute trust, in the hands of the One who knows how to guide you, protect you in the darkness, and lead you safely to your destination, in the hour before dawn.

That said, it is also important to realise that Intoxication, like every spiritual state, is capable of being hijacked and counterfeited by the *nafs*, the ego. Intoxication from the standpoint of the ego is discourtesy, recklessness, heedlessness, the rejection of Knowledge, insolent presumption upon God's favour, and the pursuit of oblivion in flight from Reality—which is, precisely, flight from Allah. It is based not on a renunciation of our claims to separate existence, but on a repression and denial of them, a glossing-over of them in a state of self-interested amnesia. It is a way of enveloping these claims with darkness and unconsciousness so as to prevent them from being exposed and dissolved.

Furthermore, with all this talk of wine and rapture and ecstasy, it is equally important to realise that neither Sufism nor the human spiritual enterprise as a whole can be strictly identified with spiritual Intoxication. The 'sober Sufis', like al-Junaid, have always considered states of spiritual Intoxication to be dangerous, and so they are; if the *nafs* gets hold of the Spiritual Wine it can go on quite a bender, even without the help of the 'real' wine fermented from the grape. The 'drunken Sufis', however—like Mansur al-Hallaj and Bayazid al-Bistami—know of a secret at the centre of Intoxication that the sober Sufis have never suspected; the name of that secret is....*Sobriety*. In the science of *Tasawwuf*, Intoxication is always paired with Sobriety, which is considered in many ways the higher state. The exclusive pursuit of Intoxication—as, indeed, the *pursuit* of any spiritual state, seeing that true states are gifts of God, not trophies of human effort—will guarantee that the traveller will fall into a false, deluded Intoxication, the ego's counterfeit. In the words of Hafez,

> No-one hunts the Anka, so dismantle your trap;
> Nothing remains in the hand of the snare
> But the wind.

Sobriety is a necessary complement to Intoxication because only in a humble, cool, self-contained, realistic and balanced state of Heart can the errors, delusions and passions hidden inside Intoxication be brought to light, understood, and dispelled. Without Intoxication, any true intimacy with God will be hard to come by, but unless Intoxication is transcended at one point, the traveller is in danger of mistaking his own intense *reactions* to God for God Himself, becoming thereby a self-idolator; the Qur'anic verse *Shall I show you one who makes desire his god?* (Q. 45:23) also applies to the science of spiritual states. When God brings us the gift of spiritual Intoxication it is highly discourteous to reject it; it is equally discourteous, however, to hold on to it when God is intent on giving us, and requiring of us, something else entirely. And Sobriety itself, to the discerning, carries a kind of subtle intoxication of its own, like breaking a long and difficult fast with a sip of fragrant jasmine tea. As I expressed it in one of my own couplets:

> Better the wine of the desert
> Than the desert born of wine.

OUR KITCHEN IN 1940s BAGHDAD

Sami Zubaida

The house of my childhood in Baghdad had two courtyards, *haush*, Middle Eastern style. The larger one was the centre of the main living area, with rooms and terraces arranged around it on two levels. The smaller *haush* was the kitchen area, *beit al-matbakh*, with a room on one side containing a range of kerosene-fuelled rings at ground level, and in one corner a wood-burning boiler for the attached Turkish-style hammam. Beside the boiler was a *kanoun*, a square frame of stone and plaster over which pots could be placed over wood and coal burning in the middle, mostly for slow cooking when the fuel was reduced to embers and ash. This is where the Saturday *tebit* of stuffed chicken and rice was cooked overnight.

In one corner of the kitchen courtyard was a *tanour*, better known globally as tandur, a clay pot built into a metal oil drum (more commonly built into the wall) with an opening at the bottom where a wood fire burned heating up the clay walls. Flat rounds of dough were stuck on the walls to make *khubuz*, flat bread, *jeradiq*, thin, crisp flat bread, and *makhbouz* or *keleicha*, sweetened and buttered dough pastries, stuffed with cheese, dates or almond and sugar. Sambousak was the name of the crescent-shaped pastries stuffed with cheese or almond/sugar (distinct from the *sambousak bil-tawa*, larger folds of dough stuffed with heavily spiced and onioned mashed chick-peas, then fried in hot oil, more akin to the Indian samosa). *Bu`bu`* (plural, *bu`abe`*) was the round bready pastry stuffed with date paste.

Elsewhere in that courtyard more kerosene rings, chopping boards and knives and pestle and mortars, *hawan*, of various sizes were to be found. There was no oven: domestic ovens are recent innovations in many parts of the world. Banquet dishes, of meat or fish, on large trays, were sent to neighbourhood bakers' ovens, also a common practice elsewhere. On special occasions a lamb would be slaughtered over the drain in the courtyard and butchered there by a hired specialist.

Between the two courtyards stood a store-room where hessian sacks of rice, sugar and flour were stored, as well as drums of oil and various packets of other provisions. We children played in that room and were once delighted to find a large cache of chocolate bars (was it forgotten by the adults?). That was during the rationing period following the Second World War and so especially welcome. Also in that room was the ice box, and later the electric Frigidaire. The ice box was a wooden cupboard with various compartments, lined with zinc, in which a block of ice, delivered periodically from the factory, would be placed, wrapped in hessian, and food and drink distributed around it in the compartments. The arrival of the electric fridge was a joy, especially in the Baghdad summer months, with unlimited supply of cold water and sherbets, as well as the coveted ice creams, previously only available from specialist shops or itinerant pedlars shouting *Eskimo!*, the trade name of the popular ice. These were the spatial parameters of my childhood food world. It was presided over by my mother and her mother, the latter a diminutive and quiet woman who seldom left the house. In her last years in the London home of her son she was bewildered, her horizons having always been domestic and local: her grandchildren took it in turn to granny-sit. She was a good domestic cook, as was my mother. They were aided by one or two resident maids (who lodged in corner spaces around the kitchen, where mattresses were spread at night), as well as the younger women of the household, in preparation of chopping, mincing and pounding (endless, loud pounding) and in cleaning and tidying up.

Shopping and provisioning were male tasks. At one point it was an elderly maternal uncle staying in our house (thrown out, we were told, by his vicious wife) who undertook the early morning trip to the markets for meat and fresh products. My father would shop for the 'dry goods' from the main bazaar, the Shorja (an Arabisation of the Turkish Carse), on his way back from work. Meat was bought from a *kasher* butcher in the Hannouni market (largely Jewish), who had a long-standing relationship with the family. The butcher would get to know your requirements and deal as honestly as possible to keep your custom. Even then, the cooks were not always satisfied with the quality or the cuts. Meat was not sold as specific cuts of leg or shoulder, for instance, but as lean or fat, with or without bone. Fruit and vegetables also came from that market.

Fish, an occasional treat, was always bought live from a fisherman on the nearby cornice of the Tigris. *Shabbout*, a kind of barbell, was the fish of choice (now largely fished out, after being monopolised by Saddam Hussein and his entourage), or slices of a very large fish called *bizz*. A large Shabbout was a banquet dish, cooked in domestic imitation of the iconic *mazgouf*, barbecued, typically by river bank eateries or fishermen, much prized in Iraq and considered a 'national' dish.

The fish would be opened flat, like a kipper, by cutting it along the backbone and gutting it at the belly. It would then be skewered on twigs, the twigs stuck into the sandy ground, so that the fish stood vertically to face the fire ignited by its side, thus grilled on the open side, it was then laid flat with the skin side on the hot ashes and embers of the fire. It was served seasoned with strong spices, sometimes curry powder or chilli, with tomatoes and onions in the middle, enriched with the inevitable ʿanba, mango pickle.

The domestic version followed this closely, except that the cooking was done in a neighbouring baker's oven. This would also be the centrepiece of dinner parties to which we were invited in non-Jewish homes, the thoughtful hosts mindful of Jewish abstention from non-kasher meats. The *bizz* pieces would be cooked as a *salona*, braised with onions, tomatoes and spices, with slightly sweet and sour flavouring. Fish was always special, not an everyday food.

Milk would be delivered from dairy farms on the outskirts of Baghdad. The quality and purity of the milk was a matter of constant concern, for good reasons. At one time we acquired a share in a cow, and the milkman would bring us our portion of the milk in an urn carried on a donkey. Did he, at one point, actually bring the cow itself and milk it on our doorstep, or is that a trick of memory? In any case I detested milk, which I was pressured to drink, largely because it had to be boiled, and the smell and taste of that boiled milk was repugnant to me. While adults drank their breakfast tea plain, with sugar, or with a drop of milk, English style, we children were required to drink boiled milk with a hint of strong tea. Condensed milk, in tins, was a boon.

Yoghurt was mostly made at home, sometimes drained in linen bags. Occasionally we bought rich, thick, buffalo milk yoghurt, as well as *gaimer*, thick clotted cream (the word being the Iraqi corruption of the Turkish *kaymak*, known elsewhere in the Arab world as *qishta*) from the Bedouin women who kept water buffaloes in the shanty town of rural migrants from the Marshes in the south. The *gaimer*, combined with *dibis*, date syrup, on fresh, hot *khubuz*, flat bread, washed down with strong tea (no milk), made a dreamy breakfast, the stuff of nostalgia. I, alongside some other Iraqis in London, try occasionally to reproduce this taste with English clotted cream and imported date syrup, on flat bread: good, but not quite the same.

After dinner of an evening, my grandmother and mother would discuss forthcoming menus and specify their shopping requirements, noted by my father and whoever was detailed to do the markets.

On school days we kids arrived at lunch time, hungry, and would walk directly to the kitchen house to see what is cooking. Almost every day, the pervasive aroma was that of chopped onions frying in pungent sesame oil. This was the final step in cooking rice. The rice would be picked over for small stones and other impurities in large trays with a servant sifting and throwing the grains from one side to the other. It was then washed and soaked, drained and thrown into a pot of boiling water, drained when nearly ready and put back in the pan. Finally, the fried onions would be poured over the rice, then covered and allowed to steam. With an aromatic, native variety of rice called '*anbar*, amber, it made for a fragrant, nutty taste.

This rice was a feature of almost every lunch and sometimes dinner. With it would be served a stew, typically of lamb or chicken with various vegetables and condiments, and sometimes with dumplings of rice and meat called *kibbah*. The simplest would be lamb, in pieces on the bone, with beans, green or white/dried, *fasoulia*. Our favourite was the lunch made every Friday, a *bamia*/okra stew with lamb and kibbah. This was called *hamidh*, sour, which was half the story, as this was sweet and sour, many families appreciating ultra-sweet tastes, achieved with sugar or date syrup. The sour would be lemon, vinegar, and/or dried limes, *noumi* basra, whole or ground. The dumplings/kibbah were made by pounding rice and a little meat or chicken in a mortar, then shaping portions into little balls stuffed with a mixture of ground meat, onion and herbs, which were cooked in the sauce. This sauce was the meat juice with tomato paste, sweet and sour agents, mint or penny royal and garlic. The meat for this dish would be typically fatty, usually ribs. The very characteristic aromas of bamia, mint and garlic, would assail the Jewish neighbourhoods of Baghdad every Friday at midday.

An occasional alternative to the bamia in the *hamidh* would be chopped beetroot. But there was always bamia, all the year round: fresh bamia in season would be threaded on strings, like necklaces, and dried for use out of season. This is done all over the Middle East and parts of Africa.

Another rice kibbah, usually of larger size and flatter shape, was put into 'sweet' stews, *helou*, as against *hamidh*, sour. This did not contain sugar or a sweetener, and was only 'sweet' in that it was not 'sour'. Typically this would be a stew of squash and/or aubergine with meat. The blandness of the stew contrasted with the sourness and spiciness of the kibbah, its meaty stuffing flavoured with ground dried lime and black pepper.

For Jewish households several days of the week were marked by dishes. Thursday evening was always *kitchri*, a spicy pulau of rice and lentils, of Indian origin. Following the Friday lunch preparations described above, Friday evening and Saturday saw Sabbath dishes, dominated by chicken. The Friday evening *qaddous* ceremony (the blessing of the vine and the bread) culminated in a dinner in which the primary dish was a chicken pulau (*plaw b-jeej*). The chicken, in pieces, was first boiled: chickens were tough, especially when freshly killed, which was the custom.

Even when modern industrial chickens arrived people could not believe that you can roast or fry chicken without first boiling it. Rice would be boiled in the chicken stock, with tomato paste (red rice) and light seasoning. The chicken pieces were then fried in oil to give them colour and crisp the skin. Peeled almonds and raisins were fried in the same pan, then everything was placed over the rice and served. Each member of the family had his or her favoured piece of the chicken: mine was the drumstick. Girls were given the wings so that they would fly to their matrimonial homes!

Saturday meals revolved around chicken, but in a different form, called *tebit*, indicating 'overnight' cooking. The chicken was stuffed with rice, chopped meat and/or giblets, seasoned with salt and black pepper. To 'extend' the chicken in some households, including ours, the bird was skinned, retaining the skin, before being cut in half horizontally into breast and back, then the skin sewed with needle and thread over each half to create two pouches, which were stuffed. The pieces were boiled in a stock mixed with tomato paste and aromatic spices: pepper, cloves, cardamom and perhaps cinnamon. When the chicken was nearly cooked a quantity of rice was added to the stock under the meat. This was done on a Friday afternoon. A wood fire was lit in the kanoon and reduced to embers. The large pot containing the chicken/rice was then placed over the embers, covered with old blankets and cushions and allowed to cook overnight. The embers were calculated to die slowly by morning or midday on Saturday, while the covers retained the heat. By the time it was ready to serve there was no fire so that cooks committed no ritual sin by handling fire on a Saturday. The *tebit* was served with portions of chicken meat and the two forms of rice: the dry, peppered stuffing rice and a pudding cake of the surrounding rice, slightly crusted at the bottom, aromatic and rich with the chicken juices. This Saturday dish was emblematic of the Jewish household, and much admired by our Muslim and Christian neighbours, who would occasionally be sent samples.

Tebit eggs (*beidh al-tebit*), were placed on the rim of the same pan, under the covers, to cook slowly in the steam, giving the resulting hard-boiled egg a mahogany colour and a smoky flavour. These were enjoyed at breakfast, when the men returned from the synagogue and before we kids departed for the morning matinee at the cinema, an indication of the mixture of religious observance and errant secularism that prevailed amongst most Jews in those days. The eggs would be eaten with bread and salad, sometimes with aubergine slices that had been fried the day before, and the quintessential Baghdadi relish of '*anba*, mango pickle from India. This pickle was so popular amongst us kids that we even ate it in sandwiches, to the concern of adults worried about our digestive systems.

GOURMET FUTURES

Colin Tudge

We're told, as a billion people remain hungry and human numbers continue to rise and the biosphere collapses around our ears (mass extinction, global warming) that we must curb population growth by whatever it takes, and that those who are left must curb their appetites. To be responsible citizens (we are told) we must learn to eat austerely. Ideally, we should all strive to be vegan. Our lust for meat (it's assumed that we have a lust for meat) must be satisfied with ersatz muscle spun from the proteins of beans or fungi and possibly microbes – or, which is the latest high-tech dream, our technologists must create a simulacrum of animal flesh in the laboratory from cultures of suitably doctored animal cells. Austerity with high-tech: that's the message from the oligarchy of big governments (like Britain's), corporates, and their supporting intellectuals (scientists and economists) who now dominate our lives.

The gentle art and craft of gastronomy – the preparation and appreciation of great food – is seen essentially to be frivolous. A luxury. Elitist. Gastronomy is taken seriously in sombre circles only insofar as it has become big business. Some chefs become celebs but the millions – billions – of workaday cooks who toil in their tiny kitchens to feed their families are seriously underrated. A whole industry has grown up to replace their efforts with whatever can be put in cans, or frozen, or de-hydrated, and sent without too much deterioration from the factory to the supermarket to be resuscitated and heated up as and when.

But as almost always is the case in all things, it seems that in matters relating to food and farming the truth is almost the precise opposite of the advice and pressure that comes down to us from on high. Rising population is a problem but there is no need to panic. The percentage rate of increase is falling and numbers should level by 2050 or so at about 10 billion –

which is a lot but should certainly be manageable. And – which is the point of this article – we absolutely do not need to be austere, or not at least in the conventional sense. People in rich societies should certainly eat less meat but that should not be a hardship and we certainly don't need to vegan. What we really do need is the very thing that is seen to be a luxury – gastronomy; that, and the craft that modern food technology seems largely to be designed to replace – cookery.

Indeed, the world's food and farming strategy should not as now be led by politicians and economists or even by scientists (though scientists of the right kind have essential roles to play) but by farmers and cooks. The future belongs not to the ascetic, to the high-tech equivalent of the Desert Fathers, living on seeds and insects, but to the gourmet – the gastronome; the person who really cares about food in all its variety and wonder, and will take the time to seek it out, and pay the proper price for whatever is good. Gastronomy isn't just for TV chefs, fat cats, and celebs but in truth is the most important human pursuit of all, at least of a material kind. Indeed, we would do well to build our entire economy around it.

All this may seem outrageous. But if we break down the issues one by one, questioning all the suppositions that now underpin world thinking in food and farming (and indeed in everything else) we see that it is so. Thus:

We don't need more food

Present-day farming strategy is geared to production: production, production, production. As is typical of the *genre*, a highly influential report from the British government in 2011 on *The Future of Food and Farming* declared that we need to produce 50 per cent more food by 2050 just to keep pace with rising numbers and 'rising demand' – particularly the supposed demand for more meat. Others since have upped the ante and call for 100 per cent more by 2100. How could it not be so? The present population stands at 7 billion plus and a billion of them are undernourished, according to the UN. But numbers continue to rise and by 2050 there will be 9 to 10 billion. Furthermore, as societies grow richer people 'demand' more meat. The big cities of China now heave with burger and fried chicken 'outlets' – because (self-evidently!) that's what people want. The traditional bowl of rice with bits and bobs is for the peasants. Backward-looking. Obsolete.

Furthermore, the vast extra quantities of food we need can be provided only with high tech, and can be made affordable to the masses only by scaling up. So we need industrial farming with big machines, industrial chemistry, and biotech (genetic engineering), on the largest possible scale. The small peasant farm is obsolete, too. The proof is in the stats. Modern arable farms in East Anglia may produce 15 tonnes of wheat per hectare (in a good year, if the price is right). Traditional Third World farms –like most of Britain's farms 100 years ago – are and were content with two or so tonnes per hectare.

But a little more arithmetic shows the lie of all this. Thus, the world now produces around 2.5 billion tonnes of cereals per year (wheat and rice are the leaders) and since one tonne provided enough calories *and protein* for three people for a year, that's enough for 7.5 billion people. Cereals are by far the most important crops but even so they account for only half our protein and energy. The other half comes from non-cereal grains, pulses, nuts (especially coconuts), tubers, fruits, fish and meat. Put cereals and the rest together and we have enough for 14 billion-plus. By 2050 on present trends the percentage rate of increase of human numbers per annum should be down to zero – which means that numbers should stabilise. After that, if the trend continues, numbers should start to go down. By 2050 humans will number 10 billion or so. So we already produce 40 per cent more food than we should ever need. The continued emphasis on production has nothing to do with real need and everything to do with commerce: profit.

In truth the emphasis must now shift, wholesale, from production to sustainability and resilience – and to kindness (to animals and people) and social justice. The key to all of these is low-input farming, which really means organic; and diversity. In general, the more diverse an ecosystem is – or a farm – the more it can survive changing conditions, and the quicker it can recover after set-backs. If farms are organic and diverse they are obviously complex and need lots of tender loving care – plenty of small farmers and growers. With enterprises that are complex and skills-intensive there is little or no advantage in scale-up so the kind of farms that really meet the needs of the present and the future should in general be small to medium sized. Thus the farms we really need are the precise opposite of the high-tech, profit-driven, huge industrial monocultures that we are being told are *de rigueur,* and in both Europe and the US are massively subsidised with our (taxpayers') money.

But can small, mixed, essentially traditional farms produce enough? Well, worldwide, they still feed 70 per cent of the world's population, even though they receive little or no support from the powers-that-be and are often actively done down. There is growing evidence to show, too, that with support – usually economic and logistic rather than technical – many or most traditional farms could readily double or even triple their present output, and still remain people and wildlife-friendly.

In addition, of course, it's now known that people in the richest countries habitually throw away a third of their food even after it has reached the kitchen – largely, I suggest, because they have forgotten how to cook (or don't have time for it) and don't know how to use leftovers. Even worse, about half the world's grain is now fed to livestock – which is why so many thinking people now suggest that we need to give up eating meat. But again, the thinking is muddled.

Meat

We should not, of course, feed more than a small proportion of cereals and pulses to livestock – staple foods that we could perfectly well eat ourselves. But that doesn't mean we shouldn't eat meat at all, or that livestock has no part to play in future agriculture.

The trouble, as always, lies with false ideals (the powers that be are trying to do the wrong things) and above all with the fixation on profit. Today's agriculture, and indeed the whole food chain, is designed not to provide everyone with good food (while keeping the biosphere in good heart, and creating agreeable, flourishing rural communities) but with maximising and concentrating wealth.

Thus, the true roles of livestock should be as they are in traditional farming. Omnivorous animals – poultry and pigs – should in the main be raised on leftovers and surpluses. They should live on the farm, cultivating the fields and eating the parasites after harvesting. In Britain and still in many traditional societies pigs in particular were kept expressly for this purpose. The meat they provided at intervals was simply a bonus. The herbivorous livestock – mainly sheep and cattle – were and are kept on land that is too steep or rocky or dry or wet or cold or hot or windy to make it possible or at least worthwhile to grow arable crops, vegetables, or fruit.

In short – very obviously – the way to ensure that we produce enough food for everyone, with minimum collateral damage, is to focus on arable (to supply the bulk of protein and calories) and on horticulture (for micronutrients, flavour, and texture) and to employ animals primarily, or exclusively, as fillers in. If animals are kept as fillers-in then they *add* to our total food supply, as well as making it more interesting. They become profligate and unsustainable only if we seek to produce as many animals as possible so as to maximise profit.

But this is where the powers-that-be become self-righteous. For, they say, if we raised animals only as fillers-in then we would not produce very much; far less than we do now, when they are given a billion tonnes or so of grain a year in industrial feed lots. But we have a duty to produce loads of meat, say the powers-that-be. For people given half a chance *demand* meat; and it is a key principle of democracy that public demand should be met. Those who call for less are elitist 'eco-fascists'.

This is yet more muddled thinking of a tendentious kind. The intellectuals who advise the world's political and commercial leaders seem to suspend their critical faculties when they hear the rattle of the till.

The great serendipities

Is it really true, for a start, that people, when un-pressured, actively *demand* meat? I have seen demonstrations the world over with placards demanding better pay and conditions, or justice for oppressed peoples or for animal rights, but I know of no campaigns to demand more meat. Of course people *like* meat. It's tasty, and quick and easy: the original fast food. It's true, too, that if you are underfed then meat – high in calories as well as protein, and able to make good various mineral deficiencies – can just hit the spot. Percy Bysshe Shelley became a vegetarian in the early nineteenth century before nutritional know-how and modern retail made this a safe option, and grew thinner and paler, until his friend the novelist Thomas Love Peacock advised him to eat 'three mutton chops with pepper'.

But meat has many other connotations that have nothing to do with nutrition – or, necessarily, with flavour. In times of austerity – as in most of China for most of the twentieth century, and as in the US during the Depression – meat becomes a symbol of affluence and success. Meat, available and affordable, was a sign that the bad times are over. Modern commercial propaganda really does work, too, which is why companies spend so much on it. The people of Beijing may well be eating burgers and fried chicken in part because they like it but in large measure too it's a reaction to their own history and because, now, it is the smart thing to do. We need not assume a positive 'demand'. Among those who are used to wealth, in California and Germany, it's fashionable to be vegetarian. Fashion – social pressure – trumps innate, hypothetical, predisposition.

If we designed agriculture as if we really wanted to provide everyone with good food then we would focus on arable and horticulture, with livestock only to fill in the gaps, and so we would produce plenty of plants, not much meat, and – because of the focus on diversity – maximum variety. Present-day industrial agriculture is almost entirely the opposite: as much meat as possible, and very little diversity. Industrial chemistry and big machinery lead us to monoculture. The apparent variety we see in supermarkets is largely spurious – artful permutations of a few crops that are easily grown on the commercial scale, including maize, soya, and rapeseed.

But here we encounter a series of serendipities. For 'plenty of plants, not much meat, and maximum variety' – just nine words – encapsulates the essence of *all* the most reliable nutritional theory of the past sixty years, which recommends diets that in general are low in fat, moderate in protein, high in fibre, and as diverse as possible. Diversity is needed to provide us not only with the minerals and vitamins that we know about but also with the newly recognised class of micro-micro nutrients which the food industry calls 'functional foods' and the pharmaceutical industry calls 'nutraceuticals' and I prefer to call 'cryptonutrients'. They include agents such as plant sterols which are not vital, but do seem to lower blood cholesterol; and all the many thousands of recondite materials produced by microbial fermentation, found in pickles and live

yoghurt and real cheese. There are far too many of these minutiae ever
to analyse exhaustively but modern studies suggest that we should seek
to imbibe as many and as much as possible – through a diet that is as
diverse as possible.

In short, good farming – designed expressly to provide us with *enough*
food without wrecking the biosphere – is entirely compatible with the best
nutritional theory. If we grow well, we can eat well.

But there is a further – very large – serendipity. For all the world's
greatest cuisines and almost all traditional cuisines *are* primarily plant-
based and use meat (and offals and bones and fish and so on) only sparingly:
as garnish and for stock. Meat is eaten in bulk only occasionally, for feasts.
This is true in general of near and Middle Eastern cuisines (Turkish,
Persian, Indian, Chinese, Thai) and of course of all of Asia and the
traditional cuisines of the Mediterranean (Italy and Southern France). A
typical meal from Turkey to South-East Asia is a pile of rice and or various
wheat-based breads with whatever nuts and vegetables grow locally and
are in season (which in the tropics means year-round) with spices and
herbs – and small fragments of meat and or fish, and molluscs and
crustaceans, if and when they are available. The result even in a modest
household is, or can be, a meal fit for a sultan.

Historically, too, even the cuisines of northern Europe were far more
plant-based than they are now, with heavy emphasis on cereals (wheat,
barley, oats) and, from the eighteenth century onwards, on potatoes –
plus a whole host of seasonable vegetables and fruits. Wheat-based pies
and pastries abounded, and thick soups. The 'roast', traditionally, was the
centre-piece of the British diet, at least for the yeoman class – but the
roast was only for Sundays. On Monday cold meats were served and any
left after that became shepherd's pie (one of my favourites). Animals still
had fat on in those days and bread-and-dripping was a treat – as indeed are
chips cooked in dripping. I am old enough to remember that tradition and
very good it was too. A fatty shoulder of lamb, raised on the hills on
natural herbs, or on the sea-shore on salt-marsh, was a thing of wonder.
Nowadays butchers and chefs (alas) favour meat that is lean, (and hence,
often, all but flavourless, or at least anonymous). Chickens were food for
the Gods. Chicken was expensive – but it was eaten only a few times a
year; a real treat.

Today's farmers could farm in the traditional ways – seasonal, local, various – if only they could be sure to sell their produce. We, the consumers – not the wholesalers who feed the supermarkets – can and must supply the necessary markets. But consumers won't take the trouble to seek out the kind of foods that are really good for us, grown in ways that are good for the biosphere, and with justice for the farmers, unless we really care about food. We need truly to appreciate fruit and vegetables grown within a few miles and in season; cattle and sheep raised on natural pastures on the uplands and by the sea; chickens that have spent fairly long lives scratching to find a more or less natural diet.

In other words, we, the consumers, have to be gourmets: gastronomes. The kind of farming we really need must be guided by principles of ecology and morality of course – but led and encouraged by a true appreciation of food. Thus gastronomy emerges not as an indulgence, a frivolity, but as the *sine qua non*; in some ways the most important pursuit of all.

Coda

Some will say that all of the above is junk. For in truth only the rich can *afford* to be gourmets. Most people need cheap food, and to keep prices down food must be produced in industrial ways and sold on the industrial scale through supermarkets. Only a middle-class elitist could write an article like this one. There are many among the powers-that-be who make this very argument. You might not like what we do, they say, but it is *necessary*. The kind of farming I am recommending here would cost far too much and would condemn many more people to hunger.

But this is perhaps the most specious and deceptive argument of all. For in truth, of all the money spent on food in supermarkets, less than 20 per cent goes to the farmer. The rest goes to the food chain itself. A high proportion – perhaps most – of all the money spent on food – the 20 per cent the farmer gets and the 80 per cent that goes to the supermarket and the middle-men – goes to the bankers, who loan the money to buy or rent the shamefully overpriced land and all the machinery needed to scale-up and industrialise. Industrialised farming depends entirely on oil and oil is as cheap as it seems to be only because the price is adjusted so that it is always just affordable. Many people in Britain can't afford supermarket food (a million resort to food-banks, though Britain is the world's fifth richest economy) – but largely because they are obliged to spend so much on housing. Food prices are adjusted, too – the 'free' market is an illusion – and it is impossible to establish a reasonable price when, as in Britain, the top ten per cent are nearly twenty times richer than the bottom ten per cent, and the top one per cent are a thousand times richer.

In short, industrial agriculture now seems cheaper than the kind we really need only because the economy is biased so strongly in its favour, making the rich richer and the poor poorer. With suitable economic tweaks food produced on small mixed farms and sold locally should be *cheaper* than the kind supported by armies of accountants and managers and battalions of lorries and fork-lift trucks *and* support rural economies and societies *and* be wildlife friendly. It's all within the compass of governments to make the necessary changes. Or, since governments of the present kind have forgotten what they are there for, and have ceded so much of their power and our sovereignty to the corporates, we can and must do what needs doing for ourselves – working in general not as individuals but as communities.

Clearly, though, we can't put agriculture to rights (or anything else) unless we re-think the economy from first principles. Certainly, neoliberalism won't do. But whether we do re-think the economy or leave things as they are (until there is a major uprising and/or the biosphere collapses) we do need to recognise that we can never have the kind of farming the world really needs until and unless people at large take food seriously and support the farmers and growers who really are trying to do the job that needs doing. Consumers do have power but they cannot use that power for good unless they know what really is of benefit, and why. In short, food will never be the quality it could be, and we will never ensure that everyone has enough and that we keep the biosphere in good heart, unless we, consumers, care enough, and are knowledgeable. In other words, we need to become gastronomes.

MUSLIM VEGGIES

Shanon Shah

My name is Shanon and I'm a failed vegetarian. And former almost-Salafi. (Ever so briefly.)

The first time I flirted with becoming vegetarian, I was in the final year of my undergraduate degree in Australia. I'd become friends with a PhD student in biology who was vegetarian for ethical reasons – she didn't like the harming of animals and the environmental damage that resulted from industrial farming practices. A gentle sense of humour informed her left-wing, green feminism and I found her convictions persuasive.

So, one day, on the way back to my student hostel, I was predisposed to be nice to someone handing out leaflets about vegetarianism. Going through my own journey of religious rediscovery, it didn't even occur to me to be suspicious of the Hare Krishna devotee who had stopped me. After a polite but slightly awkward conversation, I went back to my room laden with leaflets and booklets about the virtues of giving up meat. They were filled with illustrations in almost psychedelic colours and facts that stuck in my head. For example, you can feed up to 40 vegetarians with the same amount of land that it takes to feed five meat eaters.

Within weeks, I was having regular meals at Crossways, the vegan/vegetarian restaurant run by followers of the International Society for Krishna Consciousness (ISKCON – the official name of the Hare Krishna). They were delicious, meat-free and cheap – very appealing to a student on a budget. Soon, I decided to go meat-free on weekends – as measly as this concession sounds, back then I thought it was achingly noble. Eventually, I thought, 'Go on, take the plunge,' and decided to give up meat (but not eggs or dairy).

I explained this over lunch with a Salafi-esque Malaysian friend at university. He glared at me and said, 'Why are you rendering haram what Allah has already made halal?' I tried to explain my reasons for giving up meat – more environmental than ethical at this point – but he replied, 'Eating meat is good for us.' When he pressed me, I told him where I was getting my inspiration from – ISKCON or, as he preferred to refer to them, 'Hindu kafirs'.

I'd like to blame my friend for putting me off vegetarianism, but I can't, not even with the power of my authorial pen and the anonymity I have bestowed upon him. The truth is, staying vegetarian was bloody hard. I caved within a couple of weeks when I caught the wonderful scent of *bakso sapi* (beef-ball soup) wafting out of Nelayan, the Indonesian restaurant on Swanston Street.

This, however, was only my first flirtation – and failure – at becoming vegetarian. The next phase began when I started working at PETRONAS, the Malaysian state-owned oil and gas corporation. It felt like a part of me died when I started on my first day.

I was a PETRONAS scholar – the agreement was that they paid for my undergraduate studies and I was contracted to work with them for at least seven years afterwards. I was a nerdy, model student – the direct consequence of being the child of two teachers and the youngest of three bookish siblings. However, I had gone on to do my own research on the environmental impact of the fossil fuel industry during the final months of my chemical engineering degree. It was the late 1990s – remember dial-up modems and the browser wars between Netscape Navigator and Internet Explorer? When I came across reports of Royal Dutch Shell's complicity in the Nigerian military dictatorship's human rights violations – including the execution of activist Ken Saro-Wiwa in 1995 – I had an existential crisis. If the term 'fake news' had been in circulation then, I would have screamed it at my desktop monitor. But this was all true. When a close friend of mine hustled a job interview with Shell for me, I flubbed it by deliberately appearing bored, defensive, and inarticulate.

My PETRONAS buddies said yes, but that was Shell, whose business ethos was tied to Western imperialism. PETRONAS was different – it was set up by the Malaysian government so that we could extract our own resources responsibly and ethically. I remained unconvinced but had no choice. I had to either work for PETRONAS or repay them a colossal amount of money which I didn't have. I decided I needed to make up for it after starting work – by going vegetarian.

I never finished my contract with PETRONAS. After three-and-a-half years, I decided to quit and pursue music, human rights activism, and freelance journalism. But while I was there, working as a credit risk analyst, I was vegetarian for a bit more than two years. It was everything you could imagine being a Muslim vegetarian in a Muslim-majority oil-and-gas corporation in Kuala Lumpur to be. Colleagues teased me (sometimes mercilessly), my family often 'forgot' that I had given up meat at lunch or dinner gatherings, and I came across the usual 'why are you rendering haram what is halal' shtick.

So, I decided to become a bit more flexible. I'd eat nasi lemak, for example, that wonderful Malaysian dish of fragrant coconut rice, boiled eggs, cucumber, spicy sambal and crispy fried ikan bilis (anchovies). But then I'd invoke the ire of my more militantly vegetarian or vegan acquaintances for being a flake. And, being an emotional eater, occasionally I would crave some KFC whenever work was getting me down. After a while, it became a bit like that riddle: 'How many vegetarians does it take to eat a cow?' Answer: 'One, if no one's looking.'

I eventually chose to end the hypocrisy – I had to admit failure. I decided I was no longer vegetarian, but I would try to cut down on meat. This seemed sensible for a while, until I realised that the very idea of 'cutting down' was subjective and that it could be applied selectively and arbitrarily. So, since coming to London in 2010, I've done different things. For example, I've given up meat for the whole of Lent every year, in solidarity with my Christian friends who observe it. And, after coming across a TED Talk by Graham Hill, the founder of TreeHugger, I've now become a 'weekday vegetarian' over the past couple of years. That's a label that still provokes disgust amongst many other vegans and vegetarians I've come across and incredulity or disdain from a few meat-eaters I've met, Muslim and non-Muslim. It's hard to convince people that this does not mean I spend the entire weekend gorging on fried chicken, beef rendang, and roast lamb to compensate for a dreary week of ingesting wilted salad leaves and stale hummus. It does mean, though, that I can now quantify exactly what I mean by 'cutting down on meat'.

Maybe I needed to begin with this potted biography to seek approval from the parties across the meat-free and meat-obsessed divide, especially those who are Muslim. My hypothesis is that this need for approval is particularly strong because there seems to be very little cultural or doctrinal support for vegetarianism in Islam. Contemporary and historical evidence appears to reinforce this idea. According to Richard Foltz, the historian of Islam and Zoroastrianism, eating meat was and remains a given in most Muslim communities around the world. This is partly understandable, given the cultural and geographical inheritance of Islam – it simply wasn't tenable to have a meat-free diet in the harsh desert climate of pre-Islamic and early Muslim Arabia.

As Qur'anic injunctions enabled – and, in some passages, seemed to celebrate – the eating of meat, the cultural became sanctified with the aura of divine instruction. The boundaries hardened when Islamic civilisation spread into Asia at the start of the eighth century and Muslims encountered – and often came into conflict with – Hindus and Buddhists, whom they generally regarded as infidels. According to Foltz, the fact that many followers of the Dharmic religions were vegetarian only reinforced the idea of 'guilt by association' between vegetarianism and idolatry among many Muslims within that context.

In the modern era, several Muslim scholars have even defended animal slaughter and the eating of meat as inherently Islamic. Foltz recounts several of the more outlandish arguments in his book, *Animals in Islamic Tradition and Muslim Cultures*. The Deobandi scholar Ali Ashraf Thanvi (1863-1943), for example, claimed that slaughtering animals was analogous to punishing human criminals:

> Allah has allowed slaughtering animals in the larger interests of mankind. One should not mistake it for an inhuman act. In the same vein, capital punishment for a convict of certain categories has been prescribed in that it ensures the well-being of the human society at large. Both slaughtering and capital punishment are to be taken in the same spirit.

Apart from being opposed to the death penalty, I struggle to take the slaughtering of a cow, goat or chicken 'in the same spirit' as the hanging, beheading or electrocution of a convicted criminal.

Then there's Zakir Naik, the maverick Indian preacher so beloved of Saudi and Malaysian Islamists, who makes the intriguing claim that vegetarianism is hypocritical because plants also feel pain. Therefore, killing plants is the moral equivalent of killing animals. I'm reminded of a quote by the comedian A. Whitney Brown: 'I am not a vegetarian because I love animals; I am a vegetarian because I hate plants.'

This also recalls a scene in the film *Notting Hill*, where Will Thacker, the bumbling and adorable bookseller played by Hugh Grant, is trying to get over the Hollywood superstar Anna Scott, played by Julia Roberts. Will's friends and family try to set him up with other potential romantic partners in a series of what can only be described as middle-class English *rishtas*. The payoff for the audience comes when he's paired with a blind date called Keziah during a cosy dinner party, and she reveals that she is a fruitarian:

Will: And what exactly is a fruitarian?

Keziah: We believe that fruits and vegetables have feelings, so we think cooking is cruel. We only eat things that have actually fallen off a tree or bush – that are, in fact, dead already.

Will: Right. Right. Interesting stuff. So, these carrots…

Keziah: Have been murdered, yes.

William: Murdered? Poor carrots. How beastly.

The humour works partly because the logic is impeccable – if you believe that slaughtering living things that have feelings is wrong, and that plants, like animals, have feelings, then surely being fruitarian is the only morally acceptable way to go. But that is clearly not Zakir Naik's solution. Instead, he maintains that we might as well engage in guilt-free animal slaughter if eating plants is a problem. It's also unsurprising that he does nothing to address the lack of evidence that plants feel pain.

The clincher is the reasoning by Mawil Izzi Dien, an Islamic legal scholar based at the University of Wales, Lampeter, who states:

According to Islamic Law there are no grounds upon which one can argue that animals should not be killed for food. The Islamic legal position on this issue is based on clear Qur'anic verses. Muslims are not only prohibited from eating certain food, but also may not choose to prohibit themselves food that is allowed by Islam. Accordingly, vegetarianism is not permitted unless on grounds such as unavailability or medical necessity. Vegetarianism is not allowed under the pretext of giving priority to the interest of animals because such decisions are God's prerogative.

That's right – according to Izzi Dien, there is not only no such thing as Islamic vegetarianism, but being vegetarian is un-Islamic. Even Seyyed Hossein Nasr, the celebrated Iranian philosopher and mystic, is dismissive of vegetarians and vegetarianism.

It's not that Muslim opponents of vegetarianism do not care about animal welfare or the environment. There are increasing numbers of Muslims, for example, who despair at the inhumane and unsustainable conditions of halal slaughter, especially in the West. Many Muslims would agree that the food we consume should not only be halal ('permissible') but also tayyib ('good'), which we could interpret as wholesome, clean, nutritious, and safe. But the solutions that many ethical halal practitioners propose rarely include the option of going vegan or vegetarian. Instead, they advocate small-scale, organic farming, which is certainly worthy but emphatically not the equivalent of going meat-free.

In the praiseworthy book *Green Deen*, for example, by the African-American Muslim environmentalist Ibrahim Abdul-Matin, there is positive acknowledgement of Muslims who choose to go meat-free. There is, encouragingly, a six-page section in this 232-page volume that pays tribute to vegetarian Muslims by discussing two case studies. Alas, only one of the case studies – 'The Vegan Way' – is about Muslims who have given up meat. The second case study, 'Halal Chicken', is about a Muslim couple who have made the decision to only eat meat that is organic, free-range, and halal. Again, a laudable effort, but not the equivalent of foregoing meat entirely, so it's puzzling that it should be upheld as an example of Muslim vegetarianism.

This is not to say that becoming vegetarian is entirely alien to Islamic tradition. According to Foltz, throughout history numerous Muslims – usually Sufis – decided to give up meat, but for spiritual rather than environmental reasons. They were usually ridiculed by other Muslims for their practices. An early Sufi, Zaynab, was even persecuted for her refusal to eat meat. The eleventh-century Syrian poet al-Ma'arri was condemned for showing 'excessive' compassion to animals when he decided to go vegan later in life.

It is thus true that the idea of not eating meat because of an overt concern for animal welfare has never been accepted as a conventional Islamic doctrine. But it would be wrong to think that it is alien to the Islamic tradition. One of the more maverick examples of animal rights advocates within Islam were the so-called 'Pure Brethren' (*Ikhwan al-safa*), a radical group of philosophers based in Basra in the late tenth century. The Brethren wrote their treatises collectively, albeit anonymously – probably because of the unorthodox nature of many of their positions. Of their fifty-one works, the best known is *The Case of the Animals versus Man before the King of the Jinn*.

This unusual book centres around a court trial brought by representatives from the animal kingdom against humankind. The charge is that human beings have abused their superior position at the expense of the rest of Creation. As the trial proceeds, the human defendants argue repeatedly in support of their claims of uniqueness and divinely ordained entitlement. They argue, vacuously:

> Our beautiful form, the erect construction of our bodies, our upright carriage, our keen sense, the subtlety of our discrimination, our keen minds and superior intellects all prove that we are masters and they slaves to us.

The animals demolish each of these arguments with impeccable rationality. So meticulous are the Brethren in articulating this defence of the animal kingdom that some have even suggested that they foreshadowed Darwin's theory of evolution. In fact, at some point in the book, the humans get so alarmed and worried that they might lose the case that they contemplate bribing the judges and resorting to other underhanded tactics. The ending of the book is thus even more shocking. Spoiler alert: The King of the Jinn finds in favour of the humans, and that is that. The book's plot and structure remain a mystery. By ending the book in this way, were the Brethren trying to argue the case for human superiority? If so, why did they present such a convincing case for the animals? Or was the book meant to rouse the readers' indignation such that it would leap off the page and into the Muslim mainstream? God only knows.

This rage on behalf of animals, however, has informed some strands of Muslim vegetarianism. In modern times, the Sri Lankan Sufi mystic M. R. Bawa Muhaiyadeen (d. 1986) was an unapologetic proponent of going vegetarian. According to him:

> All your life you have been drinking the blood and eating the flesh of animals without realising what you have been doing. You love flesh and enjoy murder. If you had any conscience or any sense of justice, if you were born as a true human being, you would think about this. God is looking at me and you. Tomorrow His truth and His justice will inquire into this. You must realise this.

The Bawa Muhaiyadeen Fellowship, based in Philadelphia, is thus an explicitly vegetarian Sufi order. Its members consider themselves observant Muslims and avoid meat, among other practices, as an expression of their piety. It goes without saying that they are considered deviant by other mainstream Muslim groups, who probably regard their vegetarianism as one of several confirmations of lunacy.

In more conventional circles, the Indian Muslim scholar B. A. Masri (1914-1992) was also a strong advocate of giving up meat. Justifying his animal rights advocacy from within the Islamic framework, Masri argued:

> From the humanitarian point of view, it would be an ideal situation if all the world were to become vegetarian and all the animals were allowed to live their natural lives. Perhaps a time may come, sooner or later, when this would happen. Meanwhile the poor animals will go on having their throats slit.

The status quo in any tradition, however, has an uncanny ability to dissolve and ignore the most critical arguments, no matter how rigorous they are or whether they are motivated by conscience. Masri's ideas remain marginal, even though he was not exactly a renegade figure in the landscape of modern Islam. He trained at Al-Azhar University in Cairo and was the first Sunni imam of the Shah Jehan Mosque in Woking – the first purpose-built mosque in the UK.

Ultimately, it comes back to the Islamic tradition. If the Qur'an sanctions animal slaughter and the consumption of meat, is there really a justification for vegetarianism? What can we find in the Sunnah (Tradition) of the Prophet? The answer is not that simple. The Prophet did eat meat, but rarely. Muslim vegetarians would argue that this made him semi-vegetarian – something noteworthy in seventh century Arabia. But, the opponents of vegetarianism would argue, he still ate meat.

What about his closest companions? Again, it's not black and white. Umar al-Khattab, the second caliph, is reported to have had the following interaction:

> Yahya related to me from Malik from Yahya ibn Said that Umar ibn al-Khattab saw Jabir ibn Abdullah carrying some meat. He said, 'What is this?' He said, 'Amir al-muminin (Commander of the Faithful). We desired meat and I bought some meat for a dirham.' Umar said, 'Does any one of you want to fill his belly apart from his neighbour or nephew? How can you overlook this ayat [refer-

ring to Quran 46:20]? "You squandered your good things in this world and sought comfort in them."'

Yet again, this is not exactly an endorsement of vegetarianism. But it has deep resonance for the modern context. In this encounter, Umar seems to be asserting that eating meat is a function of privilege. And, he argues, the rich often unthinkingly consume meat at the expense of the poor. This is as true today around the world as it was all those centuries ago in Medina. Umar's concern for social justice can be juxtaposed against this more succinct quote from Ali ibn Abi Talib, the Prophet's cousin and son-in-law, fourth caliph and first Shia imam after Muhammad: 'Do not make your stomach a graveyard for animals.' (This is sometimes recorded as advice given by Muhammad to Ali with a slight variation: 'Don't make your stomach a graveyard for innocent birds and animals.')

While these nuggets of information and wisdom were sometimes surprising and surprisingly comforting to me, I was curious about vegetarian and vegan Muslims in the here and now. In Malaysia, such people were extremely rare, at least in my experience. I once made friends with someone I assumed was a Muslim vegan, but it turned out he was privately an apostate. He was a radical leftist activist whose veganism was partly a reaction against the kind of Islam he was brought up with – capitalist, conservative, and controlling. I got to know another vegetarian Muslim, but this side of her was not inspired by Islam either – her father was a vegetarian Hindu who converted to Islam and never developed a taste for meat.

I was therefore delighted to come across the Vegetarian Muslim Society on Facebook, which, at the time of writing, has a total of 4,648 likes. I was even more thrilled to discover that the founder was based in London. He introduced himself only as Shamil and we agreed to meet at Istanbul Meze Mangal, a restaurant in Colliers Wood.

Upon my arrival, the waiters in the plush restaurant area were nonplussed when I said I was meeting a dining companion. All the tables were full – no one was waiting for anyone. I gave Shamil a ring, and he said, 'Come out to the shisha section at the back – I'm the funny-looking guy in the corner.' What have I gotten myself into, I thought. Our conversations before this had been peppered with salaams, *inshAllahs* and *jazakallahs*, so I was half expecting to meet a 'funny-looking' bearded man with a shaved upper lip, wearing a turban and jubbah, and peddling 'halal and healthy' Islamic products wrapped in gaudy packaging.

Instead, I was unexpectedly greeted by a lean and fit-looking Pakistani bloke, tattoos on his arms and neck, with a chic beard and kohl-lined eyes, and wearing a denim jacket and skinny jeans. He was just about to smoke his shisha – apple and grape flavoured – that was being prepared by one of the waiting staff.

I was disappointed, however, when he declined my offer to treat us to a hearty vegetarian dinner. He only eats from 12pm to 5pm, he explained – effectively one meal a day. He said it was good for him. When I asked if he could survive on one meal a day, he smiled and said, 'lots of people do that by necessity and they survive.' Perhaps sensing that I was crestfallen or ravenous – or both – he said he would consider ordering a dessert at some point. So, I asked for the houmus starter and the falafel-and-rice as a main and merrily chomped my way through our interview.

Shamil Aloprado, 43, is from Rochdale and is of Kashmiri descent. He teaches capoeira – an Afro-Brazilian martial art that combines dance, music and acrobatics – and tonight was his night off. He is also part of Fun-Da-Mental, a multi-ethnic hip-hop, ethno-techno, world fusion band that is widely acclaimed as 'the Asian Public Enemy'.

Noticing my enthusiasm, he showed me some videos from his phone – I was impressed by his rapping and audience interaction. He told me about a Fun-Da-Mental tour in Siberia once. In the audience were two women in police uniforms. Except their outfits consisted of tight skirts, sleek boots, and shiny batons. Halfway through the performance, they started licking their batons suggestively. The band's Qawwali singer leaned over to Shamil and said, 'I don't think these are real policewomen.'

We warmed to each other quickly, and I soon conceded that I probably agreed with much of his politics. Still, I posed as many challenging questions as I could to test my own assumptions as much as his. Most of his responses echoed what I had read from Foltz on Islamic vegetarianism, but he expressed himself more earthily. There was the notion that the Prophet Muhammad was semi-vegetarian ('The Prophet *sallallahu alaihi wasallam* used to eat meat once a month, yeah?'); supported by narrations from the caliphs Ali and Umar ('Ali ibn Abi Talib said do not let your stomachs become graveyards'; '[Umar] said avoid meat because it's like an addiction'); and an overall focus on respect for animals:

There's an ayat in the Qur'an that says there's not a creature that flies with two wings, that walks upon earth that does not live in communities like you [a near-verbatim reference to verse 38 of Surah Al-An'am]. And they will all be gathered before the Lord, right? So, Islam, before all the other religions, regarded animals as communities, like us [humans]. So, if they are communities like us, they are brethren. You don't eat your brethren.

Shamil became vegetarian in 2010, after performing the haj pilgrimage the year before. The decision came amidst a personal crisis, during which he suffered from depression. But then, when visiting his old school, he had what could only be described as something akin to a religious experience:

> They'd converted the old school field into little farm allotments.... And some-body left the gate open on one of the allotments and all these animals came rushing out, sort of like so I could stroke them. It was all the things you'd expect from goats and sheep and things like that, because they're very sociable. But the chickens came over as well, and the chickens were rubbing themselves up against my leg. It's almost like they were trying to comfort me. And that really affected me.

During his pilgrimage, he had another experience – of seeing an Arab pilgrim kicking a cat in the Haram, or sanctuary in Makkah. The final straw, according to him, was when he visited Bosnia and went past a slaughterhouse for chickens. 'I could hear the chickens moaning and crying inside. I felt that it personally really hurt my feelings. I said I'm never going to eat meat again. And then I just stopped eating it.'

For going public with his views, though, he's had to endure some nasty abuse. 'People have said to me that they're going to fuck my mother and rape my sisters.' I asked if these were Muslims, and he confirmed that they were. Scrolling through the comments on Facebook later, I saw that he was not making any of this up. Another time, an imam called him a Hindu, as though it were an insult. 'It ain't an insult for me... There's a Sufi saying: Do not judge anybody's religion, because something they believe could be correct and something you believe could be wrong.'

Shamil's attitude about vegetarianism seems to be born out of a Sufi-inspired desire to be loving towards all of Creation. It's a shift I could identify with, and it came as no surprise when he confessed that he was a former Salafi – and almost-jihadi – in his youth. But – and this is part of my story, too – he became disillusioned ('Wahhabism is fascism,' he said) and wanted to explore other ways of being Muslim. Becoming vegetarian has been an integral part of his spiritual journey.

He's not stopping there, either. He said he aspires to become vegan one day, because the industrial production of eggs and dairy products also involves practices that are harmful to animals. This is a bit more difficult, he confessed, because he loves cheese. So do I, I replied. But he clearly approved when I said that I was also talking to someone from the Vegan Muslim Initiative, which was founded online in 2015 by the Australia-based Sammer Hakim and the Canada-based Elysia Ward. After contacting them via their Facebook page, I started exchanging emails with Sammer – our exchanges have been much more concise than my chat with Shamil.

Sammer decided to give up meat for health issues, but soon concluded that 'the unspeakable cruelty that occurs behind closed doors in the animal factory farming industry is just too horrific to ignore'. Like Shamil, he has very little tolerance for the argument that halal slaughter, when done 'properly', is humane:

> You know what is more humane than halal slaughter? No slaughter. How does one 'humanely' cut the throat of a living being that does not want to die? This idea has always perplexed me.... I would like to suggest however that I do not believe it is coincidental that the countries with the worst animal rights records also have the worst human rights record.

Sammer also marshalled religiously based arguments for being strictly vegan. When I asked about the requirement for animal slaughter during Eid al-Adha (the Feast of the Sacrifice), he countered:

> Slaughter is not religiously mandated. We read from the sources that many close companions of the Prophet, peace be upon him, such as Umar, Abu Bakr, Bilal ibn Rabbah and Ibn Abbas, to name a few, did not slaughter consistently. In fact, Umar forsook it out of fear that people would think it was mandatory.

That was only the first part of his answer, though. He elaborated:

> There is something else I really feel we need to evaluate. By and large, we [Muslims] have become a community obsessed with rituals but unable or unwilling to critically examine the objective of what these rituals are trying to attain. On this issue of sacrifice – the entire goal of qurbani is to feed the poor. Back in the Prophet's time, meat was a luxury. Only the wealthy ate it fre-quently. The poor used their animals for sustenance in the harsh desert envi-

ronment. Today, one acre of land will yield around 120kg of beef compared to 7,700kg of plant-based foods. There is no comparison which will feed more people. So, if the objective of qurbani can be met by far more efficient, healthier means and we can save millions of lives as well as negative impact on our planet, why wouldn't we embrace it? This is far more in line with my understanding of Islamic values.

This is why Sammer is vegan, not just vegetarian – there is no difference, according to him, between the industry that provides us eggs and dairy and the meat industry. For example:

Once cows are too exhausted or tortured to give milk due to the torrid conditions they are forced to endure, they are sent off to slaughter. Not eating meat would simply delay the inevitable for these animals. Instead of killing them right away, they would be forced to live a life of hell in a factory farm where they are repeatedly raped, have their offspring stolen from them, milked round the clock and then killed anyway.

This is hard-hitting, uncomfortable analysis indeed – on the surface, it could sound like the holier-than-thou sermonising of the Wahhabis and Salafis. The difference, though, is that people like Shamil and Sammer are not out to save others (and themselves) from a wrathful God – what Shamil refers to as the Wahhabi concept 'of some anthropomorphic being that stands outside of His creation, judging it all'. But they are trying to save *something* – and they are motivated by an uncompromising sense of social justice and deep spirituality. When I asked Sammer if he had anything else to say besides responding to my many questions, he wrote:

Do everything in your power to make this world better. You can start by what's on your plate. If you can shun cruelty from your stomach, then you will have done a great deed for countless animals as well as your own health. If that's all you can do, then fantastic. It's the cumulative effect of many doing their part that has the biggest impact. Speak out for the oppressed no matter who they are.

This is not just an initiative – it's a manifesto. It seems utopian and impossible because it calls on us to turn our backs on multiple institutions and ideologies that sustain themselves through killing of animals and – not infrequently - humans. This is not simply a far-left rant against capitalism, or a radical feminist rant against patriarchy, or a revolutionary struggle against neo-colonialism. It's all the above and more, and it's confronting because it's about Muslims striking at the heart of conventional Islam, not with terror or military technology, but by simply refusing to consume meat.

In many ways, this analysis resonates a lot with an argument that has been made by Kecia Ali, the American Islamic studies scholar and feminist – meat is murder *and* patriarchal. Ali begins with the obvious yet crucial observation that there are many parallels between our attitudes towards food and towards sex, and how they influence communal identities and the boundaries of social interactions:

> In a variety of Muslim contexts, female bodies (properly covered) and animal bodies (properly slaughtered) serve as potent signifiers. Not only are there parallels between women and animals, and between sex and food, but the conceptual utility of women and animals is linked: hierarchical cosmologies affirm male dominance in family and society and affirm human dominion over animals, legitimating their use, confinement, slaughter, and consumption.

Attitudes towards food and sex are therefore a function of power, and this is not only applicable to Muslims. Throughout Muslim history, however, religious rulings on food and sex have largely been in the service of preserving a specific social order, and not simply about obeying divine revelation. That's why it's significant that Muslim reformers and revolutionaries – from 'liberal', vegetarians, vegans, feminists and lesbian, gay, bisexual and transgender (LGBT) people, to 'fundamentalists' like the Muslim Brotherhood and Salafis – often invoke the first generation of Muslims as models to undo an unjust order and establish a new social system. Many of these movements, whether 'liberal' or 'fundamentalist', share an opposition towards external forms of oppression. However, Muslim feminists, LGBT activists, and vegans and vegetarians insist on asking difficult questions about oppression *amongst* their co-religionists. Their most radical strands want to challenge what Ali refers to as 'the truism that systems of domination are interconnected'.

This is also why, in contexts where Muslims are in a minority, Muslim feminists, LGBT activists, and vegans and vegetarians are often accused by other Muslims of betrayal. This is especially understandable when Islamophobic polemics so often target Muslim food practices, for example halal slaughter, as much as gender relations, especially the hijab and niqab controversies and homophobia, of Muslim communities. But just because this defensiveness is comprehensible, it does not make it morally acceptable.

Ali thus contends that the idea of 'kindness to animals' – for example, with 'humane' halal slaughter or organic farming – is equivalent to the 'gender complementarity' or 'gender equity' model advanced by some traditionalist Muslims. To her, they're both expressions of 'soft patriarchy'. They're not about the restructuring of an unjust system – at best, they're band aid solutions that only tackle superficial symptoms temporarily.

She's probably right. But it's an arduous argument to make, especially with those whose lives would be made much better, practically, if 'hard' patriarchy became softer. In Latin America, for example, Pentecostalism has appealed to many inner-city women not because it unravels patriarchy but because it calls on husbands to give up alcohol, to get proper jobs instead of being involved in gangs, and to help around the house. Researchers have repeatedly found that many women are relieved that their husbands are no longer violent and abusive drunkards – some even appreciate the stability and security of this Pentecostal 'soft patriarchy'.

To me, the best I can do is aspire towards fundamental change whilst taking things step by step every day. As I write this in the middle of Lent, I've extended my vegetarianism to six days a week and have even tried to go vegan for part of the week. It's challenging, and I wonder if I am disappointing Shamil or Sammer – both of whom I've developed a deep admiration for – by not going the whole way. And my intention this year is to see if I can manage to be a weekday vegetarian in Ramadan, too – I tried it last year and it was surprisingly doable. (Except when it wasn't, and I simply had to have *that* kebab or *those* peri-peri wings for *iftar*.)

I've realised, however, that my underlying motives are completely different from most of the Muslim vegetarians or vegans I've encountered. The question of animal welfare or challenging patriarchy are important, but they're secondary. And honestly, the issue of spiritual purity does not even register with me. My desire to give up meat was always primarily about being kind to the environment. And this comes from years of guilt, which I still carry, that I was once part of the petrochemical industry.

To me, reducing meat has been as important as refusing to buy a car – although I ended up driving one for a grand total of three years when I was a journalist in Malaysia – and being vigilant about switching the lights off, turning down the heating, and recycling and reusing as much as I can. When I started earning a salary after finishing my PhD, I resolved to offset every single flight I had ever taken in my life – for work, for pleasure, and for family visits. I managed to complete this in the past year or so via Climate Stewards, a Christian charity that helps people to 'offset unavoidable carbon emissions by supporting community forestry, water filter and cookstove projects in Ghana, Kenya, Uganda and Mexico'. Their website also hosts a fun calculator that you can use to measure your carbon footprint so that you can decide how much you want to offset. It's all done in an informative, non-preachy way. Their approach has helped me to commit to offsetting all my future flights.

In a roundabout way, this is the reason why I was not sure how to react when, after our meeting, Shamil introduced me to his huge, stunningly beautiful, tame, and affectionate wolf-hound. I was smitten at first sight. I had to ask, though, 'Is your dog vegetarian?' Shamil laughed and said no, and I had to wonder about this. Apart from needing lots of space and attention, dogs also need meat. Plenty of it. And it's remarkable how much you can spend on pet food – I know because I once inherited a cat a while ago, now deceased. With my climate change hat on, I just cannot make sense anymore of how having pets is good for the environment. One recent study argues that the 163 million dogs and cats in the US have the same environmental impact as 13.6 million cars. It's not that I don't love animals, but it's also about reckoning with the hard choices that confront all of us in relation to our carbon consumption. And it's not that I'm casting Shamil's ethical choices into doubt – I like and respect him immensely. I've just noticed there are some differences how I view ethical eating compared to other vegans or vegetarians.

There are also some vegetarian and vegan lifestyle choices which, to me, seem to be based more on a pseudo-scientific feel-good factor and fads than sound environmental and ethical principles. There's the whole argument, for example, about whether almond milk is as sustainable as its proponents make it out to be. There's also the growing popularity of coconut milk, suddenly marketed in the West as a vegan-friendly superfood but which proportionally contains more saturated fat than lard. One wonders at the advertising sleight of hand going on, because scientists have been aware of these health risks long before coconut-milk lattes became all the rage. In short, going vegan can be as unhealthy, unethical, and unintelligent as any fast-food, meat-laden diet – a mountain of oil-drenched French fries and a can of Coke technically count as meat-free, after all. For veganism and vegetarianism to be truly sustainable, people also need to be strict about *how* plant-based foods are cultivated, processed, packaged and distributed, and *which* plant-based foods they choose to consume.

Ultimately, veganism and vegetarianism make good moral, ethical, and spiritual sense. The stigma and disrepute that confront vegans and vegetarians in many Muslim cultures and in several strands of Islamic jurisprudence probably says a lot about the priorities and ideological baggage of their detractors. Some of this isn't helped by the quasi-religious fervour and indignation of many vegans and vegetarians. These levels of zealousness differ, however, depending on an individual's motivations for being meat-free – whether it's about physical health, animal welfare, spirituality, environmental concerns, or other reasons.

Interestingly, the hostility from some of their co-religionists means that the vegan and vegetarian Muslims I've met can sometimes empathise deeply with other Muslim *personae non gratae*, including feminists and LGBT people. The risk here is that it could be tempting to dismiss these causes because of the actions of a few condescending and self-righteous vegans, vegetarians, feminists, or LGBT activists. Let's not kid ourselves – we've all met at least one of these types (and tried to run for our lives, even if *we* counted *ourselves* as supporters of their causes). This is unfortunate, because the reasonable and evidence-based arguments for refusing meat (and patriarchy, as Ali argues) then get drowned out by moralistic tit-for-tats.

There is an alternative approach, however, manifested in the work of the scholars I've read and the practitioners I've spoken to for this article. To me, it's captured in two beautiful Qur'anic verses from surahs that are, poignantly, named after animals:

'Invite to the way of your Lord with wisdom and good instruction, and argue with them in a way that is best. Indeed, your Lord is most knowing of who has strayed from His way, and He is most knowing of who is [rightly] guided.' (Surah an-Nahl [The Bee], ayat 125)

'And for everyone (is) a direction – he turns towards it, so race (to) the good. Wherever that you will be will bring you (by) Allah together. Indeed, Allah (is) on everything All-Powerful.' (Surah al-Baqarah [The Cow], ayat 148)

As for me, I remain a weekday vegetarian. And a former almost-Salafi. (Ever so briefly.)

CLAUDIA RODEN

Boyd Tonkin

During research trips for her book *The Food of Spain*, Claudia Roden visited a cookery school outside Granada. She asked the head chef there about his cultural and culinary influences. By this time, in the 2000s, Spanish gastronomy – like some, but not all, sections of the country as a whole – had begun to throw off long centuries of rejection and persecution to embrace the nation's mixed-up multi-ethnic, multi-cultural past. A neurotic, even violent, refusal to acknowledge the Islamic and Judaic roots of so much of everyday life in Spain had given way to what Roden calls 'a mixture of denial and appreciation'. So which food styles held sway in this historically-informed Andalusian kitchen? 'Arab and Jewish,' the chef proudly replied. Roden pressed for an example. 'How to cook pork.'

Not surprisingly, that curious claim brought the revered author of cookery classics such as *A Book of Middle Eastern Food*, *Arabesque* and *The Book of Jewish Food* up short. Her wonderfully informative, but thoroughly practical, guides to kitchen history, methods and folklore across the Middle East, North Africa and the Mediterranean basin will tell you how, and why, to cook just about anything – from *kibbeh* to *kataifi*– except the flesh of the pig. Confirmed by Roden's meticulous culinary sleuthing, the chef's justification not only reveals a secret at the heart of Spanish identity. It illustrates the kind of background revelation that she uses to enrich every recipe.

After the 'reconquest' of Spain by Christian rulers, which concluded in the capture of the Moorish emirate of Granada in 1492, millions of Muslims and Jews who had lived in the Iberian peninsula for many centuries converted, more by force than choice, to the new monopoly religion of these lands. However, their customs, their rituals, their languages – and above all their food – proved impossible to eradicate. Those traces of a multi-faith history, dating back at least to the earliest Arab incursions in 711 endured long after the mass, but never-completed, expulsion of the Moriscos ('New Christians' from Muslim families) that began in 1609.

On the stove, as on the tongue, the cultures of the Moors and Jews survived in Spain even if many (though by no means all) of the people left. Roden explains that 'when they converted, they cooked the pig in the same way that they cooked lamb', rubbing the meat with cumin seeds. That uniquely 'Spanish' way with pork persists to this day. You may find it, she notes, on the menu in modish London restaurants. Meanwhile, the Muslim and Jewish cooks of medieval Spain still season evenings out on any high street. 'The kind of food they made is now the food you find in tapas bars. There's such a strong, obvious Arab influence,' she says. The spice of the past itself, those flavours preserve the taste of a contested, often tragic story that embraces episodes both of harmony and discord. 'Nowhere else in the world do they put cumin in roast pork. Just those seeds are a clue to what happened there.'

Cook with Claudia Roden and you savour history. As Simon Schama put it, she 'is no more a simple cookbook writer than Marcel Proust was a biscuit baker. She is, rather, memorialist, historian, ethnographer, anthropologist, essayist, poet, who just happens to communicate through *ta'am* – taste.' This year, half a century will have passed since she first published the collection of family recipes from her upbringing in Cairo that became *A Book of Middle Eastern Food*. Quite apart from her eminence as gastronomic historian, it's not often that you can honestly report that an author has helped to keep you alive – physically, rather than (or as well as) spiritually.

In her case, I tell no more than the truth. As a student with perennially empty pockets, and for long afterwards, her recipes taught me that good taste need not count as a luxury. Often, they showcased to mouth-watering effect the inexpensive vegetables and pulses that form the staples of the region. That lesson, gleaned from generation after generation of thrifty but resourceful cooks across continents from Tangier to Tehran, bears re-learning every day. At random, I consult one of her books: *Arabesque*, her hands-on cook's tour of Morocco, Turkey and Lebanon, and of the cultures that moulded their cuisines. The volume falls open at 'Chickpeas with toasted bread and yoghurt: *Fattet hummus bi laban*'. Each of this dish's ingredients will cost you pence rather than pounds. Yet, as she writes, 'the mix of textures, temperatures and flavours is a joy'.

I know from previous occasions that a meeting with Roden at her London home may bring some sort of delicious bonus for the interviewer. This time, we sit down during the afternoon at the kitchen table in her picturesque Arts-and-Crafts house in Hampstead Garden Suburb — almost a biscuit-box vision of Englishness, and a piquant contrast to the cosmopolitan scope of the food so lovingly prepared there. With a spread of perfect coffee, Italian fennel biscuits, semi-dried mango, *mahjoul* dates, grapes and some supremely fine chocolate as a tempting distraction from the task in hand, she tells me about her daunting schedule. Among other commitments, it takes in literary festivals in Mumbai and Dubai; a BBC World Service programme; an evening's cooking for Syrian refugees at a London synagogue; and work on a forthcoming book, a personal journey that will blend memories with favourite dishes. Her weekend dinner guests included the Iraqi-born Professor Sami Zubaida — political scientist, culinary historian and old friend — and Michael Rakowitz, an American artist of Iraqi Jewish heritage whose Enemy Kitchen project introduces Iraqi culture, and cuisine, to a public that knows the country only as a bloody battlefield. A pot of Basra date syrup sits on the table.

Younger cooks, food writers and restaurateurs beat a path to her door. Her recipes and their hinterland flavour an entire school of fashionable Middle Eastern and Levantine cuisine, light, healthy and delicious. Some disciplines do salute their source. Yotam Ottolenghi has written that *A Book of Middle Eastern Food* not only 'introduced Britons to my own cupboard staples'. As literature, it shines through 'the sheer power of her obsessive curiosity with food and its transformation' and 'her enchanted interest in people and their stories'. Ottolenghi has paid tribute to Roden as a border-crossing kitchen traveller who 'justifiably transcends national accounts but, at the same time, conveys them so plainly and so genuinely'. Others, though, have been slower to recognise their debt. Roden mentions one best-selling cookbook author who, en route to success, plundered her recipes without acknowledgement. 'Now she tells me, "You're my idol" – but she never said so before!'

Global food, as she notes, 'has become a gigantic business'. For her, a career in cookery began in a wholly different world. She was born in Cairo, in a Jewish family whose Sephardi forebears had come to Egypt, directly or indirectly, from Aleppo in Syria, Istanbul in Turkey, and Livorno in Italy. Further back, her ancestors had formed part of the Jewish diaspora from the Iberian peninsula after the 'reconquest'. 'We identified very much as Syrian Jews,' she recalls, 'but also as Judaeo-Spanish.' A grandmother, from Istanbul spoke Ladino, the vernacular language of Jewish Iberia. However, even in Cairo, the city of Aleppo shone as a beacon of civilisation to this diaspora family. Roden's great-grandfather had been the city's chief rabbi; she shows me a photograph of him in a proudly patriarchal pose. Later, as an immigrant in Paris, an aunt still cherished the key to his synagogue: 'We were so tied to Aleppo, identifying with it as the best place on earth.'

In their Cairo neighbourhood, people continued to speak Arabic 'like Syrians, with a Syrian accent. Halabis [Aleppo is 'Halab' in Arabic] wouldn't even marry Jews from Damascus, because they thought the women were flighty.' The Halabi merchants had brought their food with them to Egypt – a cuisine that still seeps deeply into the meals that she writes about, cooks and eats. For a radio programme, she has just chosen a selection of beloved recipes. They include childhood favourites such as chicken sofrito: a Sabbath dish for the Friday night meal with garlic, lemon, turmeric and cardamom. Exiled from Egypt, her mother 'carried on making that every Friday night'. As for the Passover orange cake with almonds that Roden still makes, it has since spread around the world – and sometimes mutated oddly during its travels. 'Even in India, somebody told me: "I do that cake, but I cover it in chocolate sauce".'

Alongside specifically Jewish dishes, the family loved the everyday cookery of Egypt: 'The kind of food that we were eating was a very big mix.' The household's cooks, who had come to Cairo from Upper Egypt, would make their traditional village dishes. Its comforting familiarity meant that this workaday fare was honoured only when lost. 'We didn't value all that, because it was poor or local food. But as soon as we went, this is what we pined for: *malokhia* [the basis for Egypt's beloved national broth], *foul mesdames* [spiced fava beans], falafel. We were desperate for it, but that was what the cook would make.'

As tensions between Nasser's revolutionary government and the West rose in the 1950s, Egypt's Jews began to leave. Political divisions fostered rifts between communities – Jews, Muslims, Christians – with a long history of mutual tolerance and respect. In 1956, after the Suez crisis, a large-scale Jewish exodus began. The exile of Roden's family took them to Paris, where Claudia finished her schooling, and also to London, where she studied art at St Martin's.

After these early years of displacement, now settled in London, she began to collect recipes from her own and other families. A sense of loss, of nostalgia, even of bereavement, propelled her mission. Emigrés who had taken the spicy, nourishing table of ordinary Egyptians, and of the Sephardic diaspora, for granted now yearned to keep it alive. 'At the time, nobody thought that I would do a book. It was for all of us. Everybody was desperate for our foods to be recorded… We didn't even think we had special Jewish food. We just ate what was passed down in the family.' As she says, 'The food embodies all that you miss.'

As she gathered family recipes from relatives and fellow-exiles, Roden pioneered the face-to-face research – you might call it Kitchen Confidential – that gives her books such warmth and humanity. 'Food is one of the most intimate things on earth,' she reflects. Sitting in a kitchen, preparing food and sharing its secrets, may forge bonds deeper than any more formal rendezvous. When she first harvested kitchen memories from Cairo and far beyond, she felt that 'I didn't want to lose this kind of closeness with a world that I had been born in. This was my way of not losing it.' For her, 'the first motive was loving Egypt – really loving and missing it. But also, loving the relationship we had with Muslims: missing that, and not wanting to lose them.' She adds that 'At the time I didn't think there was such thing as Jewish food, or that we were in any way different.'

In addition to this oven-fresh investigation, Roden researched the more distant history of Middle Eastern food in the British Library and at SOAS in London. In the British Library, she asked for their holdings of Arab cookbooks, 'There wasn't a single contemporary book. They were all thirteenth-century manuals!' Yet those manuals, sometimes compiled for the royal households of Baghdad, proved that an unbroken culinary lineage linked the table of the Caliphs to that of a middle-class Jewish family in twentieth-century Cairo. Her sleuthing proved that their domestic culture 'was old, and that it mattered. It made us value foods that we ate, not just because it made us happy and made us remember, but because they were part of something old and it tied us to the past.' Moreover, 'It somehow cemented us into the Arab world, that we were part of that culture.'

So, in 1968, the culinary heritage and folklore of the Jews of Cairo and Aleppo, Istanbul and Damascus, Tunis and Baghdad, found their way into the first edition of her *A Book of Middle Eastern Food*. It carries an indefinite article: 'a' book, not 'the' book. Nonetheless, chefs and menus the world over have treated it as definitive. Conversely, critics have scolded her for presenting a specific tradition, however eclectic, as the only one. Which she never did. For all its future acclaim, some of the Cairene exiles sniffed at this seeming commercialisation of their family customs. 'My father would tell them when my book came out that she doesn't make any money! He thought it was almost shameful to make money out of this. It was from the heart: a labour of love.' Others, more parochially, said that 'We're not interested in how the Doueks or the Sassoons cook.' (Roden's father's family are Doueks, a distinctive Halabi name; her mother's a branch of the Baghdadi-origin Sassoons.)

The fate of that book also suggests that experts and gourmets will label food styles as 'authentic' or otherwise at their peril. Specialists such as her friend Sami Zubaida will sometimes decry the notion of authenticity in the kitchen. After all, custom and practice inevitably change over time. 'But I must say,' she argues, 'that I knew things when they weren't changing. When people were very, very particular about how they did it. Some people have told me, "Don't ever put my name to it if you don't do it exactly like that". Including a nun in Seville.'

Roden had collected the kitchen lore of individual families, starting in the late 1950s when she was in her early twenties and her mother's generation in their forties or fifties. They, in turn, passed on recipes handed down from their own parents and grandparents. So the domestic rituals she cites stretch far into the past. Take *tabbouleh*. Roden's version, which used a lot of carbohydrate-rich bulgur wheat, essentially derived – so a Saudi-based Lebanese teacher later informed her – from 'how they did it at the turn of the century in the mountains of Lebanon and Syria'. In milder climates, it developed into a salad of 'all parsley with just specks of wheat'. Restaurants, however, have sometimes followed the rustic Roden playbook. They risk complaints that 'it isn't the real *tabbouleh* – it's got too much wheat!' In fact, it's a shade too 'real' for contemporary trends.

Roden married, raised three children, and divorced. Once a hobby, even a family duty, cooking moved from pastime to livelihood. After the Middle Eastern volume came *The Food of Italy*; *Arabesque*; *Tamarind and Saffron*; and, in 1997, her encyclopaedic, all-encompassing *The Book of Jewish Food*. This time she did, justifiably, hazard the definite article. In 2011, *The Food of Spain* allowed her to join many of the dots on her culinary itineraries. Everywhere around the peninsula, she uncovered variants of the foods of her life. 'The smells brought back my childhood,' as she told me during a previous interview. 'I could always see very well where things came from. And when I did the research, it always fitted in like a puzzle.'

Put all the pieces of that 'puzzle' together, and Roden's books channel the flavours, methods and ingredients of many lands into what can seem, or rather, taste like a single culinary space. They reveal the, often circuitous, routes that foodstuffs and kitchen techniques take, and show how culinary customs can tie cities and countries separated by vast expanses of sea and land. They will tell you, for instance, how the influence of the musician, gourmet and arbiter of taste Ziryab – a Kurdish freed slave from the court of Harun al-Rashid – brought Baghdadi refinement from Iraq to the tables of Cordoba, and thence to the rest of southern Spain. From Turkey to Portugal, she came across a proud attachment to local culinary ways, and a hospitable willingness to share them. 'People cooked what their parents cooked. They weren't in the least bit interested in what somebody from another country cooked. Nobody felt that, if you were an outsider, you were going to outshine them.'

For all its regional and cultural variations, aspects of the cuisine that inspires Roden's books stretch in an almost unbroken chain from Lisbon to Kabul, from Ankara to Agadir. The courtly kitchens of great Islamic empires – Umayyads, Abbasids, Safavids, Mamluks, Ottomans – helped to shape these styles. Thus meat dishes with soft fruit, that flagship combination of the Maghreb table, may owe their origin to the Sassanian rulers of ancient Iran.

Jews, more regularly in transit than their neighbours, often carried these culinary markers. Contrary to some assumptions, that does not necessarily mean they invented them. For Roden, 'Jews were the people who were the migrants. And somehow they brought change… from one place to another.' She cites the Spanish belief (at least in recent, more pluralistic, years) that 'aubergines and artichokes were brought by the Jews. But the Jews came with the Arabs.' The cultivation of aubergines belongs to Arab agriculture. However, Jews but not Muslims moved north to Catalonia during and after the reconquest. Hence 'in Catalonia, they think it's the Jews who brought it.'

As they travel from Anatolia to Andalusia, among Muslims, Jews and Christians, Roden's cookbooks both celebrate the uniqueness of regional cuisines and illustrate the threads that bind them. Like the food, their author also loves to cross borders. On a visit to Lebanon for a wedding she found herself in an area dominated by the militants of Hezbollah. 'I can't say I'm not Jewish, because they know about my book. But I met just friendship, and a lot of humour.' When she returned to Egypt to run seminars for chefs, 'I couldn't have had a better reception anywhere, in any country.' That, sadly, happened a while ago. Now, she regrets that political polarisation in Egypt would rule out another such homecoming: 'It's all got really poisonous.'

Not every country in the region now rushes to deny the diverse past that her books salute. She notes that 'Jewish food is now seen as one of the regional foods of Morocco and Tunisia.' In Essaouira, on Morocco's Atlantic coast, a Basque chef she knows cooked the dishes of his childhood for the Essaouira-born André Azoulay – the legendary Moroccan minister and royal adviser, and himself a Jew. 'He was very moved – he couldn't believe that she knew how to make them.'

Culinary connections, of course, can hardly by themselves wipe clean the messy spills of geopolitics. Roden mentions the dilemma faced, for instance, by the Moroccan restaurateur and food writer Fatéma Hal when she was invited to a festival in Israel. At first, she refused to attend because, she said, she wished to respect the cultural boycott: 'I didn't want to betray my Palestinian brothers.' Then Moroccan Jews kept coming to her to say 'We miss you'. She said, 'I wanted to come and tell you, "We miss you".' In the end, Hal accepted.

If the kinship of the kitchen alone can never hope to re-unite the vast empire of flatbread and hummus, of falafel and baklava, at least it can offer a brief taste of past – and perhaps future – concord. 'The condition where people cook for each other or eat together,' Roden reflects, 'is the best place for people to bond, and to empathise with each other. You're sitting at the table. You're vulnerable; you're just a person.' Recently, she has found confirmation of that belief by taking part in events to support the refugees displaced by the latest wave of conflict and turmoil across North Africa and the Middle East.

By one of history's wrenching ironies, many of these fugitives come from Aleppo itself – her own family's city of the heart. She reports that, at a local synagogue, Syrian refugees cooked a fund-raising dinner to thank the congregation for its support. And they cooked the dishes of Roden's childhood. 'That was the one thing that identified us. Now it identifies them: the food that our parents and grandparents passed on for us because they were nostalgic for Aleppo. It is quite a strange thing.'

She has herself cooked for the asylum-seekers and homeless people helped in weekly advice sessions at another synagogue. At gatherings to show solidarity with refugees, whether religious and secular, she always finds that 'There's a lot of people who want to give, who want to make bridges and break walls. And there are now opportunities to do that. Each time I think, "I should come here more often."' I want to know the menu of the meal she prepared. It consisted, she says, of an Egyptian lentil soup, followed by vegetarian couscous and a Turkish yoghurt cake. I hope her discerning clientele enjoyed it? 'We got a standing ovation.'

In Roden's cooking, and her writing, three layers of remembrance seamlessly interact. Her recipes, and the deep background she invests in them, allow personal, family and cultural memories to converge. With those memories come the emotions that particular foods carry in their rituals and their tastes, often over frontiers of time and place. Right across a region too often associated with sectarian and communal strife, her investigations have uncovered, and revived, a kind of hidden solidarity. This feels older, perhaps tougher, than the clash of ideologies. And at her work's heart lie the simple, and universal, rites of welcome and hospitality. 'The fact that you eat together and somebody cooks: it's a way of showing love.'

CAUCASUS RITUALS

Gunel Isakova

My seventy-five-year-old grandma, dusting a clean working area generously with flour, slightly patting with the top of her hand to flatten the dough she has just made, begins manoeuvring a thin rolling pin, rotating the dough with each motion. She then delicately creates intricate and tender boat-shaped pasta called *surhullu,* one of the most popular local dishes, usually served with dried meat, repeating an incantation in her native tsakhur language while she drops them into the pot. With warmth and the fondness that accompanies much-cherished memories, she reminisces about her childhood and how the family would come together to make and eat this comfort food on chilly winter days in the forbidding peaks of rural Dagestan.

Welcome to the Caucasus, a melting pot of ethnicities. This mountainous region boasts more than fifty ethnic groups with their ancient accompanying culinary traditions. A rich variety of fruit and vegetables, colourful spices, and a kaleidoscopic culinary landscape, well-preserved to this day, abound. Different species of wild edible plants, almonds, chestnuts, walnuts, hazelnuts, pomegranate, grape, mulberry, plum, apples, and pears, to name a few of the more common crops, can all be found growing wild in this rugged land bridge between Europe and Asia. I have never ceased to be in awe of the biodiversity around me, made all the more astounding to contemplate when one considers that virtually every passing empire known through the history books has conquered these people, and this land. Caucasian food culture has been influenced by the Roman, Persian, and Byzantine empires, and by the Arabs, Mongols, and Turks. The fecundity of the land has resulted in a bounty of ingredients, compounded by a few thousand years of culture and trade. Since the climate in the Caucasus is consistent across the region, many countries such as Azerbaijan, Armenia and Georgia have similar agricultural traditions, and a number of common dishes and food staples.

Food is an important link to our national identity, cultural heritage, beliefs, traditions, rituals and every-day life. Historically, the Caucasus cuisines have been stable and resistant to change. I grew up in a family who moved from a very small village in Dagestan to the northern part of Azerbaijan fifty-three years ago. We did not abandon our food traditions along the way and continue to maintain connections to our culinary heritage, to the extent that it is a defining part of our identity. The food we eat strengthens the ties with our ethnicity on a day-to-day basis and reflexively reinforces a sense of identity when we migrate and find ourselves in the midst of another culture. Food, like language, expresses us in different ways. It shapes our identity, communicates our culture, connects us to one another, forms our traditions, and symbolises our relationship with religion, ethnicity, and social class. Jennifer Berg, Director of graduate food studies at New York University, notes that food is particularly important when you become part of a diaspora, separated from your mother culture. It can play the role of a bridge that helps immigrants establish their place in a new society. 'It's the last vestige of culture that people shed,' she says. 'There are some aspects of maternal culture that you'll lose right away. First is how you dress, because if you want to blend in or be part of a larger mainstream culture the things that are the most visible are the ones that you let go. With food, it's something you're engaging in three times a day, and so there are more opportunities to connect to memory and family and place. It's the hardest to give up.' Just like my grandma who moved from her village and never stopped making those favourite traditional dishes for her loved ones. Recipes which are rooted in family traditions and preserve a family's living legacy are passed on through generations.

Cooking is indeed an integral part of everyday life in Azerbaijan. In Azerbaijani recipes, you will always hear statements such as 'weigh it with your eyes' since precision in cooking is achieved through experience, and not by following a certain recipe. Ingredient measurements are almost always approximate. Even though I have never been to Dagestan, I can make authentic Tsakhur meals thanks to my grandma. She compiled a recipe book of her own, which mostly contained instructions that she copied from her mother's extensive recipe collections, taken from magazines or notes that she scribbled down while listening to the radio. Even though my grandmother is not with us anymore, her recipes, and her incredible legacy, are alive and with us every day.

Pride and resistance in national cuisine is very common across the Caucasian countries. Increasing tensions between nations that share a troubled past often manifests itself in food related issues. The countries that have territorial disputes in the region are highly sensitive when it comes to food and vie for the recognition of certain dishes as their own. For instance, Azerbaijanis believe that the Armenians continuously attempt to steal what they insist belongs to them – not only through territorial occupation but also through food. Armenians claim that Turkish coffee does not have Turkish roots, and it is exactly what their ancestors have been making for years as Armenian coffee. Georgians and Abkhazs are vying for recognition over a sauce which is called *adjika*. Despite the many commonalities among the Caucasian cuisines, each country (and the regions) has an authentic culinary tradition of its own, as well as its own distinct tastes. The names of dishes may be the same, but the aroma and flavours reveal the cultural sensibilities and the distinctive histories of each group. Feride Buyuran, my most favourite Azerbaijani food writer, notes in her book *Pomegranates and Saffron* that 'while some Azerbaijani dishes, such as saffron-steamed rice pilaffs served with various toppings, are common throughout the country, the national cuisines vary widely between regions. Baku is known for its starchy dishes, like pasta and stuffed savoury flatbreads. The northeast is famous for its breads and pastries, while the northwest is known for its robust flavours and use of dried meat. The regions of the west are known for making use of greens that thrive in local gardens, the north in general is noted for its wide use of dried yogurt. In the southwest, the staple of choice is chickpeas and other varieties of dried beans. In the southeast, the local delicacy is a walnut filling stuffed inside poultry, fish or wild game.'

In some religions, followers avoid eating certain products, fast every year, make special dishes while practising rituals. If you were a guest visiting my family for a week, you would easily guess that they are following the principles of Islam when it comes to food. Islam's holistic approach to health, via the concept of halal, promotes treating our bodies with respect and nourishing them with nutritious, healthy food. The general idea is that by avoiding certain foods, you maintain optimum body health and repel illnesses. The consumption of alcoholic beverages is strictly avoided by some while others who identify as Muslim do not follow most of the rules on a daily basis, but pay more attention during the month of Ramadan as a sign of respect. For instance, a few of my relatives avoid alcohol during the month of Ramadan only and the rest of the months they prefer to drink once in a while. Many groups in the Caucasus region, such as the Chechens, have traditionally been enthusiastic alcohol drinkers even though they are Muslim.

The Caucasus is home to Muslims, Christians, Jews and a number of other religious groups. Islam, like Christianity and Judaism, has its own unique holidays with some customs we all share in common. Neighbours from different religious backgrounds exchange food during their religious rituals and celebrations. For instance, during the Easter holidays our neighbours would always bring traditional food and sweets, and in the same way we share our food during Ramadan and other religious occasions.

Food is clearly important for nutrition, but it is also meaningful to humans in other ways. For many of us being breastfed is the first experience that we have of being fed. That special bond between a mother and an infant is probably the primary association with family memories. To this day the scent of fresh bread, baked eggs on mini bread, reminds me of my mother's breakfast table and takes me back to childhood. I, along with my three siblings would wake up to the smell of these tasty morsels in the oven. The aroma was amazing and would always get us right out of bed. One of my most treasured memories is sharing a piece of chocolate with my mother and my siblings while my father was away from Azerbaijan earning money for the family. My mother would do her best to provide us with our most cherished food so that we would not feel impoverished. She would buy a chocolate and we would cut it into four pieces and share it in the evenings. In those days food was scarce and it was not easy for my mum, but her sun-wrinkled face beamed at the prospect of making us feel safe and happy. The food and those experiences become part of who we are and who we become. One of the more positive family traditions, a major social activity in the Caucasus, is family meals. Most families converge to take meals together three times a day. Only in a few remote parts of

Georgia, Azerbaijan and North Caucasus do men and women eat separately on a daily basis due to strict patriarchal customs.

Across the region, food is central to celebrations regardless of culture and religion. Mealtime is done family style, with shared dishes, eating, exchanging food, laughing, and chatting. Families host dinners in order to connect relatives and bring friends and family together. The etiquette of preparing the table, the manner in which food and dishes are arranged, and the types of food that should be served for family reunions all follow a timeless convention passed down through generations. Georgians have a saying that 'food in Georgia is about pleasure'. The importance of both food and drink to Georgian families is best observed during a feast called _supra,_ when a variety of dishes and drinks are prepared for the family and last for hours. Family members enjoy sipping home-made red Georgian wine, while devouring delicious Georgian dishes.

Inhabitants of the Caucasus enjoy a number of food rituals and every important occasion has its unique culinary practice. For instance, Azerbaijani women gather together every Novruz, the Iranian new year and a spring holiday, which can last a whole week, to make diamond-shaped baklava, a national dish of Azerbaijan, ensuring that the table is filled with an abundance of mouth-watering treats. A festive table called _khoncha_ is prepared: it consists of a large silver or copper tray with _Samani_, green sprouting wheat, at the centre, and with _shekerbura, bakhlava, qoghal_, nuts, and many other sweets. Breads, wheat and grains are considered attributes of abundance, so they serve as important symbols at every Azerbaijani holiday. Meeting for a tea is almost a daily ritual. Glasses of the hot beverage are enjoyed in huge numbers throughout the day. Food also plays a major role at funerals. When a person passes away, the family serves meals, tea with halva – a flour-based dessert – to everyone who visits. These rituals bring kith and kin together and strengthen family ties, providing a focal activity for those in mourning and a comforting routine for all those affected by loss.

One ritual of Caucasian families is preserving food for winter. Fresh fruits, such as berries, figs and cherries, are cooked and canned as preserves, and vegetables, such as tomatoes, eggplants, peppers, and cucumbers, are pickled and stored. Air-drying is one of the most ancient techniques of meat drying, practiced by locals for centuries. Since it is hard to obtain meat during winter months, they dry the meat and use it for soup and pasta dishes in winter. Some families hang watermelons in the coldest room of the house to preserve it for as long as is possible. Families gather together and dry persimmons, apples, grapes and other fruit, to make jam, sauces and salads for winter. These practices ensure year-round use of the country's abundant culinary resources. They make these gatherings entertaining with music, poetry, laughter, talks, and discussing superstitions based on their beliefs. In Azeri culture, for instance, people believe that if salt becomes accidentally spilled on the table it means you are about to have an argument. And to prevent the argument, you should put sugar on the spilled salt. More ominously, it is said that if you have a craving to eat halva, you must find and eat it right away, otherwise, someone in the family will pass away. In Lenkoran, the southern region of Azerbaijan, people say the same about *plov,* a rice dish which is considered to be the national food of Azerbaijan and is part of its ancient culture.

The way Caucasians treat guests reveals the culture and the spirit of their nations. In his book, *Adventures in Caucasia*, the nineteenth-century French writer Alexandre Dumas observed: 'if you knock on any door in Azerbaijan, or anywhere in the Caucasus, say that you're a foreigner and have no place to spend the night, the owner of the house will immediately give you his largest room.' Hospitality is a cornerstone of Azerbaijani culture. The guest is sacred and displaying generosity to those you welcome into your home is deeply rooted in people's everyday life. The most prominent place around the table is always reserved for guests, the eldest seated at the head. Azeri proverbs – such as: 'A guest is a decoration of a house. A house without a guest is like a mill without water. A guest brings prosperity. A guest is untouchable, even if he is an enemy. Let the houses which do not welcome guests collapse' – have passed from generation to generation. This level of hospitality can be overwhelming and seem excessive from a Western point of view. As a person who grew up in a family which hosted relatives, neighbours, complete strangers, travellers, and guests on a daily basis, it is a natural instinct for me. I remember that we always had extra portions of every meal in case of a sudden arrival. Hospitality during holidays is taken even more seriously. It is considered a duty of a family to invite guests for a meal to break the fast during Ramadan, to invite newly married couples for a dinner, distribute sacrificial meat during the Hajj holidays to relatives, neighbours, and families in need, or to visit relatives during New Year and Novruz holiday.

While observing family dinners and gatherings, I always wonder whether these rituals will continue to be practiced by younger generations. Some of the rites have changed dramatically even in the past ten years, especially when it comes to food in the major cities of the region. Here you will only find members of the older generation visiting the farmers market to bargain for fresh, locally produced tomatoes in order to cook traditional dishes. My grandfather says the younger generation is focused purely on studying and working, and has no interest in learning to cook. Ask any member of the tsakhur community to name a dish that best captures the culinary spirit of their ethnicity or family, and chances are they will name *surhullu*, the pasta meal my grandma loved to cook for us. However, now it is rarely served up by millennials who instead will seek out non-traditional food. They will only eat it when they go back to their parents' houses for meals, instead choosing to keep fuelled on fast-food options and eating out rather than labouring in the kitchen to prepare a meal of their own. Ready-made dough and flour products are now bought by families instead of making it from scratch, something quite shocking for my parents' and grandparents' generation. I remember my mother used to bake fresh bread for the family. Nowadays, everyone simply buys it from the store. The increasing number of restaurants, cafes and fast-food choices has gradually removed some of the rituals from everyday life. Despite this, no matter how much we change our eating habits, food from our culture that reminds us of family often becomes the comfort we seek as adults in times of stress and frustration. Food heritage not only encompasses the recipes, ingredients, dishes and certain food traditions; it also includes agricultural products, techniques, and table manners. It is this nostalgia that will hopefully encourage the younger generation to keep such traditions alive and pass them on to future ones.

Food also denotes status, statement of wealth and social standing in Caucasian society just like anywhere else in the world. Being able to afford food such as caviar, expensive seafood, and drinking the finest wine at restaurants is used to illustrate a person's social standing within a community. There is a commonly expressed phrase 'kids who have grown up with honey and cream' in reference to spoiled rich kids, which describes how wealth is manifested through food. My grandmother would recall: 'When I was 18, I was married and had a child and did not have a job outside the home. Back then we were on a very limited budget. So I learned to cook a lot of things with a few ingredients. As long as you had flour, water, some oil and you could make the dough, you would survive chilly winter days.' My homeland, Azerbaijan, is famous for the rarest and most expensive form of caviar which is harvested from beluga sturgeon that swims in the Caspian Sea. However, if you ask around you will find that only a small number of citizens have tried it in their life. Only those on a high-income can afford caviar as part of their diet.

Alongside wealth disparity, there are other factors that determine dietary habits. Caucasus has the reputation of being a highly patriarchal region; therefore, gender stereotypes are insidious even when it comes to food. Differing eating norms are imposed on men and women with various types of food perceived as 'feminine' or 'masculine'. 'Eat like a man!' is a common phrase frequently bandied around. For instance, *kabab,* a local dish made with small chunks of meat, or ground meat, cooked on skewers over a fire is a speciality of exclusively male chefs. It is labelled 'man's food', and is the default choice of men while dining in Azerbaijan. Society not only expects men and women to make gendered food choices, but also dictates the quantity of the chosen food that should be consumed. There exists a cultural standard that men should eat more than women, and that they need the energy because they are bigger and stronger. It is undoubtedly an archaic, misogynistic manner of thinking. If a man overeats, it is almost a badge of honour. If women engage in similar eating habits, they are considered unfeminine and vulgar. I remember my mum serving dinner in different portions for my grandfather and father, and the rest of the family. Men in the family would always get the biggest portion and a greater number of meat pieces compared to the women. Women would get a 'small feminine portion' regardless of how hungry they are.

Although a number of traditional Caucasian food choices are rich in carbohydrate, fat, flour and sugar, none of which are particularly healthy for the human body, the region is well-known for longevity. An extraordinary number of centenarians live in this part of the world. According to Caucasians, age is beauty. *National Geographic* even ran an article with photos of Azerbaijani shepherd Shirali Muslimov who, when he died in 1973, was considered to be the oldest person who ever lived. Most surprisingly, according to various studies it is not diet and exercise alone that helps people to live past the age of one hundred. The quality of personal relationships has proved to be as important as nutrition. It is clearly one of the reasons why Caucasians live to a grand age while retaining full health and vigour. What is fascinating is the high degree of physical strength found among the elders in Caucasus, and their joy in life.

The primary crops produced in Azerbaijan are agricultural: grapes, cotton, tobacco, citrus fruits, and vegetables. Livestock and dairy are also important, while rice plantations were replaced with potato and cabbage farms during the Soviet era. Due to technological advances, mechanisation increased chemical use and government policies that favoured maximising production, agriculture and food has changed dramatically. These changes allowed fewer farmers with reduced labour demands to produce the majority of food. Although such developments have had some positive effects and reduced many risks in farming, there have also been significant costs. Topsoil depletion and the decline of family-run farms has meant there are far fewer natural and organic products being grown. Living and working conditions for farm labourers remains extremely harsh, with family farms struggling to sell their wares due to lack of access to the market and high transaction costs. Changes in farming and agriculture have also affected the taste of the food we create. The small town of Zagatala, in the north-west part of Azerbaijan, where I grew up, usually has fresh and locally produced food. Freshly produced products are not so common when you move to bigger cities. Unfortunately, people have little chance to transport food from rural regions, and end up buying processed food which contains scant nutrition and more artificial ingredients and preservatives. The good news, however, is that due to concern over diet-related illnesses, local natural products are experiencing a renaissance. A friend of mine, who is passionate about community development, as well as reviving traditional tastes, has launched a start-up named ObaNatur, which is helping farmers to sell their products in the capital city of Azerbaijan. The start-up has united small and mid-size farmers on one platform and helps them to bring their products to the market and deliver to customers. By volunteering at ObaNatur, I realised that the number of people who are conscious eaters increases day by day.

As a conscious consumer of food, I prefer to eat healthily and make healthier versions of traditional food. I came to discover my passion for healthy nutrition a few years ago at the age of 20, when, after experiencing chronic pain, the importance of the right diet and nutrition dawned on me. In a short time, seeing the effects of these lifestyle changes, I was simply amazed by the power of healthy eating on my health, sleep, and emotional stability. From then on, I became passionate about promoting healthy nutrition, encouraging people to change their eating habits and consequently attain optimal health and wellbeing. My commitment to grow, expand, contribute, and thereby make a difference in our society inspires me to continue promoting healthy nutrition at a higher, institutional level. My aim is to change the eating habits, improve the health of people of Azerbaijan and reduce the burden of preventable diet-related illnesses. In order to do this, I plan to develop a health centre by mobilising distinguished experts and young professionals where potential public health programmes and policies and educational strategies can be studied and researched, and results developed into policy and behavioural recommendations. I see it as my responsibility to save the legacy of our ancestors and let other generations enjoy the food experiences and traditions we have long-treasured.

COFFEE

Tahir Abbas

Few pleasures in life surpass a cup of freshly ground, roasted coffee, whether in the form of a Turkish coffee found in the bazaars of Istanbul or an Americano served at one of the more established international coffee chains in the capital cities of Western Europe. It almost doesn't surprise me that coffee is the second most traded commodity in the world after oil. What makes it such a popular, mildly hallucinogenic, psychoactive drug that directly affects the central nervous system, encouraging hundreds of millions to prepare their morning fix without hesitation? My impression is that without coffee many individuals sitting at their office desks would freeze into a state of paralysis due to the absence of this hypnotic, elusive, high. With research indicating that coffee is addictive, leading to recognisable withdrawal systems when individuals abstain, surely therein lies the explanation for its tremendous popularity beyond the idea of a stimulating concoction that dramatically impacts the body. Is there a coffee culture that focuses on coffee drinking as a collective exercise to the extent that it is pivotal to national consciousness? How has coffee become such an essential element of any meeting involving two or more people engaged in banter that necessarily utilises the frontal cortex of the brain, enhancing short-term concentration, memory and thinking?

Having evolved from the rather bland and inferior instant range, like so many of us growing up in Britain in the 1980s and 1990s, coffee houses were a rarity among eateries in the high streets of towns and cities across the country. With the establishment of global brands such as Starbucks, Caffè Nero and Costa, drinking coffee became more than just a lubricant for exchange or a stimulant for office workers. It was now widely accessible to all, permitting an individual, or more, to enjoy the effects of partaking in a brew, not only as a social glue but to enhance ties and friendships. Coffee was more than a device to encourage individuals to start their day on an artisanal, hand-roasted, smooth, skinny high. It was now returning to its historical roots of bringing people together and engaging in thought-provoking, provocative and broad-ranging conversation, pushing forward the boundaries of thinking, intellectual development and social argument. Coffee was suddenly cool and convenient. Coffee drinkers sprung into action as social agents engaged in the process of sharing and enhancing a collective, forming an entirely new language and culture that has become firmly rooted in our day-to-day reality. It was against this backdrop in the 1990s that I too began to appreciate the nuances of the Ethiopian versus the Colombian versus the Kenyan. Each coffee brand reflected certain colour composition, bitterness or otherwise, and a preference for a fast kick-butt versus a slow high. This journey led me to eventually live in Istanbul where I learnt how to make Turkish coffee at home using the simplest of utensils, but without the refined technique, cultivated by homemakers and coffee lovers over the generations. Getting the process right was not as easy as it seemed.

Mastering this process is a prized skill, particularly as the role of Ottoman Turkey in harnessing then spreading coffee and its consumer culture is significant in the history of coffee. However, the fact remains that coffee itself came from elsewhere. Its origins lie in Ethiopia. From there, it travelled to Yemen and then to Mecca, the centre of the Muslim world, at which point the Ottomans incorporated coffee consumption culture into the fabric of Ottoman society. In my search for the perfect cup of coffee and the most enticing of coffee aromas, two countries in the world have a particular story of note. Jamaican Blue Mountain and the Ethiopian brands are undoubtedly my favourite coffee beans. I travelled to both of these countries, tasting the beans as close to source as is physically possible. It was part of a journey to explore my personal history of coffee, intertwined with a wider historical cultural and sociological analysis of the consumption of this most popular beverage that starts life as a mere inconsequential green bean.

The historical birth of coffee is well documented and it comes as no surprise that the origins of human civilisation and coffee emerge in the same place. Little else is known of this origins story other than it supposedly occurred in the city of Mocha in a region called Kaffa, in what was the ancient land of Abyssinia at some point in the ninth century.

According to legend, a herder named Kaldi noticed that his donkeys were behaving erratically after they had chewed on a wild red berry. Their frenzied activity caused a stir, prompting Kaldi to experiment with the berries himself, only to discover a similar feeling of excitement, euphoria and enthusiasm. His wife encouraged him to introduce the berry to the head of the village, who dismissed the fruit as the 'work of the devil'. He threw the berries into a fire, and the smoke began to affect the perception of those gathered around, upon which point hot water was placed over the beans, leading to a mixture, which they drank. It revealed an intoxicating but calming effect. This new-found revelation was related to others and from there the story moves to Yemen where Sufi Muslims carrying out the *dhikr* found the *qahwa*, a stimulant that allowed them to devote themselves to the chanting with greater vigour. These Muslims integrated coffee consumption into Islamic practice, which then found itself in Mecca by the 1350s. The coffee was soon transported to the cities of Damascus and Cairo by the mid-1500s, and it was in Istanbul where Venetian traders sampled the mysterious concoction and were immediately enraptured by its fine qualities. From there they took it to northern Italy, before its renown spread through Europe. From Mecca, a taste for coffee proliferated throughout the Ottoman territories, and to Spain and India.

It was during the time of the Ottomans that coffee consumption became a form of social interaction, with groups congregating to share the intoxicating drink but to also engage in discussion. Vast swathes of the different classes, cultures and religions of late sixteenth century Istanbul would come together; and, not surprisingly, such gatherings and associated activities were considered excessive by the sultans who feared political resistance or plotting. At one level, the *kavehanes* (coffee houses) were seen as a hotbed of sin because of their association with late-night drinking and opium taking. At another level, this tête-à-tête among artists, writers, *ulema* and ordinary members of the public necessarily introduced a form of 'democratised socialisation', initiating notions of leisure for the middle classes, creating a standardisation that has survived to this day. Coffee allows people to assemble, share ideas and inspire action through the intellectual and emotional responses the drink can induce. The Ottoman Sultan Murad III attempted to ban coffee houses in Constantinople, ordering their immediate shutdown, but to no avail. Even Kair Bey, governor of Mecca in

1511, tried to stop the use of coffee, but was thwarted. The Ottoman Turks could not get enough of the substance it seems. During the Ottoman era, Turks perfected the art of preparing and serving it, cultivating it as an essential component of the social fabric of daily life. Those who came to the Ottoman Centre never failed to be enamoured by its richness and splendour, and this association with coffee drinking and the Ottomans therefore remains a significant symbolic, cultural and tourist concept for the nation of Turkey today. So deeply embedded is the culture of drinking Turkish coffee, distinctively ground finely to a powder, that it is the staple drink for Turks after breakfast or lunch.

As coffee spread into Europe, it did so at a time of rapid transformation among intellectual, cultural and religious thinkers. Coffee houses became a site for the convergence of fervent intellectual ideas, sowing the seeds of rebellion and social change that would inevitably follow. These changes led to the enlightenment, renaissance and in some cases revolution. Over the years, the notion of a coffee culture has emerged, where coffee touches every aspect of our lives, from the home, to the office and to the spaces where we eat and are at leisure. The consumption of coffee is now on a global scale. It is ubiquitous in North America, where it is sometimes called 'a cup of Joe', which suggests its common appeal and expands on the idea of a national drink in response to the efforts of the Europeans who brought with them tea as their favourite tipple. However, the mass production of coffee during the 1950s by Nestlé and brands such as Maxwell House reduced the popularity of the product because of its declining standards. During the 1970s onwards, however, chains such as Starbucks embarked on a mission to provide an authentic coffee taste in a comfortable seated environment. This revolutionised coffee consumption and introduced new and decidedly more sophisticated forms of the beverage, which had otherwise been the preserve of refined Italian coffee drinkers. Choice entered into the coffee consumption world, and with rising standards of living and upward social mobility, large sections of societies were able to enjoy even more of their favourite warming drink. This reversal of fortunes for the coffee production and consumption sectors led to specialisation and the emergence of independent artisan coffee houses providing specialist beans and blends at premium prices.

It occurs to me that everywhere I have lived for extended periods has turned out to be an important site in the history of coffee. In September 2015, I had an opportunity to spend a semester at New York University. My flat was located on Fifth Avenue. Around Washington Square Park, between the numerous buildings owned by the University, independent coffee houses were on every corner on every street of Greenwich Village. Café Reggio served the first cappuccino in 1927. This coffee shop still sits on MacDougal Street. The coffee houses today not only provide directly imported, roasted and prepared filter coffee, but offer it in a variety of forms including the vacuum drip method or the Chemex filter. Some outlets provided something called 'bullet coffee', which was coffee blended with fresh butter. Apparently, the caffeine kick is supposed to be easier on the heart, but I did not notice anything too distinct. Most of the time, various blends of South American and East African beans were served to the hipsters of lower Manhattan who were spoiled for choice but without any real understanding of where these beans originated.

Turkish coffee is renowned across the world, as is the sublime preparation and service associated with it. It also carries an air of magic when grandmothers, aunts and eager sisters take their turn to read the remains of a finished cup, promising all sorts of fruitful encounters with strangers or endless bounty at the hands of divine intervention. *Kurukahveci Mehmet Efendi* is located at the back of the Spice Bazar in Kadikoy in Istanbul. When I lived in the city for six years, it is where I went to pick up my freshly roasted, ground, Turkish coffee. Locals lined up in quickly moving queues picking up their bags of still warm coffee. The effervescent aroma filled my satchel as I journeyed my way home to prepare a fresh cup. Barely through the door, I would whip out my copper plated *cezve*, and the bubbly boiling smell filled the kitchen. For a few days, the coffee smell remains intensely fresh. The process of making Turkish coffee in a *cezve* took a while to master. The understanding of how one needs to boil the coffee at a particular temperature, while removing the froth at different stages, never allowing the coffee to boil all the way, was something that had to be shown to me in the end. Convinced I had become something of an expert, I brought my *cezve* back with me when I returned to the UK. Luckily, upon my arrival I was easily able to source my coffee of choice:

Kurukahveci Mehmet Efendi is one of Turkey's most recognisable brands and a significant export, popular in the diasporas of north London and Berlin.

The Middle East, too, is renowned for its coffee but it is made in a slightly different way compared to the method championed by the Turks. In the bustling cities of Beirut and Damascus, coffee shops are everywhere. Arabs smoke the *shisha* and drink coffee incessantly throughout the day. The coffee there has some cardamom ground into the process. This gives it a mild yet distinct aftertaste, refreshing the breath and the tongue. When I asked the traders from where they sourced their coffee, the general answer was that it was a combination of South American and African, in particular, Brazilian and Ethiopian. When I purchased the blend containing cardamom from a local seller in the West Bank, the smell of the coffee engulfed the entire residence I was staying in, again for days on end. People do not really drink coffee in South Asia or Southeast Asia due to the role that tea plays there, but I had heard so much about the coffee in Indonesia that I could not wait to try the infamous *kopi luwak*, said to be the most expensive coffee in the world. Established by the Dutch settlers in the seventeenth century, the islands of Indonesia are notorious for their coffee beans today: Sumatra and Java being the two most prominent. The idea is that when the civet eats the beans, the digestive process alters its chemical composition, specifically removing the bitterness of the flavour. However, it is incredibly strong for the unassuming, and can cause an unpleasant reaction. For the dedicated connoisseur, *kopi luwak* is one for the rarer occasions.

One of the other more expensive coffees available is Jamaican Blue Mountain. Jamaica is known for its sun, sand and vibrancy. While many associate Jamaica with certain other kinds of naturally grown stimulants, coffee is not always the first thing that comes to mind. However, coffee enthusiasts are aware that there is a certain bean notorious for its pleasant flavour and limited bitterness, grown high up on the Blue Mountains on the eastern side of the island. One day, I took a bus journey from Kingston all the way to Port Antonio. In the morning before setting off, I had two cups of Blue Mountain coffee and some slices of mango. The memory still lingers of the rush of a perfectly brewed cup of caffeine tempered by the smooth silky sweet taste of a ripe mango. The eventual calming effects of these two ingredients ensured that I had a large smile on my face throughout the day. Blue Mountain coffee is exceptionally expensive because of the lofty export tariffs laid on importers due to the limited growing space high up in the mountains, ensuring that demand remains high and supply low.

Last year, I had the opportunity to travel to Ethiopia, which is the birthplace of human existence, as we know it, and the fount of coffee. Could there be a correlation between the advancement of human civilisation and coffee? Although the chances are that the bean was not roasted and consumed in a watery substance, the plant was certainly used for medicinal purposes as well as for flavouring foods. Ethiopia is undoubtedly an interesting place for all sorts of reasons, although many people associate it with famine or lack of development. Take a little time to look beyond the headlines and this country located in the Horn of Africa bestows many riches. Tomoca is the first coffee roasting company in Ethiopia, established in 1953 in Addis Ababa. Upon visiting the original stall that sold the licensed freshly roasted beans, I was taken aback by how unassuming the place looked. As I queued up to take my freshly prepared espresso, the line was littered with visitors from Europe and Asia. The balmy evening, the sun setting and the air thick with dust as I walked around central Addis Ababa, the city elevated to over 2,000 metres above sea level, I felt charged to the max, buzzing, light on my feet and with my mind racing at every observation. Boarding a local bus packed to the rafters, I could see eyes wide open, blinking in the darkened spaces of the heaving vehicle.

In my numerous travels to Europe, one place above all else stands out as the country most identified with drinking coffee – Italy. Sitting outside various coffee shops in a whole host of towns and cities over the years, the experience of sipping an espresso accompanied with a small wrapped biscuit, watching the world go by, is a sight to behold, especially in an age of frenetic activity where no one has a spare second let alone a moment to pause and take in their surroundings. Italy drips coffee culture from every pore, from Trento, Milan, Venice, Rome, Prato, Florence to Palermo and Agrigento. Against such backdrops my espressos were consumed in an enchanted state.

Enchantment is not the entire story and it must be acknowledged that coffee is a global commodity and consumer product available in every restaurant, hotel, bar or cafe worth their salt. In partaking of this international pastime, one is unmistakably connecting with a global infrastructure that begins with farmers located all over the global South, and ends with consumers in the predominantly prosperous North drinking their cups of coffee by the billions of gallons a year. What manifests is gaping inequalities embedded in this process. Farmers who supply this wonderful substance receive little by way of the gains of its voracious consumption taking place largely in the West. Countries producing coffee are some of the poorest across the globe. What's more the production of coffee has significant consequences for the environment and for the pockets of the needy.

Grande or *Venti*, single or double, with or without milk or sugar, coffee remains the number one drink of choice for so many in the global North, while in the Middle East and North Africa, it is part of the cultural fabric. I go so far as to import the green beans from an independent company emulating the Blue Mountain climate but grown in Kenya. Roasted on a cast iron pan, the beans are left to sit for twenty-four hours before the grinding and preparation commences. These beans are consumed within two weeks before roasting the next batch. My two morning cups set me up for the whole day, with no further coffee consumption unless I invite friends over for a Turkish coffee or an espresso or an Americano from my Moka pot, helping loosen the tongue and the mind for endless discussion. The roasted coffee bean needs to be ground finely when preparing a Turkish coffee or an Italian style dispersal, always using a Moka pot.

Coffee provides the stimulation, the rush of ideas and the inevitable melee of thoughts, taken alone or shared in company. It is a global commodity popular everywhere in the world. The coffee bean, from its humble origins as a wild berry, now interconnects our planet, ensuring that the process of farming, exporting, roasting, packaging, distribution and consumption remains in a natural state of flow. However, the main sources of the beans, namely farmers, benefit the least despite this thriving product being devoured in almost every community of almost every country. As with so many products consumed in the north and in the west, their origins lie in the east or in the south. It entrenches the inequalities of the world while keeping most people oblivious to the source of their elusive yet beloved favourite foods.

FRIED CHICKEN SHOPS

Hussein Kesvani

It's 10.30 pm on a Thursday night in early January 2018. Fluorescent lights beam across the city, emitted by the skyscrapers that line Canary Wharf. Look ahead and you will see the famous HSBC building, the Barclay's HQ next to it, and the flickering lights of the new residents that live between them; these are young, affluent city workers coming in from a long day at the office, or, more likely, from a night out at the latest trendy bar in the 'cool' new districts of South London.

A stone's throw from Canary Wharf, just around the corner from Poplar tube station, is Perfect Fried Chicken – written in all red capitals on a bright, white luminous backdrop. Pasted on its windows are its menu items as patrons are invited to choose from different combinations of chicken, wings, chips and burger meals. Allow your gaze to flit to the far right corner and you will see an array of Halal food signs, also a noticeboard mainly consisting of landlords letting out rooms, as well as women offering 'special massages'. Anyone living in this city would walk past Perfect Fried Chicken without a second glance. The shop looks like any other on London's dilapidating high streets. Out of the six retail outlets on this road, only four are occupied: Perfect Fried Chicken, a betting shop and a rival chicken shop that also sells kebabs, along with a new store selling vape pens and e-cigarettes. The others – a family-owned florist, and a further education centre for the area's deprived communities, all shut down in the past couple of years as a result of rising rents and business rates and the double-edged impact of the area's continuing regeneration schemes.

As a young Muslim growing up in Britain, fried chicken shops have played an important role in my life. At a time when my school friends all ate McDonalds, Burger King and KFC, obscurely named fried chicken shops were the only spots selling halal alternatives to the Zinger and

Whopper meals – a respite from days of eating *daal*, *roti* and *saag* (the kinds of food you only appreciate post-adolescence). But, beyond the satisfaction that comes with salty, crunchy, oily chicken, was also the taste of London itself. Like many well-to-do immigrant families, we moved from South London to leafy Kent. The schools were great, but, being surrounded by middle class, white families who routinely went to farmers' markets on weekends, the only fast food options that didn't have traces of pork in them were vegetarian sandwiches at Subway, or the dreaded mushroom slice at Greggs' bakery. Eating fried chicken would usually come as part and parcel of travelling out of the oppressive 'sticks' toward the bright lights that lay on the other side of the Dartford bridge – a place where things happened, where brown people weren't just provincial lawyers and GPs or oddities to be photographed for the grammar school brochure. London represented the opportunity, the freedom and the acceptance I craved. A type of liberation that, to me, still tastes like the crispy, golden batter on a freshly fried chicken thigh.

I cast my mind back to my formative years and back then, fried chicken was just another form of junk food – the type eaten by poor, working class immigrants like the ones who would hang out in the Poplar branch of Perfect Fried Chicken that I have found myself in order to satiate a sudden hunger craving. For people like Abdullah Jamaal, 48, a regular at this branch, the shop offers the only place to have a cheap, warm meal in the hours before he starts his night shift in one of the city's nearby office spaces. He came to London a few years ago from Pakistan, where he had worked for himself as a car mechanic. He lived in a small village near Lahore with his wife and her mother. His business abruptly went bankrupt at the same time that his mother-in-law had become severely ill, requiring full time care. Like many immigrants to the UK, Abdullah arrived seeking better work and more stable wages he could send home. 'I wanted to be a mechanic here,' he tells me while we eat our chicken burgers and chips. 'They wouldn't let me – they said my English, wasn't good. So, I spent three months [trying to] find a job, and then my friend said the [office] was looking for a night cleaner.' Abdullah told me that his friends all had similar stories – seeking better wages, better lives or, more common, better education, in London. They had heard about London on the TV, the radio and the internet. They, too, were mesmerised by the lights and the opportunities that lay behind the Perspex glass of office blocks they had seen on Google images – the ones they now look up towards as they eat from their greasy boxes of chicken wings and chips.

People may look down on halal fried chicken shops but they engender intense loyalty from their clients. In September 2017, there was public outcry after it became known that Goldsmiths – the renowned London arts university situated in New Cross, in Lewisham, one of the poorest boroughs of the capital, was offering its fresher students guided tours of London's chicken shops. Why are you 'exotifying local culture', one of the colleges' black students tweeted at the students' union. 'Exotify local culture and those who partake in these are racist as hell too' another student tweeted. In comment threads and on forums, others lambasted the university for its 'ignorance'. Recalling the incident, one student, who wished to remain anonymous, told me that the outrage wasn't necessarily at the event itself, but what it showed about the changing face of the capital. 'Goldsmiths has a reputation for having a student population that are mostly white, upper-middle class and live in the suburbs and home counties....for them, the campus is somewhere "cool" and "exotic", and the chicken shop issue showed that...these shops are places that people who grew up around here went to – they were the only places we could afford to go out and eat and socialise in – especially when there weren't [any] youth centres to go to or things to do. We have mates who used to work in those shops and used to go to school with them... it was seeing our community become part of this posh, white, gentrified experience that's happening all across London, that got so many of us angry and upset.'

The incident at Goldsmiths might have been the first chicken-themed backlash against the gentrification of the city, but it also indicated something larger. Chicken shops were at the heart of the battle for London – between developers and residents, between the gentrifying class and Londoners who were being forced out of the city by escalating house prices. In 2015, sociologist Sam Floy developed a mapping software comparing house prices between areas populated with coffee shops in leafy boroughs, and those depreciating in value near fried chicken joints. The accompanying explainer on Medium.com was titled 'How to know if you live in an "up and coming" area of London'.

At the same time, fried chicken has also become a staple of London pop culture; the international explosion of Grime music has put the chicken shop on a global stage. Fried Chicken's debut on the grime scene started with 2007's infamous 'Junior Spesh', by Red Hot Entertainment. The song opens with:

> Junior Spesh, 7up, fried legs
> Make sure you gimmie mayonnaise on the left
> If ya ain't got 7-up then I want Dr. Pep
> Ain't got what I want then I go HF
> Feelin' rich then I go KF
> Gimmie Jaxor, then I want side Breast
> Make sure you gimmie chips forks and pep. (Pep-ahhhh!)

More recently, Stormzy's video 'Too Big for Your Boots', the debut single from his bestselling 2017 album, was shot in a fried chicken shop. Meanwhile, some of grimes' biggest names, from Wiley to Giggs, have all referenced chicken in their music, often centred around their experiences growing up in London. From this confluence of London hip-hop and fried chicken culture, also emerged YouTube creators like 'Chicken Shop Date', in which Amelia Dimoldenberg speaks to the city's up-and-coming MCs over a box of wings, and, of course Elijah Koshie, whose YouTube series 'The Pengest Munch' sees him visiting and rating fried chicken shops in high definition with grime bangers blasting in the background. Koshie's videos went viral across Twitter, Facebook and Instagram in 2017, leading some to question how useful his videos were in presenting a true, authentic London, or, whether he had just been providing fodder for the city gents to gawk at while at their desk jobs.

Conversely, the 'fried chicken' product itself has been subject to gentrification: go to any market in London, and you'll find an array of 'posh' fried chicken shops like MotherClucker and The Fried Chicken Company, all selling 'high-end' chicken in brioche buns with a selection of expensive cheese for anywhere between £7 and £14 a head. In some cases, like the Temple of Hackney restaurant, it'll come in the form of vegan fried chicken, which has attracted hoards of the borough's hipster residents since its four-star review on the Londonist. A few weekends ago, while looking for a lunch spot in the market stall next to the Southbank Centre in Waterloo, I came across a chicken stall whose sign simply read : 'EAT DIRTY' – referring to a fried chicken dish with onions, garlic, japalenos, 'Indian spices' topped with three different cheeses and hot sauces. What amazed me was, for £8.00 a head, mostly white, middle class families who'd taken their children to see an exhibition at the centre could eat the same amount of calories as the average late-night customer in Perfect Fried Chicken as they prepared for their night shifts, or, more common, were waiting for their next assignment to come in from their gig-economy delivery job.

Debate around fried chicken isn't just restricted to class, however. A fiery debate rages within the Muslim community both about the health implications and the ethics of the fried chicken industry. It boiled to the surface during the London Mayoral election, when London Mayor Sadiq Khan – who at the time was the MP for Tooting West, home of Europe's largest Chicken Cottage – outlined his plan to ban fried chicken chains from operating within a 400-metre radius of schools. Khan was quickly called out, both by me in a BuzzFeed News article, and other outlets, after a video emerged of him praising the founders of Chicken Cottage at the Chicken Cottage Awards in 2012. Khan described Chicken Cottage as a 'beautiful thing', 'a British product...selling Islamic products, selling halal products...that is niche and general but it's gone mainstream.... When Chicken Cottage started in 1994, the aim was to be as excellent, or as good as, the market leaders...now, the aim is to be the best in its own right, and now the market leaders are Chicken Cottage'.

Khan's gaffe perfectly illustrated the contentious position of chicken shops in urban Muslim culture. On the one hand, praising the boom in halal meat industries as one of the largest employers of Muslims in Britain, while on the other, worrying that these halal meat industries, often operating using cheap cuts of meat and high levels of salt, sugar and other chemicals, may be contributing to severe health problems in many communities – particularly with illnesses like heart disease and type II diabetes. Furthermore, new concerns that have emerged as a result of the widening of global capitalism and the supply chains that fuel it, has also caused panic with some Muslim scholars, who fear that the meat isn't quite as halal as it claims to be. In 2012, Shakykh Siddiqi, a member of the Muslim Action Group, a group of leading imams in the UK, led a joint statement warning that the processing of meat by big chains like KFC didn't count as halal, because it didn't fulfil the conditions by which each animal had to be prayed over. 'With machine killing, they are not praying the prayer over each of the birds,' he told *Food Manufacturing* magazine. 'In fact, when they are machine killing, they are not praying at all. They may just have a tape recording, which defeats the whole purpose of halal.'

This is a debate that continues, as mosques, imams, various halal monitoring authorities and the government try to understand the ethical and religious positions behind the concept of halal, when confronted with advances in technology like processing machines. To this day, while the main halal monitoring organisation, The Halal Food Authority (HFA), believe that animals can still be blessed when killed by machines, the Halal Monitoring Committee (HMC) takes the opposite view – believing that meat can only be halal when an individual slaughterer performs all the rituals. While most restaurants and suppliers tend to follow the HFA, positions like that adopted by the HMC are increasingly common.

This battle, however, also points to the future of halal chicken shops. For some Muslims, whose interpretation of halal meat goes beyond the act of praying over animals, exploring vegetarianism has become a means of practising their faith. Groups like the Vegetarian Muslim Society, which has nearly 5,000 Facebook members, or the Vegan Muslim Initiative, an international campaign group started with the mission 'that if Muslims are going to be relevant and positive contributors to our planet's future, then there must be a major paradigm shift in how we view and approach food' are examples. These groups not only feature the standard Islamic reminders of living a halal life, but also feature recipes, advice and discussion groups around practising Islam while vegetarian or vegan, ranging from the sayings of the Prophet (one popular story is how the Prophet Muhammad would only eat meat on special occasions), to 'how to survive family Eid while vegetarian', and how to explain vegetarianism to your grandparents.

The issue of halal meat has also attracted the attention of far-right groups like the English Defence League and Britain First. First halal chicken shops find themselves at the forefront of extremist ire. Perfect Fried Chicken has endured racist attacks. Mohammed, the server tells me: 'We have a few drunk people come in, they say things like "go home", "Muslim scum", they shout things like "EDL EDL!" or just say things like "Fuck Muslims".'

There's been more of that recently because of the London terrorist attacks last year and the attacks in Manchester. But it's not been like other places, where they've had their windows smashed, or been threatened unless they stop selling halal food. When I ask why he thinks these attacks happen, he sighs. 'They think halal meat, it funds ISIS!... I tell them, come to the back, I'll show you where it goes. I'll show you that we don't make any money, that we spend our money in London paying rent, paying bills! ISIS! Do they know how much it costs to run all these cookers, these fryers?'

Despite these pleas, far-right groups continue to make the link between halal meat and terrorism on their social media platforms. Britain First, the far-right street group whose slogan says they are an 'Anti-Islamist Christian Movement' even made a series of videos in which they 'invaded' high street restaurants who they claimed sold halal meat, to issue warnings that they would 'return, unless they stopped funding terrorism'. The videos are bizarre, surreal and at times comical. But they are also dangerous too, especially in the wake of the murder of Jo Cox in 2016, and the attempted attack on a mosque in Finsbury Park during Ramadan in 2017.

For the most part, workers in fried chicken shops are offered little by way of protection. Most are not members of fast food workers' unions, or in a position of being able to negotiate for more secure contracts, better working conditions, or more effective safety regulations. 'Late at night, early in the morning, are the most difficult times,' Mohammed tells me while he's frying another batch of chips. 'Not a lot of police, and anything could happen. Last year, there was a man with a knife, who came in and was calling us "Paki scum" and saying he'd kill us. He was very drunk so we could hold him down until the police came but even then, the police didn't take it seriously! It's dangerous to work in a shop like this, when anything could happen...I wouldn't want my children to be working here in the future... No, never.'

So what is the future of London's halal fried chicken shops? Many of the shop owners I spoke to remain optimistic that they would survive — spurred by sales from people priced out of London's fancy cafes and bistros. Some, however, expressed doubts for their survival in years to come. 'The biggest challenge shops face today is the cost of rent in the first place. London is expensive, and for landlords, it's more profitable to turn their buildings into flats,' one manager told me over the phone. 'Which is what many of them are doing. I completely expect that if Mayor Khan wants to build more homes, he'll provide incentives for landlords to let their properties become flats – in which case, you'll see chicken shops across the city close down and high streets become extinct'.

However, it's not just development that is a threat to halal chicken outlets. They may be killed off by emerging Muslim aspirational consumers who have been instrumental in expanding the 'halal market' across the world – from clothing and modest fashion, to the kinds of food that is provided in mosques and wider Muslim communities. 'Younger Muslims are more conscious about what they eat. They want quality food that's healthy, sustainable and produced ethically.' says Ayaaz Shamim, a contributor to the halal food review blog 'Feed the Lion'. 'So you've got this boom in halal food across the UK of everything from burritos to Chinese dishes. And if you live in London then it's even more accessible to get quality halal meals. So it's in the inner cities where the fried chicken shops will suffer, not because Muslims are going vegetarian or because of ethical reasons, though some of that might be there. It'll be because tastes have changed, and you've got a generation that won't settle for bog standard chicken and chips, when they've got loads more options.'

Back in Perfect Fried Chicken, Abdullah Jamaal is finishing his meal. His phone starts to beep – informing him he needs to be on his way soon to get to work on time. He says goodbye to the guys behind the till and briskly leaves, heading through the chilly mist and toward the city lights. He'll be back tomorrow, and the next day, and the next day according to Mohammed, 'with the same meal – burger and chips, every day!'. To Mohammed, Abdullah is the reason why these shops will continue to be important to the city. 'It's not just the workers, it's everyday people. We have families come in, we have people who haven't got homes to go to. They find this shop for a place to have hot food, a drink, and just to sleep in the warm until the sun comes up'.

'This is like a home to them,' Mohammed shouts from the cellar, passing me bags of frozen chicken he'll be spending the next few hours seasoning and spicing. 'We're there when there's no one else for them...there are not many places like that in London any more'.

THE HALOODIES

Imran Kausar

Glasgow, 1994. It's raining. It always seems to be raining. But that doesn't make me love the town of my birth any less. A few months before I go on to study medicine at university, my mum had me working like her personal Deliveroo driver. On this occasion sending me to our local meat shop to collect whatever she had ordered. Driving in the incessant rain I pass our local Safeway; our usual grocery haunt. Clean, brightly lit, well stocked, hygienic, organised, with a large car park and neatly arranged shopping trolleys. In every way, it was diametrically opposite to my destination. Our local meat shop filled me with dread. I only ever agreed to go if Mum had called up and pre-ordered. That way I could keep my communication with the butcher to a functional minimum. Parking up on a nearby side-street, I plan my mission with precision. Just make sure I can see the blue, plastic carrier bags near the counter ready to be collected. But wait. Can I see the scrap of paper with the price sellotaped to the bag? Yes. Great. Go. Go. Go. I mutter a mandatory 'Salaam', then with a knowing nod, point to the bags waiting for collection. Deftly making sure I didn't collect any unwanted scraps of meat loitering on the outside of the bag or butcher's hand, I have a quick peek inside to witness the smaller bulging, white bags jostling for position as I head to the till to pay in cash. As I depart, I glance at the meat counter again. The trays of overflowing meat held in position with tight cling-film, valiantly trying to keep the contents from escaping. The morose butcher with a bloodied apron who seemed to have lost his joy for life wherever he lost his gloves. The large carcass that dangles nervously in a permanently open fridge at the back of the store and the secrets hiding in plain looking cardboard boxes. The pieces of flattened cardboard box that had somehow metamorphosed into a carpet. The wooden butcher's block that never appears to be clean. Last year's calendar with a picture of a Turkish mosque adorning the wall next to a large white plastic board,

declaring the prices in hilariously misspelled English. 'Sheep Tasticles –
£0.59'. I drive away, glancing at the shop in my rear view mirror. Medina
Halal, the sign declares. I am certain halal meat in Medina was never meant
to be like this.

The truth was that the halal meat shop embarrassed me. I couldn't
accept that something that had such a poor appearance had anything to do
with Islam or me. Islam is clean and beautiful, ordained by the Almighty
and ahead of its time. This very typical butcher shop lacked hygiene and
screamed 'low quality' with a distinct lack of pride in its mission. At this
time in Glasgow, as with most of the UK, the only outward manifestation
of Islam or Muslims were purpose built mosques and halal meat shops. In
those days you were far more likely to see a Muslim woman wearing a
South Asian *dupatta* (a long scarf, often worn over the head) than a hijab.
But for the less culturally aware Scots man or woman, the halal butcher
shop was an open declaration of how Muslims reflected their beliefs. It was
testament to how Muslims actually wanted their meat. Unclean, dirty,
cheap, with no sense of respect for the slaughtered animal, the consumer
nor their Lord. My mortification was soon compounded with the
realisation that this is what others were thinking of me. It was personal.

Like many second and third generation South Asians, my identity is as a
Muslim first and, in my case, a proud Scotsman second. Any event,
occasion or issue that affected or represented Islam, directly affected my
feelings of pride, triumph or shame. Attitudes towards Islam directly
correlated to my own self-esteem. These numerous halal butchers dotted
across the country were all my personal ambassadors. Each one of them
displaying a sticker with a verse from the Qur'an, each one of them
betraying me and tainting the beauty of halal and Islam.

The penny had dropped.
The seed of change had been planted.
The journey had begun.

Over the next decade and a half, I progressed with my education and
career; leaving my family and the damp pastures of Scotland and moving
to London in early 2000, optimistic and eager. By now I had significantly
increased my knowledge of the Islamic position on animal welfare, and the

balance between man and animal, land and grain. I had realised that the concept of halal (lawful) had to be combined with the notion of *tayyib* (wholesome). As a medical doctor, I now had a far better understanding of nutrition and the role of food in the health of individuals and populations. Although food has always had a space in the national consciousness, a number of national food scandals had made people more aware of what they were consuming and prompted them to ask more questions. From Mad Cow Disease in the mid-90s to Jamie Oliver highlighting the high fat content of Turkey Twizzlers (a staple in many UK schools), time and time again our confidence in food was being undermined. Illness and discomfort relating to food consumption saw a spike in sales of 'free-from' foods well beyond what should be expected from the rates of gluten and lactose intolerance reported in medical literature. Suddenly, it seemed as if the food we were eating was slowly killing us. The organic movement kept scaring us all about genetically modified foods and meanwhile in the West we were eating ourselves to death with spiralling obesity rates while in parts of Africa, famines still raged. Food poverty and inequality was a growing issue while we continued to over-farm and pollute our earth with pesticides and fertilisers in a never-ending zeal to increase crop yield. In the EU, we had created butter mountains and wine lakes from subsidy-driven overproduction. And halal food always had its never ending episodes of bad news stories. Often related to yet another rat-infested halal butcher shop, or a halal butcher selling meat unfit for human consumption. For a period around 2003, Muslims became concerned with the Chicken Cheats. Chicken imported from Europe pumped with water to increase its weight (and therefore price), the water being mixed with animal protein (including pork) to slow its leakage. The outrage was heard from Aberdeen to Cornwall, but as ever, little changed.

In all this time, with crisis upon crisis, I became acutely aware of the deafening answers that Islam had already provided to many of these issues. I wondered when and where Muslims would be able to turn around and show the world that the Almighty has provided us with solutions, if we would but listen. If we operated with a true halal/*tayyib* philosophy, some of these problems would never even have arisen in the first place. But, then, I realised that Muslims have remained voiceless over other significant aspects of global food production: intensive farming, caged hens, use of hormones, antibiotic growth promotion, and feeding animals other animal by-products - these practices have become so ingrained that they can be very difficult to avoid. We have chosen to become the voiceless victims of the intensive agricultural crusaders blindly adopting a new status-quo. But there were two clear issues: at the macro level, the world had much to understand and benefit from the halal and *tayyib* philosophy; at the micro level, consumers of halal in the UK were being provided a very low quality of halal, which in many instances was not halal, in the true sense of the word, at all. Halal had everything to prove.

By 2011, I had experienced careers in medicine, investment banking and pharmaceutical drug development. I had been continuously reading about the halal markets and it was clear to me, the only way to have a meaningful and sustainable impact, was to create a halal food brand and to control the quality throughout – all the way. Through a brand, education into the benefits of the Islamic perspective on food and its production could be dispersed and gradually, halal foods could occupy a new space and gain respect. Despite a brief foray into assessing demand in the market in 2006 via an advert in a trade magazine, I had made little progress. Then it struck me. The best way to get to know everyone involved in the halal food industry was to run a halal food festival. So I did. In September 2013, with help, the world saw the first ever Halal Food Festival in London. Over 20,000 visitors attended a packed Excel in East London to witness a range of halal food companies and brands feed eager customers who had come to expand their culinary horizons. Although there was nothing exceptional about a food festival per se, there was real excitement about a halal food festival. This otherwise niche, poorly understood, low value segment had come of age. Press from around the world from MSNBC in the USA, BBC and *The Nation* (UAE) had sent reporters to cover the event. Halal food was big business and everyone had to notice. To assist with social media spread and to differentiate our festival from other imitator festivals which we suspected would appear over time, we needed to create a 'tribe', a word unique to us. The word Halal and Foodies were blended to form 'Haloodies' and thus a new trend was born. Haloodies was fresh, original and exciting. An invented, culturally fluid term that was free to dictate its own narrative. Devoid of geographical stereotypes and cultural affiliations, Haloodies reflects the contemporary middle-class Muslim. Blending tradition and modernity and citizenship of the world. An exhibitor at the festival was launching a range of pre-packed fresh halal meats and had a great deal of experience in the operations and logistics of raw meats. Immediately after the festival, we met with them and agreed to re-launch the range as Haloodies. And thus, in November 2013, Haloodies was born, with the online supermarket Ocado commencing deliveries on 10 March 2014.

Although Haloodies' commercial armoury and weaponry were well equipped to compete on the retail battlefield and find a home in the fridge of the time-poor, cash-rich discerning Muslim consumer, its true purpose was to raise the profile of a philosophy that was far ahead of its time but never more pertinent and necessary than today: to reunite halal with the forgotten values of *tayyib* – wholesomeness. The driving ethos was to remind Muslims that we all have a responsibility to animal welfare, sustainable food production and environmental stewardship. To fundamentally raise the quality of the food we consume and in doing so to raise the status of halal and tayyib from a minority interest to a majority desire. These are not new concepts in Islam and neither are they inspired by secular middle-class innovations.

The first written record of halal slaughter being performed in the United Kingdom comes from the year 1600 in London. At that time the ruler of Morocco, Ahmed Al-Mansur, had sent his Secretary, Abd el-Ouahed ben Messaoud, as an ambassador to negotiate with Queen Elizabeth I. The sixteen-strong group stayed at an ambassador's residence on The Strand for six months, where antiquarian John Stow recorded: 'They kill all their own meat within their house, as sheep, lambs, poultry and such like; and they turn their face eastwards when they kill anything.' Although Muslims had almost certainly been performing halal slaughter in the UK for many years prior to this on the various trips made by merchants, there are no written records of those earlier activities.

As the number of Muslims in the UK gradually increased over the seventeenth, eighteenth, and nineteenth centuries (often from trade or due to British imperialist activity in Muslim-dominated lands), private halal slaughter would have certainly increased too although written records remain scant. By 1889 Shah Jahan Mosque in Woking, Surrey had been constructed reflecting a larger population of Muslims residing in the UK and undoubtedly performing regular ritual slaughter. As animal welfare reforms were coming into law in 1933, religious derogations on pre-stunning had already been included for certain religious (mainly Jewish) communities. The arrival of large numbers of Muslims to the UK after the Second World War (mainly from Commonwealth countries) led to a huge increase in the demand for halal meat and Kosher meat, as Kosher was often substituted for halal where it was the only available option. The first organised and large scale commercial halal slaughter was commenced in 1954 in Birmingham. As the Muslim population shifted its status from temporary migrants to permanent settlers, communities put down roots around the UK (typically in manufacturing cities where the demand for unskilled labour was greatest) and began establishing permanent social structures; mosques, halal butcher shops, Muslim organisations, printed media and charities. By 1960 dedicated halal meat wholesalers had emerged but it was only in the late 1970s and early 80s that the UK had its first Muslim-owned abattoirs. At this time Muslim migration to the UK was now mainly from countries where political upheaval and wars had created refugees. The popularity of Indian cuisine in the UK took hold when Bangladeshi refugees fleeing the war of 1971 came to the UK. Many of them entered the catering and restaurant trade and transformed Indian cuisine from sustenance for factory workers to one of the nation's favourite dishes. The vast majority of these restaurants served halal meat and this drove the demand for halal ingredients. Similar growth was observed in takeaways selling (halal) kebabs which coincided with the post-war change in social habits. Going out for a pint followed by a kebab became a national norm, which accelerated in the 80s and 90s.

However, there was an ugly underbelly to this trend. Widespread demand for halal food had now created a new set of issues related to fraud and inconsistency in standards. Imams from local mosques were being requested to oversee slaughter in abattoirs and newer technical methods developed to increase production output or to meet animal welfare legislation had led to differences in practice. Evidence of large scale corruption and hygiene failures reduced confidence in halal and served to create a sub-standard, poorly regulated impression of halal food and its methods. In 1994, the Halal Food Authority was set up, with the support of the Muslim Institute, to provide certification to slaughterhouses, wholesalers and manufacturers.

TV Asia, the first South Asian-focused satellite-based TV channel was launched in the UK in 1990. News, information and adverts about halal products and services took halal from the kitchen to national and then European prominence. Halal restaurants and establishments in cities around the country gained fame and became destination restaurants, driving the evolution of halal based cuisine and the range of halal products. By the end of the century, zabiha.com, an online database listing halal restaurants with reviews became a staple resource for restaurant discovery.

Negatively stereotyped reporting of news events of geopolitical importance relating to Muslims also began to shape national attitudes towards Muslims. The Iranian revolution in 1979, the public burning of Salman Rushdie's *The Satanic Verses*, in 1989, Iraq's invasion of Kuwait in 1990-91 and Norman Tebbit's cricket test – 'Which side do you cheer for?' a loyalty test for South Asians in 1990 – all served to create the impression of Muslims as violent, cruel, insular, ignorant and Other. The shadow of a medieval European attitude towards Islam had cast its long shadow on twentieth-century Britain.

For many Muslims, 2001 would be an epoch-defining year. From the terrorist events in the USA, leading to the death of many innocents and the retaliatory 'War on Terror'; there was another, much quieter and ironically positive change that occurred, which would have a significant bearing on the lives of British Muslims. For the first time since its introduction in 1801, the main form of the 2001 Census contained the 'religion question'. The impact of asking respondents across the UK their religious affiliation meant that for the first time, an accurate estimation of the number of Muslims in the UK could be gained to direct public resources (which had otherwise been calculated on race-based assumptions). The quantification of Muslims and the subsequent growth of the community, calculated by the responses to the same question in the 2011 Census were powerful markers for governments, policy makers and for businesses to define strategies related to meeting the needs of British Muslims.

In 2001, the number of Muslims in England was estimated to be at around 1.5 million people (approx 2.7 per cent of the population). A decade on, the 2011 census estimated the number of Muslims to have increased by 80 per cent, estimated at 2.7 million people (4.8 per cent of the population). The availability of localised data allowed businesses (mainstream grocery retailers and national restaurant chains in particular) to refine their ranges and offer relevant products to their local populations. In 2005, Tesco, a leading grocery retailer in the UK opened a halal meat shop on site in its branch in Slough. In 2007, Subway, the international sandwich chain opened its first halal store in Walthamstow, London. By 2009 KFC trialed eight 'halal only' stores in London and the pizza chain Domino's rolled out three stores in Birmingham. In both instances, any pork-based products were entirely removed from the menus. Whereas the Domino's trial was unsuccessful, KFC went on to open further halal stores and currently has approximately 100 across the UK. Tesco (under their own brand Shahada) and Sainsbury's (under the Tahira brand) experimented with a range of pre-packed raw halal meats in 2010, but in both instances the ranges failed. Very low consumer uptake meant that the supermarkets ultimately gave up their ambitions.

The largest piece of research into the English halal market also came out in 2010, from EBLEX, the levy body for English lamb and beef producers. They took a keen interest in halal due to the importance of the halal market to English lamb producers. This research provided the explanation for the failure of the pre-pack experiment. The survey responses clearly showed the importance of trust in halal certification when buying from mainstream supermarkets. The reputation of supermarkets meant that halal consumers require a higher level of certainty compared to restaurants claiming halal status. Despite numerous attempts to ban religious slaughter in the UK, the EU had provided member states the option to derogate the laws on stunning to the benefit of Muslim and Jewish communities and successive governments had debated mandatory labelling for religiously slaughtered meats although this was never put into law. In 2010, halal made the headlines when the *Mail on Sunday* ran a front page headline 'Britain goes halal....but no-one tells the public'. This headline clearly set out the media agenda against halal in the UK creating an impression that Muslims were to blame for provision of halal in iconic British institutions and that halal meat was cruel and to be avoided. Although anti-Muslim sentiment had grown significantly since 2001 and then spiked again after the London bombings in 2005, the focal point had typically been related to Islamic terrorism. This time halal was the focus of the Islamophobic agenda.

The launch of Haloodies in March 2014 via Ocado, despite the backdrop of issues and anti-Muslim sentiment, was pivotal for many reasons. Firstly, it was the triumph of capitalism over generally pervasive and increasingly xenophobic attitudes. The fundamentals of a growing and increasingly affluent Muslim population flexing their economic muscle has been a source of silent strength and influence on our journey towards establishing ourselves as British Muslims. Secondly, despite the efforts of independent halal certification agencies, the quality of halal produce in the UK will increase substantially as supermarkets enforce their quality standards onto halal producers. And finally, the shift of provision of halal meat from traditional high street halal butcher shops to mainstream supermarkets would reflect evolving family profiles from larger families with mothers as home-makers to working professional parents and smaller family units. The launch of Haloodies was a marker on the yardstick of the British Muslim journey.

For many Muslims, consuming a halal product isn't simply buying a product they need, it is the commitment to Islamic principles and teachings. Amongst those principles are the belief in the respect for animals and the environment, the benefits of the dietary restrictions placed upon Muslims (for health and other reasons) and for working towards the common good (*maslaha*).

The Qur'an, states: 'This day all things good and pure are made lawful unto you' (5:5); and: 'O mankind! Eat of that which is lawful and good on the earth.' (2:168). However, despite the frequent and combined message of halal (lawful) and *tayyib* (wholesomeness, pure), the latter concept has largely been ignored by Muslims. Halal, and its various technical interpretations, has become the only parameter that most Muslims appear to value when appraising the suitability of products. Modern day British Muslims can become passionately distracted by topics like the acceptability of stunning animals (my personal position is that animal welfare is superior with reversible stunning but ultimately it is a matter of personal preference; the choice should always be there) or which certification body is more or less credible than the other. No one is debating *tayyib*.

The characteristics of *tayyib* are a set of aligned ethical values that resonate throughout Islamic philosophy: 'O ye messengers! enjoy (all) things good and pure, and work righteousness' (23:51). The purity that we are directed towards is in the physical and moral sense. In the context of food production, *tayyib* encompasses animal welfare and farming, sustainability, environmental stewardship, nutrition and food security and safety. Various verses of the Qur'an and the sayings of the Prophet point to the importance of each of these elements and all of these combine to work toward the common good.

The history of human food production has evolved from hunter gatherers, to horticultural systems (growing in the garden), to pastoral systems (domestication of cows, sheep, goats), then agrarian (ploughing the land to increase crop yield) and then to the industrial (gradual switch from religious to scientific basis of consumption) and post-war. Each step forward has typically been in response to increasing community size and optimisation of available resources. Industrial systems had a strong focus on using machinery and new energy sources to increase output but potentiated the difference between the landowner and landworker. Post-war food production reflected increasing urbanisation and globalisation. The major benefits were significant improvements in yield (from the use of pesticides and fertilisers) and the reduction of the cost of food. The utilisation of new transportation and refrigeration methods meant food became accessible around the world and allowed communities to focus on education and empowerment, especially of women and children. Improved food sanitation assisted the significant improvements in human lifespan, one of mankind's greatest achievements. However, there were also significant costs to these gains. Emphasis was placed upon reducing cost and increasing efficiency. Environmental impact of food production was not considered by food producers and society at large had to bear these. The industrialisation of animal feed and rearing to meet demand, led to the creation of intensive farms and the introduction of hormones and other artificial methods to accelerate growth. The costs of cheaper and increasingly processed foods contributed to rising obesity and other metabolic disorders. In the most recent report from the UN Food and Agriculture Organisation, there are almost as many undernourished people in the world (800 million) as there are obese people (700 million).

The realisation that modern methods of farming and consumption were leading to negative consequences to the planet and to human health were the start of the next age of food production – the Ecological age.

Characterised by the development and growth of organic agriculture, the Ecological age is defined as 'an integrated farming system that strives for sustainability, the enhancement of soil fertility and biological diversity whilst, with rare exceptions, prohibiting synthetic pesticides, antibiotics, synthetic fertilisers, genetically modified organisms, and growth hormones.' The goal of long-term environmental sustainability rather than productivity maximisation has proven to be very attractive to consumers despite the increased costs. The organic food market is currently estimated to be worth US$77 billion (2015) but expected to reach US$320 billion by 2025. It is interesting to note that one of the founding fathers of the organic agriculture movement, Sir Albert Howard (1873–1947), a renowned botanist, was inspired into organic farming after spending time in India. Although he originally went to India as a scientific adviser to the Indian government and to pass on Western agricultural techniques, he ended up adopting Indian farming methods after observing the emphasis local farmers put upon the health of the soil. The health of the soil impacted the health of the livestock, crops and of the villagers. Sir Albert brought back composting techniques (amongst other things) and these techniques were detailed in his book *An Agricultural Testament*, considered to be a classical organic agricultural textbook and also through the Soil Association in the UK and other similar institutions in the USA. Indian farming techniques themselves were transformed in the late middle-ages and then in the Mughal era by Muslims from Arabia and Persia who initially brought in new irrigation techniques to increase the harvest potential. The Islamic agricultural practice, *filaha*, had developed over many years as expansion took Muslims to new climates and territories. Through the tenth and fourteenth centuries, these had been compiled by Arabs and Andalusians into the *Kitab-al-Falaha* with systematic and detailed manuals of agriculture, horticulture and animal husbandry. Muslims had developed advanced techniques for irrigation, crop rotation, pest management and crossing plants to create new varieties. Agricultural practice had expanded significantly as the Muslim empire grew and to facilitate trade. Crops such as wheat, rice and barley had significant value and non-cash crops such as cotton and opium were in high demand from across the Muslim world and outside it. It is not an exaggeration to conclude that modern day organic agriculture in its secular form is actually an expression of Islamic agricultural practices. A satisfying conclusion for those who support organic farming and a return to a spiritual basis of farming, production and consumption. Organic is *tayyib* by another name.

Halal food has had a long and difficult journey in the UK over the last 100 years. The next fifty years will see a new set of challenges confront humanity as the global population swells to a predicted 10 billion people by 2050. In the UK the Muslim population is expected by then to comprise ten per cent of the entire population. In order to meet the challenges of feeding the expanding global need, current food production is not sufficient. New methods are being developed to meet the nutritional demands of the world. Genetically modified organisms, meatless meats, lab grown meats and even insect based foods are all potential solutions. However, as the world gradually shifts to address significant issues in modern day food production, it has given halal and *tayyib* foods a real opportunity to demonstrate their benefits. The halal sector will also have to develop a base of experts to help navigate some of the predicted challenges on assessing the permissibility of some of the proffered alternatives.

I hope that Haloodies will be the first of many new brands proudly wearing its halal and *tayyib* credentials to populate supermarket shelves and online baskets and aid the convenience of British Muslims. More than that, I hope and pray that Muslims can take the values of halal and *tayyib* and express them in such a way that non-Muslims can value and resonate with these ideals.

LOVE STEWS

Yemisi Aribisala

My weekly blog on food and culture for the Nigerian newspaper *234Next* had earned that reputation of being an early morning table where people came, sat around and bantered about Nigerian food as anodyne for the tensions and stresses of a typical Lagos morning. Readers eagerly anticipated my Thursday offerings so they could laugh and brutally condemn what they considered my quirky twists to time-honoured recipes; my naïve questioning of our cultural practices and beliefs, of why we had to cook certain foods in a specific way. People didn't know me but they let their defences down as one tends to in the presence of a good meal. The blog was perhaps itself a kind of enchantment for people who weren't used to talking about food or thinking much about it.

On 21 January 2011, I sent in my weekly copy. If truth be told the piece was a survey masquerading as my Thursday meditations on food. I was desperate for information on the Nigerian/Itsekiri love charm called Gbelekokomiyo; the kind put in a meal that guarantees complete infatuation from the object of one's affections…if affection can be borrowed to temporarily replace an ambiguous mishmash of emotions and incentives. I was confident that the rapport I had built over two years with my readers would yield thought-provoking responses. I was hoping for unguarded confessions in the comments section, and in private emails where people typically felt freer expressing impassioned, sensitive opinions about unexpected collisions between food, life and relationships.

Gbelekokomiyo, Kop mo mi, 'Kool Aid' – that had somehow sneaked into the vernacular, past the compulsory urbaneness of men and women living in Lagos. It wasn't something you could broach head on, never confrontationally. Therein was the stout frustrating paradox: that love charms were considered old-fashioned baubles that people in villages and backwaters dabbled in, but Lagosians secretly subscribed to them and wouldn't say so, would never admit it. You couldn't just ask people if they had ever cooked a meal with something extra in it to gain another's love or obsessive attention, or agreeableness. The references and jokes made about the charms were the compromises and gaps in doors and windows that let you catch fugitive glimpses of something, but if for one minute the discussion became marginally serious, everyone sidestepped the matter like a dirty gutter and with determination slammed doors shut.

When you committed to living and working in Lagos, you signed an implicit agreement to put away actions that suggested that you subscribed to superstitious beliefs, that you paid clandestine visits to traditional practitioners of medicine. If you had ever gone to one of those medicine men who prepared concoctions, combinations of words and nebulous items that you paid for and took back to place inside a love interest's meal… husband, wife, girlfriend, boyfriend…you didn't come to Lagos and brag about it. You faced in the opposite direction and denounced the traditional as being many steps down from sophistication. People showed off their education from universities in Lagos, Nsukka, Ibadan and overseas, their general knowledge of global affairs gleaned from CNN and Sky News and holidaying abroad. We knew how our contemporaries around the world conducted their lives and we wanted to be on par with their ostensible refinement. In line with this, we reaffirmed commitments to mosques and churches and local chic waterholes, paying self-conscious weekly visits to houses of worship and entertainment. If you turned around in your expensive clothes and shoes, with your carefully cultivated cosmopolitan identity, your Sunday-school teacher's badge or mosque usher's uniform and said out loud that you had gone to one of those places where people bent down and entered dark rooms where chicken blood and strangled animals were parts of the decor of a consultation room and altar, you would immediately be classified as bush and backward, someone that couldn't be trusted to keep their solutions to life's problems above board.

A legacy of colonial rule ushers special complexity to the two outfits of cultural identity we *have* to wear, and to the divides that can never, ever be neat or un-compromised or untainted with shame. In most contexts, we had to be two people in one, speaking English and a mother tongue, eating our own food and indicating our knowledge and gustatory appreciation of foreign fares. When many urban living Nigerians get married, they have a white wedding where they go to church to take their vows in front of a priest or pastor, and then they also have a traditional wedding where they wear the clothes that were the insignia of the place they really come from, where their peoples and hometowns and lineages are rooted. The groom brought 42 yams, and 42 barracuda bellies and *Intorica George wrappers* and a goat, and a dowry. People carry out grand wedding ceremonies in these very same villages they snubbed as backwaters.

Both marriage ceremonials exhibit our commitment to keeping all relevant gods, modern and traditional, appeased. You could argue that the traditional ceremony is weightier. Many times if you had not done the traditional version of things, if you hadn't gone to meet with an extended family retinue, presenting gifts and prostrating flat on the floor, distributing gifts to distant cousins and village heads and twice, thrice removed relations, you were not considered a married couple by your people back at home. Whenever you went to visit the village you were fined for not having completed all the necessary rites.

Love charms are perhaps just a minor signification of keeping our balance between two indispensable identities, or between all the parts of compound identity. When people have initial relationship troubles, it makes sense to look for solutions locally. You go to marriage counselling and seminars and book appointments to pray with your pastor 'privately' in Lagos. When the troubles escalate you discard the airs and go 'home'. The Yoruba call it *putting the hand from home in the matter.* You seek *other* closet solutions.

My now-notorious blog was the culmination of a long-held fascination with such closet solutions, particularly the food-bewitchment tool and renowned charm Gbelekokomiyo. Love-charms say more about heartbreak and rejection than control and cynicism. When you first hear of the love charm there is no way you don't connect them to wicked manipulation, to home-wrecking women who want to get their way by any means possible with a man. The connection and imagery feels appropriate, but you look deeper and see how women's reputations and standing in local communities, in churches, mosques and in their extended families are so invested in the successes of their marriages that resorting to using a love charm shows that something has already been lost — something fundamental. Someone has been rejected. Someone's heart has been broken, especially when a love charm turns up in a spouse's meal. And when women lose, their children and dependents fall in battle with them.

It is the blatant unjust fact of Nigerian relationships that when a marriage runs into trouble, a woman is meant to do something about it. Marriages are primarily women's responsibilities. I know women who have gone to marriage counselling all by themselves, representing two parts, receiving counsel for husband and wife. Often the husband has already emotionally deserted the marriage. Sometimes he has moved on completely. Left the home. The contemporary churches and mosques that women pay allegiance to every single week tell them to submit, yield, or buckle down, dig heels in and work harder, to grow wings and hollow bones and levitate to the task of saving their marriages whatever the stakes, however impossible. To win back the dog-eared, rickety, unsavoury man even if he has remarried. To agree to house-share the malodorous life with an unfaithful spouse if need be.

Women are sometimes assaulted with the information that is meant to motivate them to fight for their homes – that there are fewer men available than women, hence the need to share and adapt, and out of that totalling of available men, good men are a minute minority. What is a good man? Good question. I've heard some good women say a good man is a man who financially provides for you and your children and doesn't beat you.

The humbling procedure to becoming a superhero is first and foremost the humble admission by the woman that there is something wrong with her – with her cooking, appearance, sexual appeal, ability to keep a man interested; ability to keep a marriage viable. From there the woman must do something that befits the superhero outfit. She must go to every extreme to make sure her house stands.

Nigerian marriages are never fundamentally about romance. They are about stunning expensive weddings with plenty of co-ordinated dancing and generous portions of food. They are endurance runs and Facebook photo-ops and rapid production of neurotypical children with no physical defects whatsoever (otherwise again the wife will pay). They are about fitting into communities, peer pressure, saving face, ostentatious marking of cultural milestones. Nigerian marriages have a unique formulation and history and dance. When a marriage is being rescued, it isn't usually about restoring broken friendship, or renewing a love affair, or tightening nuclear family ranks, or encouraging fidelity. Not about peeling away layers, allowing both parties to see the intrinsic value in the other. They are often about keeping people in their designated cultural places. Maintaining a house in superficial order so that outsiders are convinced that everything is fine. Women find themselves roughly stripped of any romantic ideals if they carried any into grand dual location wedding ceremonies.

That is why, when I wrote my blog, I put a question mark against that word 'affection'. This love charm; this carefully concocted mined meal served with flourishes in the end seemed to be only a treaty, a courtesy, an agreement to stay put and maintain a façade. My favourite response to my piece was from a woman who waited for many responses from men writing loud panicky denunciations of the practice of charming men with food. Men were jumping up and down with fear in the comments. One man wrote a response longer than my article. The woman bided her time until there was only the mere trickling of capitalised responses. She chose that moment to write quietly and anonymously two lines that just made your heart stop with their lead weight:

'Look love charms are not meant to turn men into zombies. They are only meant to make them more agreeable.'

I didn't try to engage the woman, or attempt to draw her out. There was so much in the two lines; so much pain and revelation and defeat. I saw her in my mind's eye waiting her turn to speak and then sitting with rounded shoulders and flaccid arms, mouthing the appeal for scraps of agreeableness. Why anyone would in the final analysis want a man that had to be lassoed in, deceived, manipulated, and tied down.

The tool of food plus love charm was wielded almost exclusively by women exactly because the pressure and burden to perform in marriage and to keep relationships sweet remains crushingly ours. These realities are buried in the language of the love charm. Gbelekokomiyo sounds ominous with its onomatopoeic knocks in syllables. Those knocks seem to be engineered to strike fear in the hearts of men. They seem to say power where love is denied. Yet the word has some finesse, some masquerading of intention, in fact a considerable quantity of coyness. If the contraction of the words is removed, it is in its full form *Egbele e ko ki miyo*. It translates as 'the chicken or rooster cannot refuse to eat corn'. In Yoruba, the Nigerian language I speak, Gbelekokomiyo translates to *S'okomole*. So *oko mole* on the other hand grants no shade from the direct heat of the sun. The words mean plainly *tie the penis down*.

The love charm has to be ingested along with and disguised in morsels of well-cooked, appetisingly presented food. The meal has in its own capacity to be irresistible – a kind of double-barrelled gun carrying cartridges of spiritual powder and gastronomic clout. It can be a deceptively simple fresh fish stew or a no-holds-barred pot of Okro soup cooked with a variety of tantalising cuts of meat and fish, handled with distinct virtuosity.

Recipe 1 - Fish Stew

One serving of large muscular sweet peppers that crack under the thumb from freshness
Two servings garden-fresh tomatoes with shiny taut skins
One or two small red onions
A few aromatic habaneros depending on the eater's tolerance for heat

The sophisticated witch has a smooth grinding stone that produces a sleek texture of stew that no foreign machine can replicate. The commonplace cosmopolitan witch with nail extensions is permitted to use a blender to mix the ingredients together. As to the fish and its own particularities, it must be fresh, bought while still breathing. Active, not lulled with valium. It must be young, its gills coral red, its eyes glassy and concave. It must smell like sea water, not fish, and it must not come from a stinking fetid pond in some Lagosian's backyard. The favoured fish is the black whiskered catfish called obokun caught in the sea. The sophisticated witch drives two hours to Epe and waits an hour for an old blue boat manoeuvred by a phlegmatic old man. She pays for the fish and drives two hours back to wash it, salt its skin, rinse gently and place in the stew to simmer. The stew must be cooked with first grade palm oil at least one inch thick on its face on the smallest lick of hob fire for about 30 minutes. Sputtering and not bubbling should be the attitude of the stew. The stew must not be stirred. The pot must be rocked gently from side to side to keep the fish intact.

Again the muscle that a love charm carries cannot be overstated in Nigeria. Like in many other countries in the world, divorce has been on the rise. Nigerian women are leaving their Nigerian husbands. Not in confident droves. But women's earning powers in the first instance has been stealing up on men's for years, and in many households women earn more. Women are leaving because they can. The taboo of divorce that was strengthened by tenets of Christianity and Islam wasn't always so sure of itself, so culturally inescapable. Historically, Yoruba women returned men's dowries and left if they were being mistreated; if the woman couldn't have children and didn't want to become a second class citizen when other women were brought in to bear the children she could not: if she began an affair with a man who was willing and able to take her away from her husband and care for her; for all kinds of reasons, women left. Women could leave and not be ostracised from their communities.

Women who couldn't have children, and were sure of that fact, sometimes by traditional rites married other women. The woman whose role was wife chose any man she desired, the man did not have to be identified, and allowed herself to be impregnated by the man. The child when it was born belonged to the two women who were married, to their union and their care in old age. The child's parents were two women. Only by extension did the child answer to the other union between the woman who played the role of husband and her real male husband. The man who biologically fathered the child was irrelevant. This practice was culturally allowed to ease the painful stigma of childlessness and to ensure that women had family to take care of them in their old age.

The point of citing these kinds of distinctive cultural practices is to show that things weren't so set in stone. Women could be stigmatised and disdained for being divorced but they were more likely to be disdained for having no male protector; living on their own. They could claim brother, father or uncle as legitimate protector, sometimes as cosmetic protector while they discreetly exercised their freedom to do what they wanted. Women were more likely to be ostracised for having children from lots of different men, for choosing quick successions of lovers and husbands. The strongest disdain by far was reserved for childlessness.

From antiquity it was an expedient cultural practice for men to marry many wives and have plenty of children especially if they had allotments and farmlands. Women and children were unpaid labour, emotionally capitalised in building a man's wealth, in farming his lands, in herding his cattle, in keeping his home. The women and children were fed, clothed, sometimes educated though not by right, but also significantly not by virtue of direct attention from the man. A woman who farmed or reared cattle, ate and fed her children from her labour and from her access to what was farmed or reared. She nurtured herself and her children without necessarily consulting her husband. Wives had some space designated as belonging to them and their children, depending on how wealthy the husband was. They had restricted sexual access to the husband because he of course had to be shared with other women. They belonged to a community of other women and family members. The unwritten contract said that their children would inherit and this expectation kept the enterprise oiled. In polygamous arrangements, children's rights, in-laws' rights, husband's mother's rights were usually above the wife's.

Most of the women of my generation, in their late thirties and early forties, came from the fraying ends of these kinds of cultural marriages. Their mothers were well within their truths to advise their daughters to choose the safety of power over the illusion of love. Love? What was that anyway? The problem again was the dual outfits. Choose power the mothers advised but give us still the sentimental ceremonies, the long awaited trinkets of a small community wedding where the mother of the bride gets to be queen for a day, gets to wear special cloth and sit on the high table. No matter how little these matriarchs believe in romantic love, they still crave its enactment.

A Nigerian woman never wins by sulking and being nonsensical nor by placing all her cards on the table for everyone to see. In the face of unjust odds, with no supporting legal structures, with the cultural acquiescence of family to male entitlement, infantilisation of men by sisters and mothers who are also caught in the system they are complicit in advancing, women cook and insert the mediums of compromise and right the situation in food. They apply the love charm where the prevailing atmosphere is powerlessness, not pride nor hunger for dominance. Neither are they shrugging and mourning their lack of agency. They are in stealth mode, duck legs paddling furiously under the water.

There are all kinds of pointers in Yoruba to the overpowering of men's senses with food. *Olobe lo loko* means it is the owner of the soup who owns the husband. *Sokoyokoto* means making the husband soft and pliant with the application of good food. Charms work more effectively on men because it is primal for them to gain feelings for women who cook for them and pamper them and flatter them and reinforce male/female stereotypes: a man is a man because a woman is cooking for him. A man is a man because he does not enter the kitchen or a man does not enter the kitchen because he is a man. Therefore a woman cooking for a man emphasises his maleness. Love charms work better in the employ of single, beautiful, unruffled women whose serene bedrooms are a contrast to the household where children are running around distracting attention from the pampering of an adult man. The man topples from the list of priorities in the busy household and is drawn to the opposite serenity of the single woman's home. The young lady who is hoping and trying with all her sexual appeal and natural charm to get her married lover to leave his wife and marry her instead will perhaps be halfway to convincing him, and to close the deal, she will cook an elaborate pot of Ekpang Nku Kwo.

Recipe 2- Ekpang Nku Kwo- Notorious husband snatching aid

Women who cook Ekpang (for short) do it from the moment they drop from the womb. It is food that is being prepared in the next room. There are many years of nuances absorbed through skin, without saying a single word, through eyes meeting eyes. Cooking Ekpang Nku Kwo is only easy for those who have learnt the hard work.

Special note: One has to decide on the texture of the cocoyam filling of the Ekpang; whether one wants melting delicateness or brittle sturdiness. The young cocoyam is easier to handle and so ideal for the Ekpang, but in order to get a good firm dumpling, we use a combination of cocoyam and wateryam.

Give yourself half a day plus a few hours to prepare this dish.

Slim cocoyams.

Water yams

Fresh bright green young cocoyam leaves.

Fresh periwinkles visibly moving in the seller's wares.

Boiled stockfish, boiling water discarded. Boiling must be done until soft but without allowing the stockfish to scatter in the last stages of cooking.

Good quality smoked fish – a smoked catfish is ideal. It is broken up into bite-size pieces, washed with salt and warm water.

Goat meat boiled till tender. Preferably the he-goat for its gamey aroma.

Boiled beef.

Boiled snails, water also discarded.

Ground smoked white crayfish

March gold – that's what I call that wonderful palm oil harvested before the major rains start, after the first rains have blown the chaff out of the banga (palm nut fruits).

Utensils: A grate and large bowl for the yams.

A good-sized pot with a cover for the cooking of the Ekpang Nku Kwo.

Water in two kettles kept at boiling point.

A flat wooden spatula for lifting not stirring.

The cocoyams and wateryams are peeled and washed in preparation for grating. The peeling must be done close to the tuber so that nothing goes to waste. The yams are worked against the smallest eye of the grate. Don't worry too much about the browning of the grated yams. There is very little one can do about that and the oxidation won't show in the finished dish. You can put your bowl of grated yams in the fridge while you prepare the cocoyam leaves.

The cocoyam leaves are cut into manageable pieces and washed under a running tap or in a deep suspension of water so that sand runs to the bottom of the container. The leaves must not be cut too small because you need a good size for the wraps. Make sure you get every grain of soil out of the leaves in washing.

The periwinkles have to be meticulously cleaned, individually scraped to make the protrusions in the shells blunt, and boiled several times to get them perfect. If this process is done carelessly, the whole dish will be ruined apart from the possibility of giving everyone a stomach ache.

A special steaming system needs to be built in the big pot: a layer of palm oil not water is put in the bottom of the pot. Then a generous elevation of washed and boiled periwinkles arranged on top of the palm oil. The palm oil gives more aromatics, flavour and colour to the dish. Please note that the steaming cannot be done with water. The pot is kept on the fire over the smallest hob point.

Some grated yams are placed in a piece of cocoyam leaf. The leaf is wrapped around the yams tightly. If the wrap isn't tight, it won't survive the steaming.

The wraps are arranged on top of the periwinkles. The arrangement is done concentrically. The hob fire is increased very slightly once all the wraps are in place. One in fact can retain the smallest fire to be safe and add a few drops of boiling water. Not poured directly on the wraps but in the sides of the pot. A tight lid goes on the pot, and a good book or newspaper will help to pass the hour and a half till the end of cooking time. Because the steaming is only allowed a few drops of boiling water at a time, never rising above the level of the periwinkles, one needs to remain in the kitchen, ears and sense of smell at their acutest attention. On the average the steaming needs forty-five minutes to an hour.

Don't allow yourself to feel rushed in steaming the wraps. Remember Ekpang Nku Two belongs to women who have a reputation of spending an inordinate amount of time thinking of how to bend a man's mind. But seriously, if the heat of the hob is too high, you are going to burn all your efforts. Best to keep the heat as low as possible.

The smoked fish is arranged on top of the steamed wraps, more boiling water added to the sides and the lid replaced.

This new addition can take another fifteen minutes to settle. The smoked fish should be nice and soft.

The wraps should be perfectly steamed by now. The meat, snails, stockfish, etc., are placed on the wraps and the water level is increased to cover everything. More palm oil is added to redden the face of the Ekpang. Some salt and pepper may be added at this stage but no stirring whatsoever must be done. The lid is once again tightly replaced.

The Ekpang is allowed to boil under the closed lid. I would still advise caution with the heat.

The ground crayfish and salt and ground pepper are added.

Now you can stir, but not with a spoon. The stirring is an insertion of the flat wooden spatula into the sides and raising up the periwinkles. Once you've done this round the pot a couple of times without stirring the centre, you should have moved the ingredients around sufficiently.

By now you should be able to bring up the wraps and see them perfectly formed and firm.

The seasoning can be adjusted further if required.
The water should reduce in cooking to a thick pottage-like consistency.
The finishing touch is freshly cut scent-leaf (bush-basil).

A friend of mine, an English man called Jeremy Weate, gave me a book by a scientist and sorcerer called Pierre Fatumbi Verger (1902–1996). Verger was a real life practitioner of traditional medicine renowned from Bahia to Osogbo. Born in Brazil, and a French national, Verger came to

Nigeria and studied and then wrote a book on all kinds of interesting solutions to the travails of life. And that is a polite review of a book that has recipes in it for killing one's wife's lover and *sending smallpox to one's enemy*. The book has forty-four formulae for obtaining a wife and compelling her love. The book defines its soups, that is magical compositions, as a collection of material things articulated by language. In other words, there is the making of the soup and then there is the administration of words; the speaking of spells. One recipe in the book is:

Recipe 3- To Be Loved by a Woman

Leaf of asystasia gangetica, acanthaceae
A hen's cloaca
Black soap
Pound ingredients with black soap. Recite the incantation and bathe using the soap mixture.
Incantation: Sobohee says that the woman's vagina should open completely. The hen's vagina is always completely open for the cock.

There is obviously deep confusion here on what a woman's love is and whether it is what the man who administers such a remedy wants. Opening of the vagina and love are hardly the same thing but the recipe represents the territory of the love charm possibly from a man's perspective.

The love charm in food is like the African pepper soup that has as many versions as the idea of Africa allows. Every dialect of every language of every village in every African country has its own name for it. In South Nigeria, the Efiks call their version *Kop mo mi*. In the South-West the Yoruba call theirs *Gbo temi* or the earlier mentioned *So oko mole*. The Togolese version uses the very same Yoruba words *Gbo temi* meaning 'hear my request' or 'do what I want' showing the migration of peoples and their longings along the West Coast of Africa. Gabonese love charms are famed as some of the strongest. The constant in all of these charms is food, the motion of remedy from mouth to gut. The part of the enchantment we recognise is food. The rest is speculation and darkness. A man or woman eats food or drink laced with something and does the bidding of the administrator for the rest of his or her bewildered life.

Aside from the administering of love charms, there is nothing superstitious or hysterical about the vigilance over men's mouths and guts. Control of who offers one's man a meal, if he accepts or declines, and what the food is doing in his system makes sense. If it kills him, there will be difficulties. And this is presuming that there is no love in the equation. If he is loved, there is the gruelling work to overcome heartbreak and real emotional loss added on to the loss to the household. Even if he is not loved or particularly liked, there is an arrangement that exists where he has agreed to care for his wife and children and up until the point of eating the meal in question, the meal that bewitched him because it was delicious, or because it was mined, or because it was both, he is responsible for a certain number of people. His bewitchment with food is an economic factor, a practicality that is so tangible it is insurable. His conscientiousness or lack of it is irrelevant. If what enters a man's mouth bewitches him because it tastes really good, it is the same as if there is some dark spiritual aspect to it even if it tastes rancid. A love charm goes beyond the physical because it is expedient to hold that it does. The penis is right under the stomach. They are roughly in the same jurisdiction. To hear Nigerian women talk is to understand they do not give that region any benefit of doubt, innocence till proven guilty or any other naïve default setting investment of belief like that. Like the Yiddish schmuck or the British dick, the Nigerian penis is considered wayward and troublesome, at best foolish and at worst owning a killer instinct, uncontrollable and culturally entitled. Therefore both vigilance and administration of food are women's reins to steady the already unstable world so they don't fall off.

Motunrayo Ogbara is the name of a woman who went to the same secondary school in Lagos as me. I graduated from Queens College Yaba in 1989. She graduated in 2001. She had a fiancé, and a job in Access Bank. She discovered that she had a medical problem that translated into not being able to bear children. She told her fiancé. He dumped her. And she hung herself. She was a 26-year-old whose whole identity, past, future, present, had been invested in marriage to one particular man. The man himself, it can be presumed, had been brought up in a loveless, narrow-minded society of people whose biases are daily reinforced in the portrayal of narcissistic, wicked mothers-in-law portrayed on Africa Magic. I cannot blame him for not being able to think outside the box and go against all that he had been taught, and all that he had imbibed, to love a woman who cannot bear children. My mother was in my kitchen when we read about Motunrayo in the papers. There are certain things we put in files labelled 'unheard of'. This was one of those things. Not because we have never heard of a jilted woman committing suicide but because Nigerian women for decades have been masters of adaptation. If their husbands did not love them, they loved their children. If their in-laws required that they walk on their heads, they did it with style. If their husband took on a third wife, they befriended her and recruited her into the more satisfying vocation of making the husband's life hell. Suicide had never been the immediate response to rejection. In fact, the Nigerian girl child is more than likely socialised from an early age into the reality of rejection and infidelity and polygamy and accepting all manner of unnatural and un-liveable conditions. If this girl felt so strongly compelled to kill herself, had the stakes not been raised? Had the foundations of the world not moved and we did not know it?

When I was growing up, my mother told and retold the story of an acquaintance who had married an unstable man. It seemed the man himself had doubts about his ability to live with his wife without harming her; he advised her after a few months of marriage to return to her parent's home. She attempted to return, but her parents told her in no uncertain terms that she was no longer welcome. They had given her an elaborate wedding to which everyone had been invited and it would be an embarrassment to them were she to move back home. They sent her back to her husband. And he killed her.

I suspect what lurks behind the love charm is heartbrokenness; epigenetic heartbrokenness as well as present heartbrokenness. I have an uncle whose soundbites I find myself expeditiously digging my pockets for, like that last minute dishevelled search for loose change. I wonder why I never plan for the need of coins. I always, always, always need them, but I treat small change with cynicism anyway until I'm standing in front of that homeless woman to whom they belong, to whom they are gold – who needs a cup of coffee and R5. My uncle said if a man is falling off a cliff and you hand him a single cotton thread, his fist will close around that thread with muscular hope, all the way down.

Love charms remind me of the fluff of wisdom in my pockets. They are unstable currency, buying a cup of coffee one day and a dress the next. They are irresistible strands of hope; threads that carry a thousand times their weight. A bird that flies out of a pocket when there is not one single coin there. A bowl of soup that postpones hunger. No one who is in the dark refuses the option of a lit candle. And time is distended with crazy hope and delicious fantasy.

A brief excursion back to childhood shows little girls socialised with daily doses of maternal guidelines on their worth and how a good woman always has to be married with children. Forward without delay to the marriage ceremony where dowries and yams and goats are exchanged for the personhood and divinity of a woman. The whole context, all of it, takes away more and more control from women and divorce in Nigeria is like putting salt in a wound. You've failed and now everyone knows you've failed. No matter how open-minded you were, you couldn't allow your daughters in Nigeria to be eccentric, or inordinately precocious. Even when you hated the system, you encouraged them to fit in. You would not be doing them a favour by giving them permission to revolt. They would stick out like sore thumbs and eventually they would be shunned when men their age were looking for appropriate wives. The desired virtues are agreeableness (again), a graceful acquiescence to the acquisition of dishes and glassware and pretty throw cushions and if appropriate, the ability to manage a small army of servants; a bank job, or one in a law firm, role of mentor for other women at WIMBIZ (Women in Management, Business and Public Service – a non-profit organisation for women); manicured nails, hair attachments, visits to the gym, excruciating heels. All that and a long firm chain to the sink.

Of course you turned to the comforting bowl of soup. The word Soup has a universal soothing texture in one's ears. The word hits your core. And in the end, when it enters your person, you are sated. Not sated where touch, hunger and love are concerned but limbered up to entertain postponement, or the possibility or hope or whatever fantasy may be suspended over the spooning of warmth into the room of the mouth. Maybe that is why we cannot disregard the love charm with all its figures of speech and methodology centred on food and drink. Maybe it represents the opportunity to exercise desperation; to replicate reassuring quantities of control, of feel-good. The love potion/charm goes that far. Does it in fact work? Maybe it distracts us enough so that love somehow no longer represents an ache we are actively nursing. Gbelekokomiyo is soup that postpones hunger for love.

ARTS AND LETTERS

THE KNIGHTS OF THE RAJ

Mohammed Ali

Curry culture in the UK was pioneered by the Bangladeshis, who first began to settle in Britain during the nineteenth century. The toil and dedication of these early pioneers transformed British cuisine, culture and society. For the past few years, I have been hunting down, collecting, preserving and sharing the previously unknown stories of the heritage and history of Bangladeshi-owned 'Indian' restaurants in Birmingham; those early pioneers who owned and worked in them, and their families and descendants.

It is the late 1980s. I am an early teenager. I am seated at table number 16 in my white shirt and black tie, with my dad sitting there at the opposite end facing me. The routine is the same every day; we wait for customers, on some days whole evenings go by without anyone coming in to eat. While we wait, dad reads his newspaper and I sketch something on scrap paper.

Dad reminisces on the old days: 'In my time, we had it hard, four of us sharing one room…, we would even have shifts of sleeping in beds, whilst one was working, the other would sleep in your bed.'

I have heard it all before, many times. It goes in one ear and out the other. I don't want to be in the restaurant with my dad, whilst all my friends are out having a laugh. It isn't fair. I find some solace in my pen and paper and my 'artistic creations', in which my father has no interest.

My dad had arrived in England from Bangladesh in 1957. He passed away in 2009. We buried him in Handsworth Cemetery. When you lose someone you love, your heart yearns for those memories and stories you were oblivious to at the time of their telling. When my father died, I wished I could somehow turn back the clock. The seeds for *Knights of the*

Raj were planted at that moment. I wanted to know who my dad was and how the restaurant trade had influenced and impacted him…and me.

The *Knights of the Raj* exhibition, exhibited in Birmingham Museum and Galleries in late 2017, was my attempt to reverse time and tell the extraordinary story of my parents' generation. I wanted to take the visitors beyond the table covers and the kitchen, into the lives of those individuals that brought out their favourite dishes to them.

Those families I visited for my research, who invited me in to sit and share their stories, personal archives and photo-albums, know me simply as 'the son of Watir Ali'.

I am back at table number 16.

Shalimar Restaurant, Birmingham.

Badshahi Miah – working at the Shah Bagh Restaurant in the 1960s.

Mohobot Miah (left) the kitchen of Shah Jahan restaurant,
Birmingham city centre.

Kastura Begum with her daughter Helen, at home,
77 Duddeston Mill Road, c. 1970.

Eklas Miah – owner of the Shah Bagh Restaurant on Bristol Street,
Horsefair, Birmingham, c. 1970.

Shah Abid Ali outside of his Shah Restaurant in Broad Street,
Birmingham c. 1978.

Anna Purna Restaurant menu from the early 1970s.

New Moon Restaurant, Beardwood Road, Birmingham owned by
Abdul Aziz, c. 1945.

Family birthday party at the Darjeeling Restaurant, Steelhouse Lane,
Birmingham. One of the first curry houses in Birmingham, owned by
Abdul Aziz, c. 1949.

Syed Shelin Miah. Staff quarters, Light of Bengal restaurant, 1978.

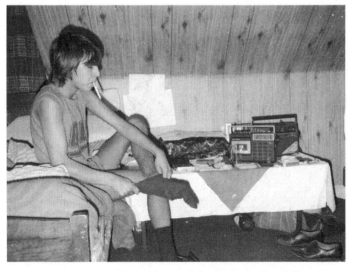

Abdul Ahad (known by his nickname Jilu Miah) in the staff quarters,
upstairs at the Light of Bengal restaurant, Smethwick,
Birmingham, c. 1978.

Mozzomil Kazi – owner of the Jinnah Restaurant.

Sitting in a Birmingham park. From left to right: Unknown, Mofiqul Ambia Choudhury and Dewan Alam Noor Raja (owner of the Raj Bhooj Takeaway in Selly Oak, Birmingham).

MALAY BONNE BOUCHE

Mastura Alatas

Nasi Goreng Tango

He danced the same dance every night, alone. In a cubicle of steel, like the rest bordering the food court. A square parade of picture frames with family recipes within.

His feet swept over the same tiles that his father's did. The same snaking eights worn into floor as he sashayed to the beat his wok demanded. For a sachet of spice to smack into the pan. A splatter of chilli. Ladle of goat broth. Salt. Pepper. Noodles, cascaded. Flipped in tsunami waves as metal grated against metal.

She'd been watching him for over three decades.

Her mother had taken her to the stall whilst it was still his father's. Master had been teaching apprentice then. And he had been a bronzed boy shuffling the floor on bandy legs. An awkward tap dance.

Her order never altered, and was spoken softly at least once a week. Yet he never remembered her, so caught up was he in the rhythm of his ancestors' creations.

Then, on one particularly tropical night, when the air was thick with dampness as well as spiced aromas, she spoke her order a little louder than usual. As if appalled by her new womanly tone, the flame beneath the wok leapt out, bit the man's fingers and slapped the woman hard across the cheek.

As quickly as it had become wild, the flame became tame.

The man clutched his hand, scolded and scorned. The woman slipped into the cubicle, unravelling the scarf around her neck as she did so, and wrapped his wound in the silk. Held his hand in hers.

Unnerved by the betrayal of his own fire, he held her waist to steady himself.

There they were. Nose to nose. Cheek to cheek. Entwined. Dancing the tango together. Into the rest of their days.

Truffle of the East

'The truffle of the east,' announced Grace. Her voice was hoarse from the meeting and greeting, and the strain of the day, and talking over the bustle of the restaurant didn't help things.

She took the only Buah Keluak seed, about the size of a walnut husk, out of the Ayam Buah Keluak (the chicken curry of their childhood with a heady flavour tasted more through the nose than on the tongue).

Eve thought this typical of her sister; Grace the First Born. She'd always taken. Taken toys. Taken attention. Taken opportunity. Taken for herself all the fermented insides of the Buah Keluk seed their mother would meticulously scrape out for them when they were girls.

Grace scooped out the seed in the same way that their mother always had, with a small stainless steel spatula. The seed's insides thrice scraped. Then the plate thrice tapped so the dark paste dropped off of the spatula and next to the rice. Scrape, scrape, scrape. Tap, tap, tap. Over and over until the insides were barren.

Their mother never noticed Grace didn't share the Buah Keluak seed with Eve.

Ayam Buah Keluak was only served on special occasions. The seeds had to be boiled, then buried in ash, banana leaves and earth for forty days to remove the natural cyanide. The seeds were deadly before they were delicious. Eve once asked their mother if she could bury Grace in ash, banana leaves and earth for forty days. Their mother had laughed.

So, Ayam Buah Keluak was a dish ceremoniously prepared for more than a month for occasions worthy of it. Some such occasions were their parent's parties, held twice a year. The lawn would be full of women wearing jewel coloured kebayas with beads that sparkled as the sun set. Men would huddle around the periphery of the colourful mass, whispering seriously to each other and glancing to admire the display every so often. The palm leaves would hiss in the tropical breeze. The cicadas would join them once darkness fell.

Their mother was known as a glorious hostess so she would quickly scoop out the seed for her girls to keep them quiet and get back to her duties before noticing Grace had taken the entire pile of dark paste for herself.

Eve had only tasted Buah Keluak because she had eaten it off the used plates abandoned by party guests.

Grace continued to scrape, scrape, scrape, tap, tap, tap.

They could have ordered more seeds. The menu said one dollar a seed. Eve didn't think one dollar was a bad price but Grace was so outraged that the restaurant charged extra for more than one seed that she refused to indulge the owners.

When Grace finished scraping Eve watched her gather up the dark paste and transfer it onto a soup spoon, ready to dollop onto her rice and stir in. Eve considered sucking the seed shell out to at least get a taste of it, but a middle-aged woman slurping and sucking in public just didn't seem polite.

Grace lifted up the spoon laden with the dark paste and moved it towards her own rice. And then beyond her rice. And then across the table. And then to Eve's plate where, with a final tap, the insides of the only Buah Keluak seed were deposited. Eve looked to Grace for an explanation. But Grace didn't look up as she busied herself serving out the rest of the chicken curry.

For a few heartbeats Eve just looked at the dark paste, deep into the dark paste, and heard the hiss of the palm leaves, and the cicadas, and saw the colours, and smelled their mother's perfume from the frangipani flowers she wore in her hair. Then Eve stirred the paste into her rice, which turned as black as the dresses the sisters were wearing.

The Tea Man

The Tea Man pours the tea (he also pours the barley water, lime juice and beer as weak as his finances). And when he pours the tea he pours it from such a great height that frothy islands appear.

He stares into them and lets the canteen chatter of the hawker centre take him far back to his school days, to the dull clatter of plastic crockery and the sticky aroma of vegetables slicked with starch. And the great map of the world that stretched along one wall in that dining hall. There was a little red dot on their Little Red Dot. 'You Are Here.' From there he had plotted journeys in longitude and latitude, longing to tread those paths rather than just trace them with a fingertip.

People often pay for their drinks in rounded up quantities. People. Locals. Foreigners. Travellers. Backpackers. The Tea Man pockets those excess coins.

The Australian backpackers he poured the tea for pay him two dollars instead of one dollar and eighty cents. As the Tea Man weaves between tables, on his rounds, the two ten cent coins rub together beneath the surface of his shorts. He hears them whisper promises of adventure.

Back at his station he finds the empty jar of a malt-chocolate drink. It's emerald, like the hills of New Zealand, or the lagoons of Fiji, or the skinny evergreen trees of Sicily. He cuts a slot in the plastic lid of the jar and slips the coins in. They clatter excitedly on the bottom.

The Tea Man pours the tea. And when he pours the tea he pours it from such a great height that frothy islands appear.

One day an air stewardess wrapped in batik will pour tea for him, from a trolley she has just trotted up the aisle. And when he takes the cup from her they'll be islands far below him, out the oval window, as well as in his cup. One day. Penny by penny. Hopefully.

THE RIVER AND THE TREE

Wasio Ali Khan Abbasi

Paras left his village and walked down a well-trodden path through the farms. On his left and right green fields spread as far as eye could see, a small puff of dust rising with his every step. The path soon opened up to a well-travelled road and his school was right in front, a small building with peeling paint and barely legible board with school's name. Paras turned towards the river on his right.

The river was visible, water flowing with a gentle glide. Paras approached the bank, picked up a stone and tossed it over the surface of the water. It bounced a couple of times before plunging into the river's depths, the ripples quickly fading. He sat down on the roots of the large banyan tree, said to have been planted there by his great grandfather many decades ago.

He gazed over the flowing river, an occasional fish jumping out and disappearing back with a splash, leaving behind a spreading ripple that would disappear before reaching the bank. The sound of the river flow soothed him, making way for tranquillity. The birds chirped on the branches, an occasional bark from stray dogs and shouts from shepherds as they guided goats and cows back towards the village.

Paras simply sat there and watched the river flow. He once heard from a village elder that fairies lived in the water, coming out at night during full moon. If one saw a fairy, she would talk to him and tell him about the secrets of the hidden world. If that person ever told anyone he saw the fairy, she would never appear to him again. If a bad person ever saw the fairy, she would drag him into the river and hand him to the crocodiles, his body never to be seen again. The justice of the mighty river was swift. It blessed people with food and bounty, those with the good hearts, and it drowned the ones who sinned.

For people of his village and beyond, for those in the north and those in the south, the travellers from the east and the travellers from the west, the mighty Indus River was the King and to his judgement they all submitted.

The sun was now lower in the horizon and Paras came out of his reverie. He got up, dusted his clothes and saw the river once more. His father, Nabi Bakhsh, once said that grandfather used to come here, to sit under the shade of this tree and write poetry. Father himself never held any fascination with poetry or the river, though he always had fun when he brought the cows to the river for a bath. They would glide down the river bank, half submerged in the water, and happily moo for half an hour. Paras also accompanied father for these trips and played with calves that would dart in and out of the water, not big enough to venture deep and not brave enough to stay long. Like his father, Paras never held interest in poetry beyond the textbooks, though he once tried to write words to describe the river and his feeling of tranquillity.

He described the flow of the river, how it resembles the blood flowing inside your body, how the sound settles your nerves and enchants you, how birds sing happily and crows caw happily and cows moo happily … how the river turns everything into happiness.

He showed it to his teacher who, after reading it, thought Paras was on some intoxicant and told his father to stop his daydreaming hours by the river. His father was concerned and Paras decided never to write such nonsense again. He was the only son of his parents and anything was better than to see them worried.

Paras set off on the homeward path.

***

Exams had ended and summer holidays just begun. The sun beat down upon them and twice a day Paras would head out with friends to jump into the river. Older boys made sure they didn't go far into the water, lest the river flow drag them away. *Only sinners go that far and never return*, it was said, *and their families would be shamed for life.* He would never shame his family by going far into the river.

They occasionally felt fish bumping past them. Older boys often managed to catch one or more as they passed by, including Palla fish. Paras tried a few times but never managed to catch one. He once grabbed a Palla fish but it slipped away easily, leaving behind his bewildered self.

Daily he helped his father with cleaning out cow dung, checking on hens in the morning, delivering milk around the village and making sure the chicks stayed within the shelter. He also kept fresh water for chicks to beat off the heat; they died pretty easily whenever a heat wave hit the village.

Paras didn't know what his future would be. He would be starting his matriculation (junior high) soon, choosing between arts and science. His teacher once said science was for geniuses and arts for losers. Paras didn't much like science but he would never be a loser. He did his best in all mathematics and science subjects; still it was the languages that came easily to him.

You'll be a teacher somewhere, his friend had once teased, *a grumpy teacher drinking tea all day and beating kids in class for spelling mistakes*. Paras didn't want to be a teacher; he wanted to be a respected person, a scientist who will do miracles.

Miracles, just like magic. Before falling asleep each night he would imagine how his miracles would change the world. A bullock cart that would drag itself; seeds that would plant, germinate, grow and the crop would cut itself down in neat rows to be picked up and stacked with ease. Watermelons that would always be sweet; cow milk that would taste like honey, each cow bearing milk equal to five cows without compromising health and milk quality. Donkeys as strong as horses which would eat less than half of what they do now. Water canals diverting themselves when pointed. Fish jumping out and falling into waiting hands without need of fishing line and bait.

Such ideas often swirled around his head as he fell asleep, and sometimes his dreams would be just like his thoughts … miracles and magic.

On one such night Paras dreamed about meeting the fairies of the river. Beautiful women, wearing thin veils across their faces that partially hid their lips but made their eyes prominent, rising out from the river. Their flowing dress, made of light, would be untouched by water as they stepped onto the river bank and approached the banyan tree. Elegant as queens and honey-voiced, they would tell him how to achieve his dreams and be the genius he wanted to be. They would tell him secrets of miracles, of creating magic and changing the world and becoming the best scientist there ever was.

He thought about his dream the next day. It all felt very real, as if the fairies were waiting for him at the river bank. He went there at his usual time and found no sign of their presence, not even at the banyan tree. He dove into the water, hoping to catch a glimpse of light of their dress, but found nothing. He even thought about asking his parents before realising what would happen. His father would be worried he was daydreaming again and his mother would throw a tantrum. She would think he was having bad thoughts about girls; the river fairies always brought out a carnal viciousness from village women, as if those fairies were sworn enemies. He never understood why, and was too afraid to ask.

One day he decided to go and see if the fairies did appear at all or not. No one left home in the night and only the lord's guards patrolled the perimeter against dacoits. He crept out and silently passed through houses, then out into the fields on the walking tracks. Despite the dark he kept his walking swift, mindful of the muffled growls of stray dogs out into the fields. He reached the road and could barely make out the school building, let alone the river. He walked, blind as a bat, towards the river and in the darkness of the night managed to locate the tree.

That's where his tracks came to an end. The tree, so peaceful and a blissful relief against the harsh sun, was a towering lock of witch hair waiting for its next victim. He remembered the stories around night fires, of elders and travellers, about witches and spirits and djinns that inhabit the trees and attack those in the night who would dare to touch them or sleep beneath their branches. For the first time in his life, Paras felt afraid of the banyan tree. He felt it rising out from the ground, its branches spreading like wicked claws and the eerie silence with which it stood like a patient hunter. The leaves ever-so-slightly moved in the light breeze, teasing Paras, urging him to come closer.

With wobbly legs he traced his footsteps, going back into the village, avoiding the guards somehow, entering home without alerting his parents and falling to sleep on his small bed in the corner. He dreamed of darkness, of witches with twisted feet descending from trees on him and tying him up with roots and branches. He was suffocated, squeezed, drowned and trampled by evil horses. The laughter of the wicked witches sounded in his ears. He woke up, his body burning, his limbs shivering. He had fever that burned to the touch and scared his parents upon discovery.

Nasreen, his mother, stayed home as Nabi Baksh ran out to find the Pir, a holy man, devotee at a saint's shrine, with intimate knowledge of herbal medicine. Wearing beads made of brown wood around his neck, shoulder length loose hair, rings adorning his fingers and a shock of henna-coloured beard, the Pir sat at his usual place in the shrine, reciting the verses by an old Darvesh named Arab Saeen. Nabi Baksh approached him, thanking God that he was alone and not surrounded by people clamouring for his advice and attention.

'Saeen baba.' Nabi Baksh addressed the Pir, folding hands together in greeting. The Pir looked up, a smile lighting up his face as he returned the greeting, palms pressed together.

'Nabi Baksh, what a blissful sight.' The Pir began to rise.

'No Saeen, please sit down. Don't rise on my account,' Nabi Baksh protested.

'Nonsense,' Pir hugged him. 'Your name is Nabi Baksh, Blessed by the Prophet. How can I be a scoundrel and remain sitting when you arrive.' Nabi Baksh hugged back with some embarrassment and they sat down on the straw mattresses.

'What brings you here today?' The Pir asked.

'My son, Paras, has a fever. It is very strong and burns to the touch,' Nabi Baksh said.

'Burns? Is he delirious?' Pir inquired.

'He doesn't respond to our words, as if the fever has taken him away to another world,' Nabi Bakhs said.

The Pir frowned, his eyes questioning. He stood up and began gathering a few things, small bottles of coloured powder and brightly coloured thin clothes.

'Let's go,' the Pir told him as Nabi Baksh began to lead him home.

They reached to find Nasreen placing towels drenched in cold water on Paras's forehead. The Pir asked her to stand aside as he removed the wet cloth and dried the forehead. He placed his hand and felt the fever, then took out a thin blue silk scarf and sprinkled white powder over it. He placed the cloth on Paras's forehead, the powdered side above, and waited.

A few moments later specks of red appeared. The white powder was turning crimson.

'Paras has the witch's fever,' Pir informed. 'He has been affected by evil beyond the veil.'

Nasreen muffled her mouth, horrified. Nabi Baksh was shaken, his eyes wide with fear.

'Has he been out somewhere recently? To a graveyard? Any place that may be an abode of evil?' The Pir asked.

'No, he doesn't go anywhere without telling us,' Nabi Baksh replied. 'He has been a good boy, an obedient boy.'

'It must be that witch Gulain,' Nasreen said venomously, tears streaming down her cheeks. 'Her face drips with hatred at my boy's good fortunes. She must have put the evil eye on him. I know she dabbles in black magic.'

'No sister, this is not the evil eyes,' Pir said in a measured tone, 'they don't cause fever but loss of heart and bring waywardness in life. This is a pure witch's work, an evil that is boiling your son away from within. Bring me boiling water and add this herb in it.'

The Pir prepared a concoction using various herbs and crushed powder, making Paras sit up and gently pouring it in his mouth. Paras drank it in small measures and was laid back once the cup was empty.

The shivers in his body began to die down, his eyes no longer darted around behind the lids and his breathing stabilised. A few minutes later, he was sound asleep.

'He will be awake in six hours. When he does, give him milk and warm bread, then send for me.' The Pir left for the shrine while Nasreen sat down beside his son. Nabi Baksh began his daily chores, delivering milk and eggs to the village followed by cleaning of the livestock shed. He was worried but much less so than in the morning. The Pir's knowledge was extensive and no one was better equipped to help his son than him.

He entered his house and took the place of his wife, who began her chores; she cleaned the house and began cooking for the afternoon. She brought him tea as he took out his beerhi (cigarette) and lit it up, sitting closer to the window so the smoke went out: he wouldn't want it to affect his son in any way.

***

Paras dreamed of the river, the water lapping the bank as boats floated down and away. Their occupants, faceless people with robe-like dresses, looked downriver. Paras saw them sail away, one after the other, in a never ending chain. He looked towards the banyan tree, a thing of beauty and terror, towering over the river bank. The branches waved in the air, wind whistling past that often broke leaves and made them float around the sails of the boats before falling onto the water.

Come to me, a voice sounded in his head. The tree branches moved as if inviting him. Paras shook his head.

Come to me, the voice sounded again, more insistent this time. Paras again shook his head.

Come to me, the voice commanded with intoxicating authority. Paras wavered and took a step. He felt an inner resistance that broke the spell, and he shook his head again.

A cracking sound came and roots erupted around him. Snaking up and tying his body, the roots silenced him before he had the chance to scream. The ground began to break as the giant banyan tree uprooted itself and began to move towards him, its massive bulk moving with precision.

Before the tree could reach him, the occupants of the sailing boats stood up and pointed towards the tree. Water erupted like vines from the ground and shackled it, making it immobile. Water rose around Paras and locked itself in a battle with the roots. The sound of wood cracking dominated the air, as if the tree was screaming at the intrusion of the river. It shook violently to break the hold, but the water held.

Soon the cracking sound of wood began to die out as the sound of river-flow rose. Paras, despite being trapped, began to relax under the hypnotic effect. The sound of river-flow brought him tranquility and it seemed to have calmed down the tree as well. It no longer fought the water vines, but the roots held tightly as ever.

A figure stepped out onto the bank. It was one of the faceless people; but feminine features began to appear. She moved closer and placed her hand onto the roots trapping Paras. She gently pulled, and the roots began to let go. She unwound them until Paras was completely free of them and he gingerly stepped out.

The water vines around the banyan fell, and it began to lumber back to its place. The roots dug themselves back in and the tree stood as solidly as it always had. It no longer had its earlier threatening presence.

The figure began to walk back.

'Wait,' Paras said.

She stopped, turned around.

'Who are you?' He asked.

She stood there, a small smile on her face.

'What's your name?' He inquired.

She turned back and started walking towards the boats.

'Stop, please!' Paras shouted. 'Tell me who you are. Why did you help me? And why was the tree moving?'

She climbed into the boat. The figures sat back down and the boats began to sail again. Her boat also started drifting into the water.

'Please, stop, please,' Paras pleaded. 'I want to know what just happened. Why did you save me? Why did the river rise? And who are you?'

The figure turned towards him, her face still smiling. Her boat stopped in the middle of the river and she pointed at the sky. Paras looked above, the sky darkening as if it was night … a full moon shone, its reflected image lighting up the stationary boat.

Paras felt his world going dark. He saw the woman standing in the boat, waiting for him and he didn't know if he understood any of it.

Darkness enveloped him and after a few moments he opened his eyes.

Paras rose groggily and Nabi Baksh placed the empty cup down. He called for Nasreen, to bring milk and bread, which she quickly did. Paras seemed ashen, his eyes red and skin dead as he started chewing on the bread on his mother's insistence. Nabi Baksh went out and sent word to the Pir that Paras was awake, and came back to sit near his son.

They asked him gentle questions, if he ate anything out of home or something that may have caused the fever. If he had drunk anything that was offered to him, probably infused with black magic to make him ill. Paras shook his head in response. He spoke few words as his throat was parched, yet he couldn't drink much either, except milk in small measures.

The Pir arrived at their place a short time later and proceeded to sit next to Paras. He checked his fever and the rate of his heartbeat, then grunted with satisfaction.

'You seemed recovered, your strength is still away though,' the Pir said. 'Sister, give him food that he can easily eat. No meat for now, just vegetables and dairy and make him drink this first.' He handed her a small bottle of a white powder.

'Mix a quarter teaspoon in a glass of water and make him drink that, then give him food. His strength will return faster.' He instructed, then asked them to give some privacy while he talk to the kid.

Once the parents went out into the livestock shed, the Pir turned to Paras and asked, 'What did you see?'

Paras looked at him quizzically and asked 'What, baba ji?'

'What did you see that gave you the fever?' Pir asked again.

Paras was silent for a moment. Then he told him about the first dream, of seeing the banyan tree, the witches torturing him. The Pir listened, rapt, not interrupting. Paras told of everything he saw, of waking up with fever and burning body.

The Pir was silent for few moments before asking, 'Is that it? You only dreamed of it? Nothing else?'

Paras shook his head.

'You do know that lying about witches will bring them back, worse than before, eh?' Pir asked, a knowing look on his face.

Paras was about to shake his head, then stopped and simply looked down in embarrassment.

'You went out into the night to look at the tree, didn't you?' Pir asked. Paras nodded his head in acceptance.

The Pir sighed, placing a hand gently on his head.

'Son, why did you tempt fate? The forces that balance this world should not be taken lightly,' the Pir said. 'Every year I treat young men like you suffering from witch fever, all trying to show they are the bravest of the lot. You chose the banyan tree by the river, and tomorrow you would try to hit a nail in its trunk during full moon. Do you know what the witches do to you then?'

Paras shook his head.

'Better not find out, it's not for the faint hearts like yours,' the Pir said. He began to rise up.

'What does happen during full moon?' Paras inquired. The Pir stopped in its tracks.

'Why do you ask, boy?' Pir gently asked.

'I don't know. I hear so much about it but don't know why.' Paras replied.

'Full moon is a foul time, particularly on the longest night of the year,' Pir replied. 'It lets forces play out their games on people, wicked ones, and it is never a good thing. Never trust a stranger you see during full moon.'

'Are you afraid of the full moon?' Paras asked.

'No longer, but I don't trouble the forces either,' Pir said. 'Harmony is the answer to life and its challenges.'

Paras looked at him as if struggling, then blurted out.

'Can you take me out, during full moon?'

'To where?'

'The tree by the river.'

The Pir looked at him, his eyes going wide.

'Didn't I tell you not to tempt fate?' he asked, his fists on his sides. 'Have you heard nothing?'

'I am sorry, I heard you well,' Paras mumbled. 'But I want to go and see it during full moon.'

'Why?' the Pir asked, his tone harsh.

'I dreamed of answers … answers that I will find only at the banyan tree during full moon,' Paras replied.

'Answers to what?' Pir inquired.

'I don't know, only that I have to be there during the next full moon.' Paras replied.

The Pir looked at him … then he looked at him again. This time it seemed he was looking past him, right through his soul, breaking apart secrets.

Paras gulped.

'You haven't told me everything,' Pir said, looking at Paras. 'What else is there to know? What else did you dream?'

Paras remained silent.

'The dream you told me, it holds no questions nor answers. There is more you have seen, what is it?

Paras remained silent.

The Pir waited for few more moments, Paras only looked down. The Pir sighed and looked out of the window, into the livestock shed. Both Nabi Baksh and Nasreen were tending to the chickens.

'You have a beautiful life here, don't waste it chasing after mirages,' the Pir said, a hint of smile on his face. He turned and began to walk away.

'Full moon is in three days, find me at the shrine in the evening,' the Pir said. 'Convince your parents yourself, that's not my headache.' And he walked out of the house.

***

For the next three days Paras was constantly fussed over by his parents. They made sure he ate plenty, drank the foul medicine regularly and they didn't let him out of their sight. He kept worrying how he would ever manage to get out without arousing suspicion.

Finally, on the morning of the third day, he asked his father if they could go to the shrine. He told him he wanted to spend some time with the Pir, to thank him for saving him from the affliction. Nabi Baksh said he hoped he wasn't planning on becoming Pir's disciple, his Murid, and taking up his place at the shrine. Paras assured him he wasn't, and he walked to the shrine in the evening with his father.

There they paid their respects to the deceased, a great man of wisdom and knowledge, and sat down with the Pir for some talk. With some understanding with the Pir, Paras managed to convince his father to let him stay here for the night as he felt peace in this place. The Pir assured Nabi Baksh that he would take care of it, and Paras would be safe. After a while, Nabi Baksh agreed and left for home as the sun started to disappear.

Paras stayed at the shrine, his back to the wall, and recited poetry from a book the Pir gave him. They ate the dinner together and when dead of the night approached, the Pir asked him to perform ablutions.

'Purity is the first step towards every goal, and we need to be prepared for the folly that'll befall us,' the Pir said. Paras performed the ablutions from the nearby water drum and submitted himself to checking by the Pir.

'Thankfully, no nails in your pockets. I hope you don't plan on doing that, it'll be suicidal for both of us.' Paras assured him that wasn't the case.

They walked out near midnight, the moonlight illuminating the surroundings. The path ahead was clear and he could easily make out the route leading out towards the river. They walked in silence, their steps the only sound breaking the racket made by crickets. The Pir carried a staff this time, adorned with ornaments Paras couldn't make sense of. He decided not to ask as they approached the road. The school stood right in front of them, structure clearly visible. On the right stood the tall banyan tree, not as intimidating as before, though darkness still gathered under its arching branches.

The Pir took the lead, this time intoning words Paras didn't know. They walked, slowly, towards the tree and came to stop about ten feet from the shadow of its branches.

'What do you see?' The Pir asked. Paras looked at the tree, realising how intimidating it looked in the night but not as terrorising as before.

'I feel a gathering darkness in the branches, but nothing much else,' Paras replied.

'Then you are lucky. The tree doesn't mind your presence. Me, however, it is ready to kill if I get any closer,' the Pir replied.

Paras looked at him, question in his eyes.

'What dwells upon it doesn't like me. We are, no longer, on friendly terms,' Pir said.

They stood there in silence, the looming tree in front of them.

'Do you know where your answers are?' Pir asked.

Paras nodded assent. The Pir simply gestured to go ahead while he stood on guard. Wind picked up speed, the branches began to dance in the air; the Pir began to recite words, louder this time, which Paras did not understand. He took his steps gingerly, afraid of roots popping out to grab him.

But the darkness merely shifted around the branches and stayed there. Paras walked slowly, his heart thumping and palms sweating. Soon he stood under the tree, close enough to touch the trunk. Wind whistled past the tree.

'Ignore the seductive sound, do not touch the trunk,' the Pir said, his voice firm. Paras nodded and walked past the tree, going near the river bank.

He looked at the sky, the full moon shining brightly, and he looked down at its reflection in the water. It was about the same place where the reflection had appeared in his dream. He looked around, hoping to find what he came here for.

But there was no fairy. There were no sailing boats, no faceless people and no woman waiting for him. He kept looking around, walking up and down the riverbank to no avail. He moved a few steps away, where he stood in his dream in relation to the tree, and checked the riverbank. Nothing appeared.

He felt his spirits plunge. His answers eluded him. He no longer knew why he was here, with a priest who kept looking at the banyan tree as if it was all that mattered. He stood up and turned back towards the Pir.

A reflection caught his eye.

It was small, very minute, but he felt it clearly. He turned back towards the river and walked at the bank. It was a tiny light, barely visible. It was hidden in the water at the very edge of the bank. Paras sat low and looked at it carefully, trying to make sense of it in the dark waters. He brought his hand forward to try and touch it ...

The glow moved and a fish jumped out and hit his hand, hard. It stung so badly he nearly cried out. The creature was gone in a flash, the light nowhere to be found. He felt searing pain at the back of his hand and he tried to rub it. He gingerly walked back to the Pir, whose eyes were still locked with the tree.

'Found anything?' The Pir asked.

'No, but a fish hit me quite hard,' Paras replied.

'Good, at least you are alive. Let's go.' The Pir slowly backtracked, his eyes still on the swaying tree. After a few steps, the wind began to die and the tree stilled. Pir let out a long sigh and turned back to walk properly. They reached the shrine in silence and there, using an oil lamp, the Pir examined Paras. There was swelling at the back of his right hand.

'Looks like a very strong fish, to leave such a mark. Unusual,' Pir said as he rubbed an ointment on it. Paras winced at the heat it brought, following by instant relief. Pir tied his hand with a clean cloth, crushed leaves pressed on the swelling to heal it.

Paras slept a dreamless sleep at the shrine that night.

When he woke up at the crack of dawn, the swelling was gone, leaving behind traces of lines that resembled slivers of moon. Paras thanked the Pir and walked back home, finding his mother awake and waiting for him with his favourite *Besan Jo Chilro*, pancake made from gram flour. He sat down, tracing the sliver of moon on his hand. When Nasreen asked if he was fine, Paras smiled in response and began eating his breakfast as Nabi Baksh joined them, the shape on his hand growing into a full moon.

THREE POEMS

Shadab Zeest Hashmi

Terms of Tea Tasting from
The East India Company
Book of Tea

Appearance
Tippy: *indicates the presence of the golden*
or silver coloured leaves
from the tip of the budding tea leaf

Tip of the tea-tongue *Mowgli*
Budding Mughal prince swathed in silver
and gold
When you see your reflection
you see an unclothed jungle boy

Wiry: when a leaf is tightly twisted
it resembles a piece of wire

Remember twisting
those Enfield cartridge ends
with the teeth?
Your *sepoy* blood boiling over paper
greased with beef tallow and pork lard
Taste of sacrilege
in your brown mouth
wired to orders in your ears

Bright: after infusion the leaf has a good, pronounced colour,
usually orange or coppery
The one in the copper-bordered sari

and marigolds in her hair
is the groom's mother
It is their last photo together
Tomorrow she will lose him in the first
of many massacres

Liquor Body: the sensation of weight
of the liquor on the palate

or of a verse in Urdu
(sudden gravity, sudden flight)
Ghazal couplet midstream
stops a *yekka* carriage in the street
for an empire to alight

Plain: lacking in desirable characteristics

It is 1912, you must get into your khakis
Khak is dust:
camouflage for the sons of this soil
Nothing
and everything

Point: a pronounced favourable sharpness of flavour

The trader who folds his legs on the velvet divan
for a royal portrait
has designs
on his host's empire
Tyrannies will, in the end, be punished
But what of *your* glass-bangled Dalit wrists?
Your untouchable hands?
The sharpness of your slap across empire's face?

Simla Club dining-room is built,
as all the world knows, in two sections
with an arch-arrangement dividing them.

Arches all the world knows
dogs and Indians don't.
They eat rubies, they eat bones,
rub their fancies in boot blacking
in yearly Simla snow.

Come in, turn to your own left,
take the table under the window,
and you cannot see anyone who has come in

(though the window is wild abandon
and a golden sparrow flew
straight in from the lime tree
bit the dust in the soup
just this morning)

turn to the right, and take a seat
on the right side of the arch.

where the banana leaves graze the bricks,
the clock reflects the castor oil
plant in the pretty poison garden

Curiously enough, every word that you say can be heard,
not only by the other diner, but by the servants
beyond the screen through which they bring dinner.

Gossip jigsaw
Spy boomerang
Chain of command

This is worth knowing. An echoing room is a trap to be forewarned against.

(Note: The italicised text is from Kipling)

Proust's Cup of Tea: A Concussion Study

*The tea has called up in me, but does not itself understand, and can only repeat
indefinitely with a gradual loss of strength, the same testimony;*
Pinch of memory
from the canister with tea for an answer,
whir of plaza pigeon, ghost of child pidgin
hopping mad in the mouth like masala jaggery,
cup after cup
of receding birdsong
by the same window

*I hope at least to be able to call upon the tea for it again and to find it there
presently, intact and at my disposal, for my final enlightenment.*
Pool of turpentine, wick
of unsurpassed flame,
(same room in the old house lit up by the same lantern),
dear brain cell,
foot-bridge to tomorrow,
bring back my earliest China,
settee with monarch design, condensed
milk, burnt lip, dawn and lawn and primal lizard,
sorcery of sameness I drank again and again

I put down my cup and examine my own mind.
I say: curator of exquisite ruin, why
did you bite me like that?
And, where do you hide that morsel? And, who will I plot
my revenge with? And, let the rest of me go too.

What an abyss of uncertainty whenever the mind feels that some part of it
has strayed beyond its own borders?
I've outgrown your delicacy
like the catgut that took to my hand at two,
something fattens, glows neon with stolen thoughts
You
island in the night of Spinal storm where a quiet thought

meets a cold shoulder,
be the one room with switches that turn on light and fan,
be the lasso of lost time.

(Note: The italicised lines are from *In Search of Lost Time* by Marcel Proust)

ZERESHK POLOW

Mimi Khalvati

One couldn't see through the glass doors,
the glass being frosted and endowed
with fruit and flowers, but the odours
of cooking seeped through and the bowed
figures of aunts bent on their task,
positioning spoons, plates, cast shadows
against the panes, humped and grotesque,
like kindly, harmless Quasimodos.

Unlikely loves! Like Stevie Smith's
lion aunt who gave her the lion's share,
my aunts, great-aunts, who always came
in twos, the way fruit and flowers pair,
if love was the dish, ladled out rice with
barberries, cumin, then called my name.

REVIEWS

METAPHORICAL MUNCHIES

C Scott Jordan

My seat was in Iraq. It sounded like as good a place as any for me to colonise my Made in the US of A posterior for the evening's performance. I cannot believe this act of irony was the product of chance alone. Ticket in one hand, a paper cup of steamy mulled wine in the other, I pondered the meaning of this unusual seating categorisation. I was assured this was a fine seat. I revelled in the creative way of dividing seats into refugee contributing countries. How immersive of the show runners! I didn't have a clue. The long hall took me not only to the Iraq seating section, but beyond the simple theatrical construct that was the Young Vic Theatre. Step by step, layers of ignorance thawed as I moved from the stage which was the West to what appeared to be the backstage area. The seat appeared to be the left-over scrap from the set designers. I was in Calais. This was the Jungle.

I feared I had taken a wrong turn, for this was not stadium style seating. In fact, I wasn't sure where the stage was, perhaps it was the fourth wall of this square room, but it was a bit small for an elaborate production. Rows of tables and pillow cushions for seats. Had I stumbled into the green room? No, this all was to be the stage the players would perform upon. My mind moved at a million miles a minute trying to decipher what must have been a puzzle. My seat was on a nice raised bench, looking in through a window, into this shanty world. Dirt made the floor. Graffiti and trash the interior décor. There I was, an American in a sports coat, sipping mulled wine, looking in on the Jungle, a refugee camp. My seat of course, was on the far end, so I, as us Americans are all too familiar in doing, had to inconvenience the rest of Iraq to find my proper seat.

The informality of it all was beautiful. It took me back to my primary school days, and the lay out was that of a school cafeteria. But how do you have a performance in a school cafeteria. As the room filled and filled, there appeared no place for a play. Are they going to dance on the tables? Is this going to be a recitation of monologues? Then suddenly, a beginning. I hadn't even taken notice that the play had begun, for it might well have just been a fellow audience member speaking too loud. Then the lighting changed, ever so slightly. The speaking grew louder, and we, the audience, grew quiet. People began pacing about. Shouting in foreign languages and one of them seemed to be collecting the information about, I suppose, all of us. After all, we too were refugees as far as anyone was concerned. We thought we were here to watch, but, in fact, we were part of the show.

We are thrust into a cacophony, or is it a parliament, or perhaps a tribal council. Brits bounce about, somewhere between the words they carry on paper and the updates their phones deliver. Elder refugees stand firm in place and position as they discredit promises made before our arrival. How like life, that one day we are born but the story began long before our arrival. Just the same it will continue long after our exit, stage left. The damned French have done something. The courts are, well the courts. A boy is dead. It is apocalypse. Just as the gates of hell open up and the final battle plays out before us. A thunderous calm delivery: 'Stop!'

The utterance was delivered by our narrator, Safi Al-Hussein, thirty-five years young, a Syrian. He appears taller than his frame. A hefty jovial type, with long, yet controlled, hair and a kingly beard. Where was he during the emergency meeting of this mock council? Is he an elder, or a child caught in a memory? Perhaps he is an angel, or at least the ghost of Christmas Present here to reveal that we mustn't just repent, but truly change! He reveals to us that we are in the dismal lacklustre present of Calais, France. Once a place fought over by the kings of history, now a sandy heap, a refugee camp, a leftover. What is our setting, a UN centre, a war room, a city council hall? No, a restaurant at the table scrap edge of France. A restaurant called Afghan Flag.

McDonaldisation has vulgarised the concept of restaurant. A quick stop between important life points. Order, pay, consume, dispose. In as much time. Rinse and repeat. Afghan Flag is no restaurant by contemporary Western standards. Here turnover is not the demanded outcome. Afghan Flag is a place to eat, a place to meet, a place where happenings happen. Afghan Flag is home. It is our, the audience and players, home for the next couple of hours. So, get comfortable. This may be difficult, after all this is not France. This is Zhangal, or as the Brits call it the Jungle. Naan and rice are always close at hand. Thanks to your proprietor, Salar Malikzai of Karz. For generations his family has defended their home in the graveyard of empires. Salar himself, the quintessential father figure, is a natural leader, a fighter who will survive. Afghan Flag is a new symbol of his strength and resistance. It is in this most indispensable hub that this story will play out, a house of community and of all things food.

The Jungle by Joe Murphy and Joe Robertson, Directed by Stephen Daldry and Justin Martin, a co-production of Young Vic, the National Theatre and Good Chance Theatre, Young Vic, London, 7 December 2017 to 9 January 2018.

The rules are simple. Afghan Flag is a traditional Afghan restaurant serving traditional Afghan food. It is a place of peace, a place for all tribes. No smugglers allowed. No alcohol. Before my mind can comprehend Salar's commands, I find myself putting the mulled wine under my seat. Dancing and celebration accompany high quality food which is indeed distributed to some of the audience. This structure is where Zhangal will survive and thrive, without it, as Mohammed, the Sudanese representative expresses, 'there is no hope.' Food is that one thing that drives humanity together, for it is necessary for survival. Furthermore, it is interesting that every culture has ritualised eating, from grand ceremonies, to simple yet foundational moments of time in the day that need be scheduled around. Food is also strange. It depends on the place and time, yet because of this it makes for a myriad of dietary diversity from person to person. It is a wonderful cultural appendage that we often leave unthought.

Food is a part of life and, sometimes unbeknownst to us, slips into our cultural and artistic expressions. Food causes a blending of the senses and because of that has the ability to control humans. Not enough of it drives desperation, an overabundance can create an agonising joy. Made just right, it can cause transcendence inspiring love, peace, and camaraderie. It permeates religion. Catholics eat the body and blood of their saviour so as to imbibe the holy spirit. Other Christians eat bread and drink wine or juice to symbolise sacrifice and spiritual cleansing. During Ramadan, Muslims fast, denying the pleasures of food, for an entire month to practice discipline and modesty. Various religions the world over offer food or sacrificed meals to their god(s). Food permeates government and diplomacy. It could be said that it is the original diplomatic ritual. HBO's *Game of Thrones* revives the medieval practice of sharing bread and salt as a symbol of protection to foreign guests and the blasphemy of breaking such a sacrament. State dinners are a must when two governments meet. Dinner parties are an act of bringing people together and the delicacy of the meal makes for better relations, be that of state or business or otherwise. We give travellers a meal or welcome our neighbours with a small food offering. All of this finds its way into art and especially seen throughout all schools of film.

Film takes overt and subtle approaches to food. Sometimes it is a simple prop. The Warner Brothers mascot Bugs Bunny always totes with him a delicious carrot, just as Homer Simpson is at his best with a donut, complete with sprinkles. Other times food is a deep thematic symbol. Chocolate symbolises love as berries tend to represent lust. *Willy Wonka and the Chocolate Factory* (1971), while taking on a multitude of themes, doesn't pull any punches on commenting about child obesity, addiction to sugary sweets, and other mindless practices of consumerist society. In *Sideways* (2004), issues of aging and fame are taken on as the main character Miles is compared to a bottle of pinot noir. A delicate grape that requires ageing, but has one perfect peak period, before it begins to go downhill thereafter. Food can be the punch line of a joke, or the victim of pain and tragedy. This can be a simple slippery banana peel, or a Baby Ruth candy bar looking like something much more nefarious in a swimming pool in *Caddyshack* (1980). In *Ghost Story* (2017), a pie given in sympathy after the death of her husband becomes the female lead's victim of anger and loss as it is viciously eaten only to be immediately thrown back up. It is the revenge of a victim of bullying for his whole town during the famous pie eating contest scene in *Stand By Me* (1986). Food fights are the expression of childhood innocence as seen in *Animal House* (1978) and *Hook* (1991). Food often times moves beyond the simple background of film, becoming a key part of a scene, even a sort of character.

Food can be a key figure in the progression of a story, even a symbol of power. In the series of films featuring Anthony Hopkins' portrayal of Hannibal Lecter, his genius knowledge of cuisine gives us insight into the psyche of a killer. Counterpoised with his cannibalistic tendency the story is made more complex with love, psychology, and horror. The TV tray dinner, perched before the all glowing and all-knowing television set, was America's destruction of the communal dinner model and was portrayed in all its grotesque misfortune in *Matilda* (1996). A chocolate cake appears later in *Matilda* as a disgustingly large morsel is fed to one of the school's children as punishment for thievery. The symbol of oppression, meant to kill the poor boy, is turned into a symbol of triumph as he finishes it to the standing ovation of his fellow classmates. An apricot becomes a key element behind the romance of *Call Me By Your Name* (2017). It is first used to test the etymological knowledge of the newly arrived doctoral student, Oliver. A pop quiz to see if he is worthy of the study he is about to undertake. Later in the film, the fruit is used as a shocking visual metaphor for childish lust and longing. A sort of dimension of the forbidden fruit of the Abrahamic Adam and Eve.

Cuisine in film can help transport you to other worlds. In *Indiana Jones and the Temple of Doom* (1984), the offering of a platter of bugs by a poor village in India and the Maharaja's banquet of fried snake, eyeball soup, and chilled monkey brains show the audience that Dr. Jones is a long way from Princeton. The mystical mandrake root and the Pale Man's dinner table take us from Spain in the midst of war to Ofelia's fantasy world in *Pan's Labyrinth* (2006). Quite literally, the peach in *James and the Giant Peach* (1996) takes James from a seaside village in England across the Atlantic to the Big Apple, New York City. Even Salar's Afghan Flag restaurant brings the audience from South London to Calais, or rather Zhangal. In a few films, food takes centre stage, becoming the setting or even the story in and of itself.

Cuisine is a place of refuge for the characters in *Julie & Julia* (2009). By day Julie answers calls for the Lower Manhattan Development Corporation concerning the September 11th tragedy and on future development of the area. To move beyond the gloom of the day, by night she slowly begins working her way through Julia Child's famous *Mastering the Art of French Cooking*. Alongside this story, the audience watches Julia Child as she attends the Cordon Bleu in Paris during the 1950s. Separated by time and brought together through a similar challenge and art, they both overcome the mundane of life to achieve something greater.

In *Chocolat* (2000), a single mother and her daughter arrive in a small French village at the beginning of Lent in 1959. As the pious town attempts to uphold this season of abstinence and reflection, the single mother, Vianne's, chocolate shop presents a threat. The temptation of the chocolate as a symbol of sin is countered by the ability of Vianne's influence to bring people together long separated by time and improve the overall wellbeing of all her patrons. Even the most outspoken against Vianne's shop, the mayor Reynaud is turned to her side by the slightest taste of her chocolate. Symbols are challenged and hearts are changed.

The life of a chef and the struggle between fame, fortune, and the artist's pleasure are explored through *Chef* (2014) and *Burnt* (2015). Both films depict a chef that had reached the top of their game and fallen from grace. The protagonist stands as the metaphorical creature that easily sells out talent for more money, and despite a stubborn and misanthropic attitude, struggles to refocus their love and art while salvaging their personal relationships with friends and family. Food here is not something you simply eat, but another window through which to see culture, family, and love.

Finally, one of the greatest culinary and spiritual films of all time is *Babette's Feast* (1987). Babette is a refugee fleeing counter revolutionary France who works as the cook of two sisters in Denmark. Slowly, Babette wins the pious village over by twisting the bland cuisine of the land into something stupendous. Every year as she works for her employers, Babette has her French lottery ticket renewed. When one year she wins the lottery, instead of returning home, she sacrifices her wealth to throw one large, authentic French dinner for the sisters. Babette's forfeiture makes her seem a saintly figure to the two women, but she is pleased to be an appreciated artist. Food can be divine and a path towards truth and beauty in the true chef's, rather artist's, eye.

In many films, food is seen as something higher. It is a reprieve from the chaos of everyday life. These stories show that any person can become an artist. Any ingredients can be transformed into an ornate meal. The spirit of the chef is the spirit of all humans, to create. To take the raw materials around us and make something greater. Much as Salar, Mohammed and the other first arrivals in Calais transformed an overgrown patch of coast into a safe haven. Their goal was to seek asylum in the UK for there they can communicate and function without having to learn yet another language or deal with the tension that already exists within France and other European states. What they actually created was something new entirely, and potentially a permanent settlement, a new home. The question still remains, but for how long, after all the French do not intend for this to be a new home. The French prefer that they seek asylum or move on, for they have their own internal problems to deal with. At a point where they can almost see the UK, but not legally get to it, the UK comes to them.

Just as Zhangal begins to look like its own functioning society, the West in all its ugliness arrive to save the poor refugees. A drunk, a foul-mouthed patriarchy-damning independent woman, an aid savvy veteran of global calamity, and two millennials, one who knows nothing and the other with far too many assumptions about the world outside their dorm rooms. Their rapid approach to action and change is met with confoundment by the refugees. Despite Salar's initial hesitant reception of the Brits, Afghan Flag is a place of peace and all tribes of man. Together they are all fleeing something whether it is as simple as the banality of modern life or the terrors of war. They all seek refuge in this restaurant.

We the audience also seek refuge. Be that a moment to enjoy something expressive and beautiful in a world that is otherwise – well – not. It is easy to lose sight of life as it seems to be the breathes between tube stops, bus stops, traffic lights, boarding calls, time clock punches, or deadlines. For a couple of hours, we the audience are refugees with these poor souls in Zhangal. The Players respect us, teach us, and feel with us. They offer us food and demand we pay for it as well. There is no such thing as a free lunch. We walk through the dark with them, hide from the authorities with them. We choke on the tear gas with them, tremble as the restaurant is shaken from its foundations. We cry with them. Will we grow with them? Are we simply props, like the food, or are we characters? Can we be something greater?

The Jungle does a wonderful job of using a confined space to metaphorically demonstrate the need for people from around the world to come together and cast away their precognitions of each other. The racism between refugees, the animosity between piety and contemporary habits, the enmity between the West and the rest, and the simplest of all conflicts between love and hate. The ignorance of each character keeps them authentic and real, and the dissection therein provides for wonderful arcs.

The play ends with the apocalypse it began with. Our saintly narrator, now stripped of even his coat, which he has given to someone in need, stands shivering. The cold eats at him as do the visions of the war he ran from. In conduct unbecoming of his character, he takes the smugglers' onion, its smell keeps the search dogs away, and makes his way for the UK. His journey is almost complete, but in order to do this, he had to take that journey from another. But, even logic crumbles with the other structures of this old world. The other refugees and the Brits finally stand with Salar as the bulldozers come for his restaurant. A boy dies. A girl seeks asylum in France. Victory in and of itself becomes a meaningless concept. Petty and temporary. After all, Zhangal was never meant to be the end of the journey.

The play itself does not have a conclusion. The story is not over. This is also not the beginning of another story. Now the story is ours. The authors give us the option. We hear that Zhangal is rapidly erased from the map bit by bit, evicted by the French. We hear that global attention waxes and wanes with the media's need for a story. We learn that the refugee crisis is still far from over. Once we stand from the uncomfortable wood benches or the pillows on the floor, what will we do?

No answers are provided. Not even guidelines of where to move next. Do we the refugees return to the trials of everyday life; do we continue to flee? We are challenged to, in our own special way, keep the story alive. In Western consumerism, the formality and beauty of a meal has been distilled out. Eating becomes a chore like cleaning the bathroom or laundry. Have we forgotten the ritual? Can we appreciate the art that forces us to act? The meal that brings us all together to love and be merry, and, just maybe, begin to save the world.

Tomorrow is a new day. For now, the meal is finished, but there are still dishes to do.

COLONIAL FANTASY

Becky Trow

Unemployment does a funny thing to a person. In the quest to save money, staying home to watch television doesn't seem such an unappealing idea. So there I was, settling down to watch BBC's Question Time whilst snacking on those amazing biscuits advertised as more chocolate than a biscuit, you know the ones. I was soon grateful there was chocolate at hand. Watching #bbcqt should come with a health warning as it never fails to fill me with despair at the state of humanity, and this edition was no exception. Already experiencing a mix of horror coupled with the car-crash inability to switch it off, David Dimbleby ramped up my indignation by seemingly mocking Shami Chakrabarti on her appointment as Baroness. She retorted with exasperated irony, 'How dare I take my place at the table as well.' It made me think of the power dynamics that endlessly play out in our post-colonial world, when we continue to question the legitimacy of a person's role because of who they are rather than what they do. A few days later I found myself watching *Victoria & Abdul* and was reminded of this encounter.

Directed by Stephen Frears, whose other works include *My Beautiful Laundrette* (1985), *High Fidelity* (2000) and *The Queen* (2006), *Victoria & Abdul* is an adaptation of a novel written by Shrabani Basu and based on a true story, well mostly as the screen reads. It's 1887 and Abdul, a young but tall prison clerk in Uttar Pradesh, is requested, much to his delight, to present a ceremonial coin to the Empress of India, Queen Victoria, at her Golden Jubilee in England. This is how the film starts its journey: with Abdul and his smaller coin-presenting-counterpart Mohammed, travelling for months on end in squalor and stormy seas with the simple goal to present her majesty with a gift from India.

For all its beautiful cinematography and the quiet anticipation one feels when you settle down in your seat and the first scenes roll in, I couldn't help but feel a little apprehensive. Why was Abdul travelling all this way to deliver a coin to the Queen of a country that had imposed its rule on his own? More worryingly, why was he okay with it? At this point India had been under British rule for decades under the expansion of the British Empire. With the spread of imperialism came the violent suppression of local people through systematic policy-making and violence. Anybody who dared to retaliate was brutally wiped out.

A YouGov survey carried out in 2014 shed light on the general thoughts of our nation on its problematic history. The survey found that 59 per cent of British people were proud of our record of colonialism with just 19 per cent regretful and 23 per cent remaining ambivalent. Not surprising when you consider the British school curriculum. I don't remember ever learning about the atrocities committed in India, Sudan, Benin, Jamaica, Canada to name just a few countries on the receiving end of our quest to rule the world. In fact, ten-year-old me was under the impression that it was quite amazing that such a small country could amass so much power. Stories of Christopher Columbus' great voyage to the West Indies or Captain James Cook's 'polite' negotiations with the Maori to claim New Zealand for King George III were cloaked with romanticism and adventure, almost as if taken straight out of a fairytale.

Victoria & Abdul, directed by Stephen Frears, Screenplay by Lee Hall, BBC Films/Working Title Films, UK, 2017.

This rose-tinted and jubilant view of the colonial era is, likewise, conveyed in *Victoria & Abdul*. Not least because we see England and the monarchy through Abdul's eyes and he happens to hold these people and the role he has been given in great reverence. It is easy to see why. When the beautiful stately homes and Downtown Abbey-esque type banquets light up the screen you can almost feel his awe. The splendid clothes and intricately crafted wobbly jelly Abdul so precariously carries to the Queen's table brings a world most of us have absolutely no experience of to life. Such wonderment is soon brought down to earth, however. The reality of the times is quick to pervade and the niceties fall away when

Abdul comes into contact with the Queen's council. They despise him from the moment he steps out of the carriage, because of course he is Indian and a low born Indian at that.

Frears does moderately well to mock the superior British attitude, for example when Abdul learns the jelly is made from a by-product of cow bone to which he exclaims 'barbarians!' Or when numerous racist remarks are bandied about, it is telling that few laughs are elicited from the audience. But eventually these insults become wearing. I couldn't help but detect an attempt to create a contrast between the Queen's council and the Queen herself, portraying her as 'woke' and politically enlightened, whereas this engenders a mockery out of everybody else. Using racism as a tool for entertainment within the film only diminishes the real problem of such attitudes that sculpted the colonial agenda and continue to bubble up in today's society.

Racism and classism are crossover themes in the film. 'Whatever you do, you must not look at her majesty.' A low born cleric should not be looking into the eyes of the Empress of India; this is emphasised time and time again but of course Abdul disobeys, because otherwise there would be no story to tell. Inevitably, Abdul is reprimanded, yet it is clear that the Queen does not mind. In fact the bored and weary widow takes an immediate shine to the cheerful, rule-breaking coin bearer. So much so that he rapidly becomes her personal footman and, following this, her *munshi,* personal teacher. Much to the rest of the court's scandalised irritation, of course.

As the story goes on the relationship appears to be promoted as an unlikely love story between two people separated by a class and racial divide. Much remains ambiguous, particularly as to whether there is in fact any hint of romance involved. Frankly, the whole thing actually made me feel a little uneasy. Not because of the age difference, rather the undeniable power imbalance in the relationship.

Despite this you can't fault Dame Judi Dench in her portrayal of a character with which she is supremely familiar. Appearing as Queen Victoria in *Mrs Brown* in 1997, also a film depicting a love affair across class divisions, it is safe to say Dench settles into her role with ease. Even with the lack of material to work with, she portrays the cantankerous, messy, snoring and farting widow without reservation. Dench's on-screen presence evokes, for me, distant but fond memories of sitting by the fire on a late December afternoon wrapped up in woollen blankets, the smell of Mum's cooking thickening in the air. For a moment you are lost in the guilty pleasure of resigning yourself to an afternoon of watching films, writing off any tasks that you had to do that day. I am transported to the world of feigned magic of the old British aristocracy, complete with opulent ceremonies, the grandeur of the gardens, and old books lining the study. I would go so far as to argue her recognition as British film royalty. Casting Dench was Frears' saving grace.

Beyond Dench's formidable performance, the other half of the relationship sees Abdul appearing just a bit meek. Played by Bollywood actor, Ali Fazal, it was during a scene featuring his character that I actually fell asleep towards the end of the film. Now this is no slight against Fazal, he did a tremendous job with the script he was provided. It was Abdul who, unfortunately, had less substance than a gram of dust. His dialogue was bland, the pinnacle of which was him reciting some platitude about how life is like a carpet and we weave in and out to make a pattern. Whilst on a stroll around the gardens with his new bestie we are regaled with his description of the wonders of the Taj Mahal and his favourite Indian dishes, which sounded more to me like he was reading from the local takeaway menu. Despite his philosophising on the beauty of life, Abdul appears full of superficial anecdotes and clichés.

This stereotypical representation of Indian culture is prevalent in the world of British drama and film. The Brits' fixation with the colonial relationship is depicted on the screen in all its 'othering' glory. The fascination only lies within the nostalgic, fantastical relationship not the inconveniently unpleasant imposition of reality. The way Abdul appears to be amazed and impressed by all around him gives him a childlike air, reinforcing the concept of the naïve native; a simple, unsophisticated man easily captivated by the glitter and grandeur of British royalty. He oozes one dimensionality, but I wouldn't be surprised if the real life Abdul turned out to be far more complex.

Abdul's counterpart, on the other hand, I found infinitely more interesting. Mohammed was the only one with something legitimately interesting to say. On the initial journey to England, Abdul's excitement makes Mohammed appear cynical and a little jaded. Upon his appointment as the Queen's munshi, it transpires that Mohammed becomes Abdul's servant. Dazzled by the special treatment he is receiving, Abdul is blissfully unaware that his 'friend' isn't faring quite as well and in fact ends up perpetuating Mohammed's misfortune. He even fails to notice when he grows increasingly unwell, eventually culminating in his untimely death. The story of Mohammed is a tragedy. Frears not only missed the opportunity to work with an interesting, dynamic underdog but also to use his character as a vehicle to explore the issues of power and racism in greater depth.

Racism and classism are still prevalent in today's society, despite the efforts of elements within the right-wing media to claim we live in some sort of post-racist utopia, or worse, a world in which 'political correctness has gone mad'. We saw this in action during the pantomime that is Question Time. Regardless of how well Dimbleby can roll his R's, such comments that throw shade on Chakrabarti's right to be a baroness and the trajectory of her appointment, whether he meant it or not, are received with a sting. Could this be because we are fed a discourse that perpetuates the idea of male, pale and stale superiority? This narrative is reproduced in the news, school curriculum, television, books and film, and across all our institutions. It is here that the premise of *Victoria & Abdul,* a film about the relationship between two people who are part of larger dynamic between an oppressive empire and its colonial subjects, written by a white British man and recounted through his prism of experience and perspective, is laid bare.

BLOOD-SOAKED BUDDHISM

Laych Koh

The plight of the Rohingya in Myanmar has been covered considerably – denied citizenship and reviled by the country's majority, the stateless Muslim minority are persecuted, raped, killed and dehumanised, all because of their ethnicity and religion. Since August 2016, some 600,000 Rohingya Muslims have fled to Bangladesh and thousands more have sought refuge in neighbouring South East Asian nations.

What is less known is how the Rohingya became targets of such great hate and violence. Who are they exactly? Where do they come from? What forces are fuelling such slaughter? When did their position in the country become contentious? Why have they been targeted by Buddhist monks, hitherto considered proponents of peace and pacifism? These are questions that journalist Francis Wade attempts to answer in *Myanmar's Enemy Within*, a timely book which presents the myths and falsehoods that are key to understanding why this Muslim group is facing the threat of genocide.

I read this book alongside Azeem Ibrahim's offering on the same subject: *The Rohingyas: Inside Myanmar's Hidden Genocide*. Upon finishing Ibrahim's book I realised how thoughtful and important Wade's take is on the crisis. Both books wrestle with the history of the community in Rakhine state, and the controversies surrounding their identity and status. Both present the devastating abuses and violence perpetrated against the Muslim minority in Myanmar. Ibrahim ploughs through page after page debunking claims that the Rohingya are mere recent additions to the Rakhine state, but even he acknowledges that history is irrelevant to their entitlement to citizenship in Myanmar today. At some point it all feels somewhat immaterial, with the hatred and turmoil seemingly impenetrable.

Crucially, it is Wade, a seasoned journalist, who presents the eye-opening and chilling views of Burmese Buddhists, revealing their cold dismissal of the Rohingya as 'Bengali immigrants'. He conveys Rakhine perspectives as significant and vital to understanding how things have deteriorated so gravely.

Deep resentment towards the minority group has existed for generations. Wade says some responsibility for the stark racial divide lies with the British, who ruled from 1824 and brought with them their obsession with racial classification. To compound matters they encouraged immigration to Myanmar from India and Bangladesh, a source of great rancour. Ethnic tensions were present but, generally, both communities continued to co-exist peacefully. Official documents throughout the 1950s, 60s and 70s referenced the Rohingya as inhabitants of the northern Rakhine state and permitted the community to organise politically. Members stood as politicians, formed student associations and ran a Rohingya-language radio broadcast.

Wade's book details the way in which the status of the Rohingya grew increasingly precarious as the military regime sought to promote an exclusive Buddhist identity in the 1980s. It played up the majority's fears about their dominant position, especially in areas such as north of Rakhine state, where Buddhists are a minority. Under General Ne Win's citizenship criteria detailed in the 1982 Citizenship Law, an ethnic group must have had a presence in Myanmar prior to British rule in 1824. This should have covered the Rohingya, but due to its absence from British records, the regime had a pretext to exclude the entire group as it pursued an ethno-religiously 'pure' Myanmar. The 'Rakhine Muslim' category was removed from the 135-strong index of ethnic groups created by Ne Win. This compelled the Muslims of the state to cling more tightly to another label – Rohingya, 'one that had a history in Myanmar going back to at least the eighteenth century, and one that, at least initially, the government recognised,' writes Wade.

According to Ibrahim, the Rohingya were in the state before 1784, linking them to Indo-Aryan groups who arrived from the Ganges Valley as early as 3000 BC. But Wade explains that public opinion is completely against the notion that anyone within the Rohingya group might have had such longstanding presence in the Rakhine state. '(Rohingya) is a "new" label, and therefore its members must be new. Opponents of the label claim it gained traction in the 1950s as part of a fib by Bengalis who crossed over the border and settled on the land to support the separatists' ambitions of the Mujahids,' Wade writes.

Illegal immigration from Bangladesh had indeed taken place throughout military rule, exacerbating the siege mentality felt by Rakhine Buddhists, who came to perceive all who identified as Rohingya as interlopers. The Rohingya label was a lie, it was asserted, and the people who identified with it were there to support the campaign for a separate Muslim state.

Francis Wade, *Myanmar's Enemy Within*, Zed Books, London, 2017
Azeem Ibrahim, *The Rohingyas: Inside Myanmar's Hidden Genocide*, Hurst, London, 2018.

Wade dismantles these fallacies, and addresses preconceptions about Buddhism in Myanmar. He shows not only how Buddhist extremist groups like Ma Ba Tha fomented fear and hate towards Muslims, but how its adherents justify violence and murder. Wade is careful to question how Ma Ba Tha came to be so influential. He acknowledges they could only reach such heights with the backing of elements within the state, but says the connections are unclear and there is much speculation in the absence of facts. One theory, he notes, is that hardliner factions within the military and political elite wanted the Buddhist group to warn about the dangers of a democratic opening led by the National League for Democracy.

The stories told by Wade are incisive and intriguing. He describes the way in which two artful non-Buddhists infiltrated the ranks by lying about their ethnicity; a young monk who marched in the Saffron Revolution but remained sceptical of the goals of his colleagues, saying they did not really understand democracy; an interview with monk U Parmoukkha, who seemed to suggest 'an on-off switch available to Buddhists' so they could step outside their faith when committing a violent act in service of the group. Wade says we are guilty of simplifying and essentialising belief systems, and coming to the conclusion that people have just broken with their teachings. 'But Buddhist history carries the same tales of blood-soaked conquest as do all other religions, from the Zen masters of Japan to the Sangha in Myanmar today. ... Like all other religions, when Buddhism deploys violence it does so with a powerful sense of righteousness, of a "just" battle being fought to ensure its longevity.'

He paints a depressing picture when it comes to showing just how Buddhist extremist elements have inflamed fears about Muslims trying to 'purify the land' or build 'the (Islamic) bridge between Bangladesh and Malaysia via Burma and Thailand'. On 8 June 2012, mobs of Rohingya attacked Rakhine houses in retaliation for a bus attack five days earlier, during which ten Muslims were beaten to death by Buddhist mobs avenging the alleged rape and murder of a Buddhist woman, Ma Thida Htwe. Chaos and violence ensued between the two communities, and a popular Bamar journal, *Weekly Eleven*, sensationally reported that these were 'Rohingya terrorist attacks.' Later, the same publication stoked fears of ethnic cleansing or genocide perpetuated by the Rohingya in an attempt to eliminate the Rakhine.

After these attacks, things got exceedingly worse – anti-Rohingya material produced by local political parties, community groups and monk organisations was distributed in greater frequency. Since late 2011, a plethora of seminars, leaflets and other materials casting the Rohingya in a sinister and subhuman light proliferated.

There was no condemnation by the government over such demonisation, and the denigration of the community was becoming normalised, even outside the Rakhine state. A popular Burmese comedian, Min Maw Kun, called the Rohingya 'black-skinned, big belly, and hairy *kalar* who marry many Burmese women' in a sitcom directed by one of the country's best-known directors Maung Myo Min. Wade describes the force of propaganda to mobilise the Rakhine against the Rohingya as being so great that this transformed 'a floating sense of fear and resentment … into something more concrete and deserving of action'. There was no mental space left, Wade writes, to consider the Rohingya as anything but menacing. Sympathisers and moderates were now regarded as traitors and would need to be weeded out: a National League for Democracy (NLD) officer was arrested for 'outraging religious feelings' for speaking out against the fusion of violent nationalism and Buddhism; a Rakhine man was beaten to death for selling rice to a Muslim customer.

Against this backdrop, both Wade and Ibrahim juxtapose the expectations of Aung San Suu Kyi and her party as the just and democratising force in Myanmar. Prior to the 2012 violence, Suu Kyi and the NLD's position was sacrosanct, writes Wade, that criticism of them felt treacherous, even for foreign journalists writing on the country. Suu Kyi's reluctance to condemn the racism and violence against the Rohingya has been disappointing and deeply problematic, but it seems she is far from the only one who may harbour less than friendly views towards the community. Wade gives the example of Ko Ko Gyi, a leading opposition figure who is revered in Myanmar and spent seventeen years behind bars for opposing the junta. He has said the Rohingya were 'absolutely not an ethnic race of Burma' and that 'if powerful countries are to keep pressuring us, then us, the democratic forces of Burma, will view this as a national affair and will resolve this issue by joining hands with the Tatmadaw (the Myanmar army)'. Wade says that Suu Kyi's silence also hides a more significant problem – that the plight of the Rohingya had never featured in calls for equality between ethnicities in a post-junta Myanmar, and this looked like a certain continuity. 'They had no voice, and no presence. It seemed as if they were ghosts – people who lived in Myanmar, but who didn't quite exist. I grew to wonder after 2012 whether, if left long enough, these prejudices could grow even more entrenched, particularly given the absence of any countervailing narratives that might de-stigmatise the identity of the Rohingya.'

The country may be undergoing changes under Suu Kyi and the NLD, but no one was willing or able to rein in the vicious hatred directed at the community. Wade acknowledges that if she were to condemn the Buddhist movements, she would be depicted as pro-Muslim and lose support. He cites a campaign of vilification conducted against Suu Kyi in the lead up to the 2015 polls, where doctored photos of her in a hijab were circulated, and accusations were made that the NLD was focusing too strongly on universal human rights and too weakly on protecting Buddhism. Her refusal to use the name Rohingya in public, however, preferring to use 'Muslims of Rakhine' is a serious and significant form of persecution. It not only rejects their identity, writes Wade, it places them outside the purview of the state and the security it is obliged to offer. This legitimises the violence against the group by the Rakhine, who 'interpret the continued subordination of the group as indicative of the subhuman nature of its members.'

This means Suu Kyi and the NLD helped strengthen what Ne Win began by creating the 'national races' index and the tiers of belonging – the equating of foreignness with threat, whether in appearance, belief or practice. According to Wade the NLD could have cultivated a nationalism based on civil values rather than exclusionary ideologies, and this could have strengthened their ability to govern effectively. Instead it has chosen to go with this toxic 'us' and 'them' trajectory, leaving the military's blueprint for society unchallenged. Perhaps this was unsurprising, Wade says, considering the NLD's ranks are mainly Bamar, a privileged group in the country's ethnic make-up. Improving livelihoods for both the Rakhine and Rohingya by developing infrastructure in the state is often argued as a solution to the ongoing unease. Wade argues this can only go so far in defusing tensions. 'Without any effort to de-stigmatise and depoliticise the Rohingya identity, and to make clear that identity should not provide a basis for discrimination by the state, these cycles of violence risk repeating themselves.'

Wade interviews both communities, and in descriptive and depressing scenes notes how the separation of the two peoples has proved calamitous. Pre-existing divisions become entrenched, both cliques withdraw further, and rumours of attacks whirl and gather more force and venom without any counteracting information to correct them. There is little chance at reconciliation or peace when both communities are torn apart and segregated. 'Friends quickly became enemies because the actions of a few were portrayed as indicative of the intentions of many, and so the measures needed to address them were rolled out to all. As the communities grew further apart, there was nothing to correct these thought patterns, and they had a circular effect: the security measures could be read as evidence that Muslims had been allowed to roam free for too long, that they were always threatening, and that action was finally being taken to remedy that threat.' While Ibrahim makes his arguments forcefully – that the violence against the Rohingya is not a predictable side-effect of Myanmar's move to liberalism, and that global indifference supports the regime and is leading to genocide –Wade gives us pause to consider how the situation looks like for the ordinary man and woman on the ground.

Perhaps the most horrifying of all the accounts Wade relates is the story of Aarif and his family. Images conjured up by the description stay with you because it deals not with mobs and machetes, but how basic lifesaving services can be so cruelly and coldly denied. It is at once completely relatable and devastatingly unimaginable. In 2012, Aarif's wife developed complications during the labour of their fourth child in Kyauktaw – the baby was breech and required an operation. Unable to go to the hospital they usually went to, they were directed to another one, a three-hour drive in the opposite direction. Five minutes after finally arriving, they were told to leave. The doctor said it was too late – the baby would die and so would Aarif's wife. They were separated and police ordered Aarif back to the ambulance, which drove him to his village without his wife. He never knew what happened to her, except that she had died. He is not granted permission to travel for her funeral in another state. He is unable to visit her grave site. Through these stories Wade illustrates what it really means to be stateless – to be one who exists outside the law and all it entitles, with no recourse to legal action and no avenue to air any grievance. It is important to remember that it was not always like this.

Ibrahim says the military and notional opposition must be challenged, or the world will one day wake up to outright genocide. But Wade suggests that without addressing the longstanding prejudice in the country itself, there is little hope for any improvement to this complex crisis. So is there any chance of an end to the suffering? There are moments, brief flashes of optimism in Wade's book. He gives examples of the brave activists who are working against all odds to bring people together. A gathering to watch football. A simple meeting attended by different ethnicities to discuss the administrative affairs for a local community. Ibrahim reminds us that orchestrating a genocide is not easy. For the situation in Rakhine to now resemble, 'almost a text-book case of pre-genocide', he writes, different forms of repression have to have occurred. Myanmar has experienced the usual precursors, he argues: the creation of a racist culture that rationalises or encourages discrimination, systemic legal discrimination, and abuse of the historical record to construct a narrative in which mass murder becomes desirable or even imperative. He surmises that only a final trigger – arising from conflict, economic crisis, natural disaster or political events – is missing now before full-blown genocide takes place. Reading Ibrahim's take on things leaves one feeling helpless – that genocide is imminent. We can only stop things if we put international pressure on its government and Suu Kyi, but after everything that has happened and as both authors have shown, this seems hardly enough in the face of such deep animosity and resentment.

The two books are worth reading together to get a sense of how dire the crisis really is, and what needs to happen for any hope of improvement. Ibrahim's firm focus on the possibility of outright genocide is understandable. But are his suggestions realistic? Wade's demonstration of how entrenched the feelings and fears are within the communities and groups on the ground shows that this is problematic and inadequate. Unless something extraordinary happens, should the focus now be on the Rohingya's fate outside of Myanmar? And if the focus must be on its leadership, then could the observations in Wade's book prove useful in forming a more persuasive approach? Whatever prejudices towards non-Buddhists are held by figures within the NLD and the democratic movement more broadly, he says, there still remains the fact that harmony between the country's many different communities is politically beneficial for a civilian government, while violence will eat away at its legitimacy. 'If the primary goal of the party is civilian governance, then its interests will not be served by the kind of divisions that its silence has encouraged.'

A CUP AND FILL IT UP!

Irum Shehreen Ali

On a New Year's Eve in Dhaka, Bangladesh, many decades ago, my cousins and I, already giddy at being allowed to stay up past the magical hour, stealthily ran around the living room draining the dregs of the celebratory champagne from the grown ups' abandoned flutes. Back upstairs, we giggled ostentatiously and staggered around in an innocent facsimile of what we took to be inebriation. In this officially dry corner of the world, it was a truth secretly acknowledged that alcohol existed and that people drank it, at times to excess. Growing up I was surrounded by many a devout gentleman who enjoyed a hearty peg or two and saw no conflict between their identities as whisky connoisseurs and as Muslims. We knew that some of our white-collar parents partook at parties and corporate events, where white suited bearers carried around silver trays lined with regiments of glasses. We also knew that even though men were allowed to discreetly imbibe, the same rules did not apply to women. Girls were told with depressing repetitiveness that a drunk young lady was unacceptable, unattractive and downright unmarriageable. However, once in possession of the social legitimation shield of marriage, women could daintily sip cheeky glasses of wine, safe in the knowledge that everyone knew that they weren't really 'drinkers'. There were of course those who among us deeply disapproved, deeming it impious, offensive and unIslamic, but they existed peaceably side by side with those who deemed a nightly beverage a right.

Fast forward three decades, and *plus ça change*! While the country is still officially dry, shining a light under the hood shows us that the reality is still less straightforward. The upper classes still imbibe with ease in their homes and their elite institutions; safe in the access and protection afforded them by their money and power. In the villages, many farmers still drink their homemade toddy after a hard day in the fields; and in the cities, shops in the know still sell cheap hooch to the hard working common man. The increasingly religious middle class, attempting to hold the moral fabric of the nation in their hands, decry the ruinous effects of alcohol and 'too much' modernisation. In keeping with winds of Islamic conservatism sweeping many secular and tolerant Islamic majority countries, these latter voices seem louder of late.

Muslim societies have long railed vociferously against the monolithic view of our cultures as immutable theocracies. We are not iron bound orthodoxies of obedient would-be radicals, but rather possessed of overwhelming diversity of thought, appearance and lived experience in our midst. But even the most open among us still speak of alcohol in hushed tones. While drinking has no doubt been a part of Islamic societies since their very inception, the Qur'anic directive to avoid intoxicants meant that since the advent of Islam, debate has raged for centuries as to whether this is a mere suggestion or direct prohibition. Thus, it might shock some to learn that some of the greatest bacchic poetry was written in Iraq during the Abbasid Caliphate, known as the Golden Age of Islam.

Al Hasan ibn Hani, known as Abu Nuwas ('He of the dangling hair-lock'), wrote Arabic *khamriyyat* (wine poetry) of divine linguistic mastery and extraordinary range. In the 1200 years since his death, he has been both revered and reviled in the Arab-speaking world, but is unknown to the rest of us. His poems range from paeans to the joys of drunken excess, dissolute nightlife and sexual experimentation to satirical digs at religion, the idealisation of the past, the moralising clergy and the overtly pious. In *Vintage Humour*, Alex Rowell, an American translator and journalist living in Beirut, presents 125 of Abu Nuwas' best works grouped thematically in the original mono-rhyme scheme. They are accompanied by an impressively researched history of the poet's life, as well as commentary on and introduction to the variety of poetic styles, themes, motifs and references, be they literary, historical or religious. It is an illuminating work for both the casual reader and serious student of Arabic literature and Islamic history alike.

The virtuosity of Abu Nuwas' verse lies not only in its technical brilliance, but also in its humour and ingenious interplay with the established poetic canon that preceded it. As a young poet, he was mentored by renowned literary scholars and poets of his time who insisted that he have a thorough understanding of both the Qur'an and the classical Arabic literary cannon. While this provided the technical grounding for Abu Nuwas' work, the subject matter was his lifelong immersion in the night life of his cities, most importantly, Baghdad. Rowell's description of him as a genius who excelled at every style of poetry he attempted seems apt given the range of his work on display. While he shone at everything from love poetry to heretical verse and all in between – 'lampoons, panegyrics, ribaldry, pious odes' – it was his *khamriyya* (wine poems) that were his most revered. His bacchic odes chronicle a dizzying variety of words for wines, receptacles and wine related festivities, and employ a specialist vocabulary to describe drinking wine at various times of the day and night.

Alex Rowell, *Vintage Humour: The Islamic Poetry of Abu Nuwas*, Hurst, London, 2018

At their most elemental, these are masterfully penned verses to the varied joys of wine as a bulwark against the overwhelming complexity that defines the human condition. Knowing that 'For your world's a fleeting dwelling', he says 'For the joy of gathering is repelling pain' and thus instructs us to 'Have an early drink, and enjoy yourself/And defy those, ignorant of love, who berate'. These poems are a glimpse into the intense pleasures of a life fully lived, a mind constantly searching and a heart forever open. In a rare, deeply autobiographical moment, Abu Nuwas admits: 'I ran with youthful passion like a wild horse/And the choice of wickedness came easy', closing the poem with the admission: 'And I'm aware that the distance shall/Be great between my soul and my body'. Here is a man who is profoundly aware of the choices that he has made and how they, in turn, have made him. In any time or place, such introspection and self-knowledge are inspirational. In his many lighter moments, he advocates wine's ability to create generosity, authenticity, openness, tolerance and good humour, all virtues to be prized and striven for, with or without the help of a libation.

His dedication to his chosen lifestyle of drunken licentiousness intertwined with satirical poetic output did him no favours with the rulers and clergy of the day. Abu Nuwas was thrown in prison repeatedly by Caliph Harun al-Rashid for public drunkenness and religious offence, and less often by Rashid's son the caliph Muhammad Al Amin. The latter, often exasperated at Abu Nuwas' inability to toe the line, was still his dear friend, drinking partner and protector. Now that Islam is so often portrayed as dogmatic orthodoxy that seeps into every corner of social and cultural life to the exclusion of all else, it is hard to imagine a world where believing rulers allowed the expression of anti-Islamic sentiment and patronised those who engaged in it. Abu Nuwas' life is a testament to how steadfastly being true to one's genius can win you the forbearance of two Caliphs and the deep love and friendship of another. When he heard news of Abu Nuwas' death, the reigning Caliph Abd Allah ibn Harun al-Ma'mun (Al Amin's half brother) is said to have exclaimed, 'The charm of our time has departed … Allah's curse on upon whoever disparages him.'

Abu Nuwas' life and poetry during the Abassid Golden Age is evidence of the pluralism in religious thought, interpretation and lifestyle present in these early days of Islam. In these pre-orthodox times, religious dogma was yet to be enshrined in stone and Rowell argues 'the creedal topography … of Islam during the poet's lifetime differed almost unrecognisably from today's'. There were massive leaps made in all conceivable areas of human knowledge, especially philosophy and medicine, and the creation of brand new paths of learning, such as algebra. The Abassids oversaw Islam's most important intellectual awakening, and indeed, one of the world's most significant, predating the Western Enlightenment by centuries. It is in this fertile cultural ground that Abu Nuwas penned his verses, taking full advantage of the intellectual freedom his world presented.

In an Islamic society where diversity and tolerance was the norm, Abu Nuwas' poetry celebrates what Rowell dubs 'cosmopolitan humanism'. His poems are standard bearers for diversity and tolerance, peopled by a diverse cast of Christians, Jews, Persians, and folk of many different sexual mores. Abu Nuwas casts an affectionate and non-judgemental eye on them all, penning celebratory odes to vintners ('Many a vintner I've come to, unguided/Except by royal Persian wine bouquets'), tavern keepers ('How many a tavern keeper I've frightened/Waking him while he's wrapped in his sheets') and wine producing towns ('By God I dearly miss/Al-Hira, and its wine'). His world is one where all are equal before the opportunity to imbibe, converse and carouse.

Running through his *khamriyyat* is a vital progressive energy that eschews blind obedience to tradition. He constantly mocks an old trope in Arabic poetry, *atlal*, which describes mourning the remaining traces of a lover's campsite. Inherent in this is his lack of veneration of the Bedouin ways of life and refusal to pay empty obeisance to cultural history. He does not weep for what for he considers a stultifying manner of living, but rather luxuriates in the life of choice offered in his favoured cities. Abu Nuwas' poems are a political endorsement of cosmopolitan living, where humanity is varied and experiences endless. His verse is a rebuttal to those of today who equate Islam with racial, ethnic and religious purity, falsely harking back to a past that never was. Both jihadists and Islamophobes alike would do well to note that the Islam and Middle East of old was always a flourishing bazaar of people, ideas and ways of being.

For me, the most radical and pertinent aspects of the poems presented here are their satirical engagement with Islam and his attempts to reconcile drinking with Islamic practice. Rowell's introduction intricately explains Abu Nuwas' continual engagement with Qur'anic precepts and literary style. Many of the poems presented in the section entitled 'Pour me the *Haraam* before the *Halaal*', subtitled 'Poems (un)concerned with piety', rail against unquestioning religious observance, the imposition of piety on others and the judgement of another's actions. He writes: 'Tell him who covets holiness/I sold mine for depravity' and that 'rebuke brings me naught, save/Desire for the beaker's rim' and encourages his readers to take all the pleasures that this transient life has to offer. In an exhortation to go big or go home, Abu Nuwas pleads 'Aim, if tempted, for the nobler/A sin that costs its buyer dearly/Never losing its flavour'. As someone who broke every social convention of his time and then some, he was a living rebuke to the intolerance of difference. In one of the most oft-quoted lines from Arabic poetry, Abu Nuwas urges folk to 'Cease your reproach, for reproach is but temptation/And cure me with the very cause of my debilitation'. This message of tolerance feels essential in a time when societies both Islamic and otherwise react to the diversification of ways of being with the threat of ever more righteous religious and cultural purity.

More controversially, Abu Nuwas seeks to integrate the drinking of alcohol with life as a practising Muslim. These poems remind me of all the people I knew and know, who refuse to demarcate an artificial line between their culture and religion. Abu Nuwas repeatedly questions the use of spurning wine during one's life on earth when Allah himself has promised it as a reward in heaven. He notes 'These rebukers bring me nothing but resolve/To grant wine my lifelong dedication/Shall I spurn it, when God himself hasn't', while in another poem he promises that wine 'abounds in the hereafter'. Over and over he argues for God's ultimate forgiveness, *ghufran*. According to Rowell, Abu Nuwas at times explicitly advocates for the Murji'a doctrine of *irja'* (postponement). This now long gone Islamic faction believed that one could delay the question of whether a person could indulge in sin and still be a good Muslim until the afterlife, whence God himself would make the final judgement. They believed that divine forgiveness was available to true believers no matter their level of sin. Abu Nuwas states 'Given God's a pardoner/would forgiveness be created/But for those who err?' and 'You've tried to make me fear God but/My fear's offset by his mercy'. 'Cease your Reproach' concludes: 'Don't forbid forgiveness if you chose to abstain/For that forbiddance is, of faith, desecration'.

The world often sees Islam as unforgiving and binding, and Allah as an angry immutable force. Abu Nuwas' impassioned advocacy for a God of Forgiveness, and his reproach to those who in his eyes desecrate the religion with their refusal to acknowledge this, highlights a lesser-seen side of Islam. At the very least, it reminds us that orthodoxy is not set in stone. Explaining his decision to call Abu Nuwas' poems *Islamic Wine Poetry*, Rowell cites the poet's deep engagement with Islamic precepts, practice and mores of the time and his continuing influence in the Arabic world. The drinking of wine predated the Abassid Islamic world and flourished during and after it, as I have seen all my life. Denying this would be churlish and reductionist.

Reading poetry from another time and in another language as a casual reader can sometimes inspire the same feeling as arriving at a party where we don't know anyone else. Not to say that there isn't immense value in reading dispatches from an unfamiliar time and place. However, as someone unschooled in the historical intricacies of the time, the cast of characters of the world and the literary conventions of the form; going back repeatedly to Rowell's brilliant introduction and thorough notes was at times the only way to unlock the verses. The linguistic virtuosity of the Arabic completely escaped me, as did the daring significance of his panegyrics and the literary brilliance of his interplay with Qur'anic verse and form. At times, it felt that I was being told of Abu Nuwas' genius instead of feeling it first-hand. In fact, if there is a critique of Rowell, it is that the thoroughness of his introduction makes the reader feel they are undertaking a guided tour of Abu Nuwas' greatest hits rather than on a self-directed journey through the poet's oeuvre. Rowell's guidance is the vital key that unlocks Abu Nuwas' world, but also at times makes it hard for the reader to see past the thematic threads, comic motifs and historical interconnections that he shows us.

Abu Nuwas' body of work, as presented by Rowell, is a vibrant argument against the ossificiation of tradition, the worship of a past that never was and for the recognition of a present that is far more complex than many care to admit. His poetry beautifully advocates for a life truly lived, for pleasures truly experienced, for complexities truly embraced and fights for an eschewal of the simplistic, the unexamined and the unquestioningly labelled. Through his main metier of the *khamriyyat*, his overarching message celebrates diversity of thought and existence. Abu Nuwas risked his freedom over and over to do the things he loved: drink, write and entertain. Now, more than ever, the West needs be reminded that Islam and Muslims are diverse, culturally varied and averse to simplistic categorisation. It is the Islam that is my lived experience, one where plurality, ambiguity and rebelliousness live side by side with observance and piety. It is fitting, perhaps, that the 1200 year-old work of this literary genius who was so unwilling to be told what truly constituted the highest virtues of humanity speaks so eloquently to our times.

HORRID NOURISHMENT

Misha Monaghan

Ugly food is not a concept I grew up with. I have mixed Scottish, Indian and Pakistani heritage so it was not unusual for me to be served up haggis bonbons, *paya* (trotters), any offal that could be procured and I have, on more than one occasion as a child, been tricked into eating cow brains by my grandfather who convinced me that what I was eating was scrambled eggs. I also grew up in a family where the aesthetic qualities of food were only commented on when one was discussing the way a dish should look at certain points in the cooking process. To add to this, from a very young age my grandfather would take me to halal butchers and abattoirs where I observed first-hand how the food that was such a pivotal part of my life ended up on the dinner table. A cardinal sin for my family was waste. My grandfather would come home with a whole lamb, which he then butchered theatrically and there was absolutely no question that every last inch of it would be eaten. What was not being eaten now would be frozen to be eaten later, a habitual family trait that has led to my inherent distrust of ice cream boxes in freezers, which in my house would be more likely to contain left over *kheema* (mince) than my favourite chocolate ice cream. I would not have had it any other way, though. I remember visiting a Malaysian friend's home for dinner as a teenager and a fish head curry being placed in front of me. Thanks to my grandfather, I did not even bat an eyelid as my friend's grandmother poked out the eyeball and put it on my plate explaining that it was the best part. I can confirm that it was.

Given this eclectic background, you can imagine the confusion I felt reading *Ugly Food: Overlooked and Undercooked* by Richard Horsey and Tim Wharton. Ugly food is the latest 'hipster' trend that seems, like a turmeric latte and the 'discovery' of avocados, to be somewhat culturally appropriated. Middle class men and women wearing their undersized beanie hats walking around fashionable areas such as Shoreditch, London, explaining how the world needs to eat more ugly vegetables for sustainability is something that I have personally witnessed many times. I, along with countless other people, can confirm that much of the world is eating 'ugly' food. Horsey and Wharton have written a book that sheds light on a wide array of issues that surround food consumption in Britain. Their perspective is that of two ivory tower academics who have developed a love for food through a lifetime of travel and new experiences.

The purpose of their work is to highlight why it is that we (specifically the British) have such an aversion to food that we do not perceive to be attractive. Why is it that squid is deemed more acceptable than octopus despite its similarity when on a plate? On the other end of the spectrum, why do people avoid eating rabbit on the basis that it is far too cute when those same people would not flinch when offered up the leg of what was a formerly bouncy, jovial lamb? Through the medium of historical analysis, anecdotes, folk lore, recipes and beautiful photographs taken by Tanya Ghosh, Horsey and Wharton are attempting to take us on a journey through our understanding of these foods.

Ugly Food by Tim Wharton, Richard Horsey and Tanya Ghosh, Hurst, London, 2016

They do present an excellent point, although I personally devour whatever I am given regardless of how many eyeballs are staring back at me from my plate; one only has to watch an episode of 'First Dates' on Channel 4 to see the intense aversion that people have to food that they may not see on a regular basis on their supermarket shelves. Part of the explanation that is given in the book for this is a psychological phenomenon called Introspect Illusion, something that was discovered in the 1970s by two psychologists who found that although humans are very good at knowing what they do and do not like, they are significantly less proficient at explaining how they have reached that conclusion. In the proceeding six chapters the nuances between the British population and octopus; cheeks and feet; ugly fish; rabbits and squirrels; ugly vegetables; and giblets are discussed in detail.

The importance of the topic of sustainability and the future of eating habits is hard to get away from, and so it should be. Netflix alone has commissioned or aired at least twenty documentaries in the last five years on the topic and in one of their most popular – 'Cowspiracy' – showed that veganism is potentially the only solution for the catastrophic damage that is being done to the environment through mass commercial farming. By becoming vegan you reduce your carbon footprint by 50 per cent and in a world where 51 per cent of global greenhouse emissions are as a direct result of the farming of livestock and the production of their by-products this is most definitely a figure we should be acutely aware of.

On the other hand, many studies have been done into the practicality of vegan diets for people across the world. It certainly can be a significantly more expensive way of eating and therefore not universally appropriate. Under some circumstances a diet completely devoid of animal products can cause severe tooth decay; a lack of high quality protein leads to liver detoxification being limited and eventually toxicity; not to mention the fact that effective Vitamin A can only be found in animal products and has a direct influence over thyroid function, hormone production and fertility. So, it would seem that Horsey and Wharton would have provided us with a pragmatic approach to these issues in a healthier and more sustainable way.

In the introduction to the book we find a list of 'maxims': quality, purity, availability and sustainability. On the whole, I do not have a problem with this. They are tools being employed to approach a somewhat non-academic subject in an academic manner. Broadly the maxims are used to define the parameters for their study and justify the food choices that have been made. In a perfect world the maxims that Horsey and Wharton present are ones that many would enjoy abiding by but are at their very core ignoring a deeper issue. They claim that buying an ox cheek will cost you less than a leg of lamb. A brief exploration into the local butchers on my high street in Clapham allowed me to verify this. It also allowed me to clarify that the butcher's shop was entirely empty. I asked the two men behind the counter of the family run shop whether that was the norm on an otherwise packed street on a Saturday and they confirmed my suspicions. It was. Through our chat I found out that they had to move out of their previous – significantly larger – shop because they were no longer attracting enough clientele, a story that is more often than not mirrored across the country.

Difficulty continues to rear its ugly head when you delve deeper into the rationale behind what the authors refer to as 'the core techniques'. It is from this point in the introduction that there is an inherently arrogant approach to the preparation of food. When asked their opinion on people who never follow recipes but still manage to cook food that is delicious, their response was that 'more often than not they are the only ones who enjoy the fruits of their labour'. As someone who has eaten plenty of food cooked by fantastic cooks who have never followed a recipe, I would like to wholeheartedly disagree. There is also a significant amount of time dedicated to debunking the use of 'heavy spices' as a device to mask the purity of the high quality, readily available and sustainably sourced items you are encouraged to cook with. I have to say that it was at this point that I became quite frustrated with what I was reading. I grew up being told I smelled of curry and the only reason Indian people used so many spices was because they were trying to cover up the poor quality of their food while in the same breath being asked for my korma recipe. So the accusation of spices being used to cover rather than enhance food is one that was not unfamiliar, what was also not unfamiliar was how it smacks of an unnecessary loftiness of people who have not been taught how to use spices correctly.

The hubris exhibited in the opening chapter only worsens to the point of elitism throughout the book. So that by the time I got to Chapter Three where they begin discussing the importance of Marie Antoinette, the poster girl for a bourgeoisie lifestyle, in the ugly food movement of France I could not help but laugh audibly in the middle of a crowded train.

There are deep-rooted issues in this book, although I will readily admit to the fact that visually it is beautiful. The artistic quality of the photography is stunning and would not look out of place on the walls of a high-end restaurant. On the surface, this book also seems to be achieving what it feels it should be, providing a light-hearted but academically-fuelled approach to a much more serious issue through the medium of stories and pictures. *Ugly Food* has done an excellent job of identifying an issue which should be discussed in depth. The writers claim that their purpose is to encourage people not to avoid foods that they do not see on their supermarket shelves. This is genuinely a fantastic concept, people should be more aware of what they are eating, sustainable alternatives and where their food has come from in the first place. Unfortunately, the book falls short of its ultimate goal. Yes, I was given an insight into the potential origins of the fear of eating octopus – they specifically reference the myth that it is a particularly difficult meat to cook but I also went into three supermarkets and two fishmongers within walking distance from my home to buy octopus and it was nowhere to be found. I was also laughed at quite viciously when I asked a local butcher whether he ever orders squirrel – another 'cheap' and easily acquired meat that had been promoted in the book. I also searched everywhere for salsify and burdock root; not even Wholefoods the most elite of all high street food shops could help me here.

My question to the authors is who is their book for? It does not seem to be for the average person who acquires most of their food on a strict budget from their local supermarket. Often their purchases are based on what will go the longest way, be easy to cook or particularly simple. On the other end of the spectrum are the people who would potentially pick this book up and consider changing their buying habits according to what they are reading. As I have already pointed out, squirrel can be particularly difficult to come by and although it may be possible that this is an issue affecting my particular corner of London, a cursory glance on the internet does seem to indicate a similar issue is also plaguing the rest of the country.

Ugly Food is aimed at the very people who are least likely to have a problem with eating so called 'ugly' food: those who have a selection of other coffee table books, and would like an additional prop in their home to prove how progressive and committed to a sustainable lifestyle they are. Another issue is that I really did not feel that I emerged at the end of the book with a deeper understanding of British eating habits, although I do now have some interesting anecdotes for the next dinner party I am invited to about Ancient Greek soothsayers and their relationship with giblets.

What would have potentially been a better use of paper would have been a thought-provoking analysis into why less attractive and more sustainable foods do not make their way onto supermarket shelves where they can be purchased by the average consumer. How can we help people understand what is seasonal and what is not? How practical is it, in a globalised world, for people to entirely abstain from using products that are shipped from abroad? Why it is that ideas for cooking sustainable foods do not end up in recipe cards distributed for free at tills or on websites for people to peruse? The fact remains that the 'ugly' food they are talking about is not as widely available as they claim it is. It all seems to me to be a futile academic exercise.

ET CETERA

THE HALAL SNACK PACK

Vicky Bishop

My mother is a Cambodian. My father a New Zealander. I am Australian. My mother's background shaped much of my early life compared with my childhood peers. Little things, like setting the table with a fork and spoon, taking off my shoes before entering the house, speaking in Khmer to one half of my family and English to the remainder. I lived in the same room with my mother's mother after my sister was born, and spent most of my time with her while my parents worked and cared for the new baby. Instead of play dates and after school sports, I would be practising maths and English, poring over textbooks far exceeding the year of school I was in. Every night, I ate dinner at the table I always either set or cleared as a chore, then shared out rice, soups made of chicken necks and oxtail, daikon, stir fries of vegetables with thinly cut steak dripping with oyster sauce and garlic, out of communal sharing plates, now a trendy concept in casual dining in Australia. As a young adult, my life in suburban Melbourne consisted mostly of eating out with friends, peeking into the world of other cultures through its food, and the customs surrounding them. One dish in particular that I would enjoy, usually late at night and out of a styrofoam box was the Halal Snack Pack – a uniquely Australian dish from the same stable as our famed Chiko Roll; another fusion bite attempting to consolidate mainstream Australian culture with 'foreign' influences.

Going to school in the mid 2000s, even though there were many other children with East Asian backgrounds, I lived in the firm belief that my home life was not the norm. I would gaze upon the white bread, crustless, Vegemite and tasty cheese sandwiches or individual chip packet lunches of my schoolmates with the same curiosity that they must have looked upon mine – novel desire; one that has now manifested in my pursuit of a career in the kitchen, learning the ins and outs and history of European Cuisine in the UK. In retrospect, I understand now that my upbringing would have probably been familiar to many more people than I ever dared to imagine as a child. Mainstream media, Australian supermarket advertisements and the British-centric culinary traditions I was introduced to throughout my education (Shrove Tuesday pancakes, scones, ANZAC cookies and eating cut oranges at school sports day) all left me with the impression that I was somewhat of an alien in Australia, as I knew nothing of these 'classic' traditions before being introduced to them at school. Perhaps not singled out as much as my darker skinned South Asian peers were, but certainly enough that I was acutely aware of my Asian-ness, aware of the notion that when I got home what I experienced was not what I watched on *Home and Away* and *Neighbours*, and certainly not in line with what people spoke about in 'Show And Tell' at school on Monday. I had never been yabbying or camping at the weekend, my Dad didn't drink beer, my Mum didn't referee netball games. What my mum actually did was cook (the now ultra-cool) Mi Goreng brand fried noodles for all my teachers as a gift at Christmas break and parent-teacher meetings, earning me a kind of status that the food I ate at home was exotic and enviable. Had I grown up in the decade before – closer to the peak of national fears that Australia was in danger of 'being swamped by Asians', a quote from an Australian Senator in her 1996 maiden speech to the House of Representatives that called upon a 'radical' review of immigration policy, my school life would have undeniably been impacted by bullying and more overt racism as a result of the fried noodle offerings and stir fry and rice filled lunchboxes.

Growing up in a society that, while perhaps not treating me in a way that immediately and overtly outcast me, but definitely labelled me as 'other', the food scene within that culture became utterly re-defined so as to make communal eating, small plates and 'Asian fusion' buzzwords. Ironically, this has led to fine dining and European restaurants falling out of vogue and unable to survive in the current hospitality climate. Australians, buoyed by social mobility and in possession of disposable income are increasingly adventurous in their culinary consumption, now exploring cuisines that are not limited to British and Italian dishes. The frequency of white-washed Asian recipes in food magazines and stay-at-home suburban mums making rice paper rolls for school lunch continues to cause disdain amongst some Australians still hankering for the days when immigration policy was designed to ensure a 'White Australia'. A section of the population is horrified that the British-centric culture of white homogeny may be dying out, with the appetite of the nation one of many indicators that the tide is turning.

Unlike art, music or the media, food is not something you can point a political finger at. It has the power to promote or protest change in an almost organic manner. It is a bandwagon that people jump on through the most primal of needs, which is to eat, but the social and economic power that we exercise with our food choices is palpable. To me, food conveys acceptance, on both a macro and micro scale. When I visit another person's house, if I eat and enjoy their food I am both welcomed into their culture, and myself welcoming of it. On a wider social level when I see that the food I grew up eating is now being celebrated and enjoyed by my fellows compatriots, I feel understood a little better. It seems as if eating another person's food may ignite a curiosity about the history of that cuisine and the people who made it. Perhaps this may even develop into a deeper understanding about the culture, beyond merely how the food tastes. The complex politics of appropriation aside, eating, whilst motivated by basic instinct, opens us up to much more than the act of putting food in our mouths.

A brief glance at Australia's food culture or, some would argue, lack of food culture, offers an insight into the country's history. We love a pint, thanks to our English ancestry, and a pub meal of a Parmie (Chicken Parmigiana) and pot is all too familiar. Barbecuing makes sense here, because why on earth would someone, on a 40-degree day, not take full advantage of the back-yard that nearly every property in Australia boasts and the alfresco-social dining opportunities that may ensue? The (in)famous phrase 'slapping a shrimp on the barbie' makes complete sense despite the Americanised use of the word shrimp (we actually call them prawns) – firstly, because of our love of alliteration in slang, and secondly, we are, and are reminded every time we sing our national anthem, literally girt by sea. Sprinkling colourful sugar on bread for children's parties to make a much loved dish known as 'Fairy Bread', lava-hot meat pies at AFL matches, and stealing credit for desserts from our next door neighbours in

New Zealand (Pavlova anyone?) are seemingly the only other parts of the otherwise bare canvas of our food landscape, the barrenness of which we have started now to define ourselves by and build on. The short two hundred odd years ago since Federation, followed by apparently just battling with nature to create society, has left us with a scarcity of traditions to abide by. Fusion cuisine is so popular in metropolitan areas because it fills the void created by such lack of tradition. The quick uptake of a multicultural food scene offers a wealth of history as well as documenting the different waves of immigration Australia has witnessed in the last hundred years.

Travel to Melbourne and in one suburb you can be immersed in strip grocers selling durians, pak choi, lychees and live crabs spilling out onto a street where every shop name is in Vietnamese. Wander down the road into another suburb and get ushered into a red and green awninged restaurant for a free glass of red or a Negroni alongside a plate of fresh pasta, rolled by Nonna out the back. In Melbourne, one can often find nestled in otherwise non-descript residential areas, small family-run takeaway shops making food that enjoys a cult following. I grew up in a suburb that housed an Indo-Malaysian take-away called Rich Maha, secretly known as the best place for curry by the South Asian diaspora in Eastern Melbourne. I went to school in a heavily Chinese area of the city; everyone I went to school with knew that this one shop, David & Camy's, served the best plate of $7.50/15 piece dumplings you could lay your hands on in all of Australia. Getting a table in the tinted window hole-in-the-wall was impossible between the hours of 5pm and 9pm, so we all knew to go straight after school or late into the night. Similarly, everyone from my city has a complete local food knowledge of Melbourne mapped out; where to go for the best of a certain culinary tradition – and particularly where is the best eaterie for the food of their family's culture. The existence of these different boroughs in which you can experience specific cuisines, like many metropolitan cities in the world, has become a celebrated part of the Melbourne experience. The notable absence of indigenous cuisine, however, speaks volumes about how far we as a country have to come in our understanding of the culture of First World peoples in mainstream Australia, so weighed down by a dark history of atrocities, genocide and child abduction.

It was in 2016 that Iranian-Australian Senator Sam Datsayri made a speech in Parliament about a fusion food called the Halal Snack Pack (HSP). The HSP is a dish consisting of chips topped with, in this order: a layer of cheese, shaved doner kebab meat (chicken, lamb or mixed), and the specific combination of sauces known as the 'Holy Trinity'– garlic, BBQ sauce and chilli sauce, artfully patterning the top of the steaming concoction with such generosity that the sauce has to make squiggly lines on the meat as it comes out of the bottle. A political and culinary masterpiece, it is a dish that would earn you the lifelong shame of being named a 'haram dingo' if you dared put tomato sauce or god forbid, salad, on top of it. The Halal Snack Pack is a phenomenon that has, in just existing, bridged the sometimes inexplicable connection between food and politics in this country. It is a huge 'fuck you' to the clamouring calls for the banning of Halal certification. It is a 'fuck you' from the Muslim community to the casual anti-Muslim sentiment permeating conversations played out in modern Australia media and a 'fuck you' from the literally crowds of people lining up for delicious meat and chips at 2am outside outer suburban food trucks and local grocery shops. The comical refusal of Senator Pauline Hanson of the One Nation party, the person also responsible for the 'swamped by Asians' quote, to eat or even be near a Halal Snack Pack hilariously parodies the growing fear of 'terrorism', and love of keeping our borders closed that both major parties have mongered in recent times. Such sensationalism only vaguely shadows the insecurity that traditional white Australian culture is becoming less and less relevant, and perhaps soon will not be automatically considered the majority norm in a contemporary, globally connected Australia.

A modernised anxiety with echoes of the archaic Gold Rush era fear that Asian immigrants and Chinese labour would somehow take over and ruin the country, gave birth to the 'being swamped by Asians' mantra. Far right-wing notions that our recent British Colonial History will be overtaken by, heaven forbid, people of colour, has taken many forms and pointed fingers at various races throughout Australia's relatively short time as a federation: Chinese, East Asians in general, South Asians and now Muslims. The nation's Members of Parliament are still living so firmly under a rock as to mistake the world's second largest religion as a race. Politically, fear-mongering is the government's way of excusing itself for a frankly abysmal effort at refugee resettlement. Australia is accepting shockingly low numbers of asylum seekers by global standards and has a policy so poorly executed that the UN are calling Australia out for human rights violations in its treatment of destitute people in off-shore detention centres. It is convenient that in the midst of all-time high Islamophobic rhetoric in Australian politics, there is a refugee crisis in Syria and other parts of the Muslim world. Elections are now won and lost over which party will show the most strength against the peer pressure of every other first world country to accept a humane number of refugees. The argument is that immigration will endanger the 'Australian way of life', water down the culture into something unrecognisable, threaten job opportunities for 'real Australians' and introduce Islamic extremism to the country and its children. The facts are laughable: that a continent larger than Europe and boasting a population of around 24 million would 'run out of space', lest we keep the boatloads of those seeking refuge from war at bay.

I was introduced to the HSP on a second date. The way to the heart is through the stomach, as everyone knows, and correctly so, in my case. It is interesting to see the Halal Snack Pack function both as a political statement, literally spoken about on the floor of parliament as a much needed marriage of cultures in the current fraught global mood, and in a personal way, as a silent and delicious way of saying that you are on the same page as someone. To be invited into the world of the Halal Snack Pack was momentous, as you needed approval from an existing member to be let into the 188,000 strong 'Halal Snack Pack Appreciation Society' Facebook group. I was told by my date how to properly place an order: greet the shop owner by calling him 'brother', and don't even think about ordering sauces other than the Holy Trinity. We waited a good 40 minutes for our late night dinner in suburban Melbourne that Tuesday night. There was an epic wait to order, and I watched styrofoam container after styrofoam container lined up on the counter ready for cheese and meat to be dropped on and sliced from the spit for each one. The workers masterfully cross-hatching tri-coloured sauces on each hot pile of chips and meat. Couples and groups of every ethnicity were gathering to enjoy in what seemed to be a shared weeknight tradition. Such is the affection for the Halal Snack Pack in the Australian psyche that one fish and chip shop on the Mornington Peninsula, a two hour drive from metropolitan Melbourne, was in the local news when a man popped the question to his partner with an engagement ring hidden within the layers of a Halal Snack Pack.

There is no doubt that the HSP has become truly embedded in Australian popular culture. What better way for Senator Sam Datsayri to fuel a now infamous rivalry with Pauline Hanson – the latter famously, visibly shocked by the reveal that Datsayri actually identified as Muslim on Australian television. This to her, and probably the more ignorant sections of Australian society, was inconceivable for a person with his qualifications and who was so integrated into Australian society.

Is the phenomenon of the Halal Snack Pack, and other popular culinary and otherwise fusions of culture, the first step towards inclusion? The way to the heart is through the stomach… Euro-centric cultures have been quick on the uptake to Middle-Eastern cuisine and the many unfamiliar flavours it brings. Could it be that Australia is, for the most part, actually more willing to be open-minded, embracing diversity and less resistant to change than the mainstream media and governing bodies care to represent? I find it difficult to resign myself to the idea that this country is incapable of acceptance when every local kebab shop is bursting with people of all backgrounds arrived to engage in the community of this pointedly contentiously-named food item. Food is extremely important in my life, not only because of my occupation as a chef but as an everyday way to connect with other people, who sometimes don't share a common language or even age range as me. For me, food has always functioned over that bridge, over a language barrier, and perhaps it could be the bridge over a country's borders, over Australia's problematic policies.

In the middle of a parliamentary sitting in which one Ms Hanson parades a burqa purely to incite, you can step outside and walk down the road to the local kebab shop and find an eatery where the 'Halal-ness' of a dish is widely and passionately celebrated. Where the owner speaks to everyone with a warmth eclipsed only by the steaming plastic bag of meat and chips he's just handed over. Media outlets run by those with political agendas will never be a place to look for hope, but the places where one can enjoy a $12 box of carnal joy might just be.

SEVEN WONDERFUL
FUTURE FOODS

Not so long ago, a prawn cocktail was the height of futuristic sophistication. Radioactive-looking frozen curries would be thawed out on a Friday night and, according to legend, washed down gullets with a swig of 'Blue Nun'. Pre-packaged and icily-preserved ready meals felt so very high-tech as we watched BBC's *Tomorrow's World* speculate what weird and wonderful offerings would adorn our plates in the future. Would we swallow a daily magic pill that would provide us with all our nutritional needs and satisfy every hunger pang? The possibilities seemed endless. Food of the future continues to enthral and amaze with its limitless potential. Technology, climate change, a growing population, and scientific discovery are all combining to enact a dawn of the weird and wonderful on our dietary horizon. Sit back, tuck into your en vogue organic quinoa, lentil and feta salad, and ponder what you'll be eating once you emerge from your cryogenic slumber a few decades from now.

1. Locusts

Deep-fried locust is a much-loved delicacy in South East Asia. A rich source of protein, this nutritiously generous creature offers an environmentally-friendly alternative to traditional types of protein. Not only do locusts provide five times more protein than an equivalent unit of meat, but their carbon emissions are significantly lower in comparison. In a world increasingly impacted by climate change, this makes them a welcome edible delicacy that could soon become as commonplace as grilled cheese. The taste of locust has been compared to eating walnuts, although we will need to see it on Instagram to believe it, when people actually reach for a slice of coffee and locust cake with their afternoon tea.

2. Jellyfish

Would you like ketchup with your plate of jellyfish chips? Can you imagine hearing these words uttered at your local chicken 'n' chips outlet! As impossible as it seems, it could one day become a reality. The need to reduce meat consumption and the consequential harm it wreaks on our ailing planet has inspired increasingly imaginative food solutions; jellyfish being one of them. Overfishing has lead to traditional seafood becoming gradually depleted while jellyfish numbers continue to thrive. Climate change has caused the oceans to become warmer and more acidic; both perfect conditions for jellyfish to bloom in chaotic proportions.

At The 62nd Biophysical Society Annual Meeting in San Francisco, California, a team of Danish researchers presented their study on the transformation of jellyfish filaments from soft and gel-like to hard and crunchy – like chips and with a taste that was not at all dissimilar to the potato version. Someone pass the ketchup.

3. Ants

A traditional English fry-up could one day consist of eggs, chips, beans, and no, not hash browns or vegetarian sausages, but ants! Apparently, the taste of flat-bottomed ants is eerily similar to smoky bacon – not that halal-only consumers would know! The King of the Jungle confirmed exactly this fact in the 2016 film the *Legend of Tarzan*, so obviously it must be beyond doubt. Other types of ants reportedly have a lemon flavour while Australian honeypot ants, as the name suggests, taste sweet, due to the nectar they consume. Mexico is already ahead of the game with pan-roasted, fat, red ants with huge wings, known as *chicanatas*, submerged in lime and then served in the form of a paste with chilli, salt and garlic. High in protein and plentiful in supply, the greasy spoon on the corner will be placing orders at its local anthill in due course.

4. Lab-grown meat

The thought of meat being cultured in a lab has a somewhat Frankenstein-esque ring to it. But needs must and with methane from cows obliterating our precious ozone layer, extreme remedies are being sought. Culturing meat from cells has the unique advantage of creating food without any need for animals to be involved in the production process at all. The ecological advantages are endless, with the financial and environmental costs commonly associated with meat production of land, water and feed being drastically reduced or even eliminated altogether. Using tissue engineering techniques was first developed in regenerative medicine; lab-grown, or in-vitro meat still has a way to go before the stigma surrounding its synthetic origins is swallowed by the meat-eating public.

5. 3D-printed food

Food is all about how it looks and not how it tastes, wouldn't you say, particularly in our social-media obsessed age. And, convenience of course, is tantamount to everything. Wouldn't it be amazing to cut out the necessity to cook altogether – and we are not talking microwave meals for one. So, let's disregard all those people who claim they love to cook, and instead service the needs of the more lazily-inclined among us: what if you could switch on your 3D printer, feed in some edible paper and print out the most exquisite, mouth-watering, visually-stunning, food image imaginable. As with most innovations, food-printing was first developed by NASA to enable astronauts to create food in zero-gravity conditions. The precision of printing has led mechanised food 'printing' to find its way into restaurants and homes. No more fighting among the kids for the biggest cupcake, because soon they will all be absolutely identical.

6. Algae and Seaweed

Algae languishes pitifully at the bottom of the food chain, yet could revolutionise our eating habits in the future. The green murky mulch and seaweed are known as sea vegetables and are rich sources of potassium, calcium and zinc, as well as one of a rare number of foods that are a source of B-12. Already prevalent in Japanese cooking is the purple-tinged seaweed nori. Highly nutritious, it is used to wrap seaweed rolls as well as added as flakes to soups or stews. Algae can also be eaten as a snack; grilled seaweed on toast could be the ultimate solution to midnight munchies.

7. Fake fish

We're on the cusp of a fake meat trend, so why not conjure up some fake fish too. Throw some red algae into a pot, shape it into the form of a shrimp and there you have a highly plausible imitation shrimp that only the most eagle-eyed shrimp fanatic could tell from the real thing. Using much the same technology as synthetic meat, fake fish is transforming the gastronomical options of vegans and vegetarians as well as those concerned with overfishing, farmed fish and mercury poisoning. In the not so distant future, you'll be wrapping your fake fish and jellyfish chips in 3-D printed newspapers.

CITATIONS

Willowbrook Farm by T. W. Bartel

The Willowbrook Farm website – www.willowbrookfarm.co.uk – offers a broad spectrum of further information on the farm, from visiting opportunities – visitor days, school and group visits, volunteering, camping, and the Arts and Music Festival – to a detailed explanation of their method of slaughter.

The quotation from Pope Francis is taken from his encyclical letter Laudato Si': On Care for Our Common Home (London: Catholic Truth Society, 2015), para. 19. I regard, and recommend, this work as one of the most valuable contributions in recent times to Christian reflection on the ecological crisis.

Lutfi Radwan himself has contributed helpfully to Muslim reflection on the crisis in an article titled 'The Environment from a Muslim Perspective', in Norman Solomon, Richard Harries and Tim Winter (eds), Abraham's Children: Jews, Christians and Muslims in Conversation (London: T&T Clark, 2005), pp. 272–283.

My discussion of prophecy as both purging and refurbishing the imagination is heavily indebted to the work of the New Testament scholar Richard Bauckham, especially his The Theology of the Book of Revelation (Cambridge: Cambridge University Press, 1993), pp. 9–10, 17–20, 150–151, 159–160.

The quotation from the obituary of Jennifer Swift is taken from the contribution of Youçef Nedjadi (Church Times, 16 October 2009, p. 23).

Celebrity Chefs by Jeremy Henzell-Thomas

In discussing the gastronomic legacy of the celebrated French chef Paul Bocuse I have referred to the articles in the *New York Times* and *Japan Times* of 20/1/18.

John Bagot Glubb's ideas about the distinct ages of empires are set out in his *The Fate of Empires and Search for Survival* (Blackwood, Edinburgh, 1978). See https://runesoup.com/2014/07/fate-of-empires-archonology-part -8/
On Obsessive Chef's Disorder, see Tim Garman's article of 7/11/2008 at https://www.washingtoncitypaper.com/food/article/13036518/ obsessive-chef-disorder

The revival of fine Ottoman imperial cuisine at Asitane Resturant in Istanbul is described by Constanze Letsch in her article 'Ottoman imperial cuisine back on menu in Istanbul' on 15/7/2011 in *The Guardian* – see https://www.theguardian.com/lifeandstyle/2011/jul/15/ottoman-imperial-cuisine-istanbul. See https://www.asitanerestaurant.com/ English/ for menus.

For the article on famine in parts of Africa and Yemen in the *New York Times* of 22/2/2017 , 'Why 20 Million People Are on Brink of Famine in a World of Plenty', see https://www.nytimes.com/2017/02/22/world/africa/ why-20-million-people-are-on-brink-of-famine-in-a-world-of-plenty. html. On hunger amongst Rohingya refugees, see the article in the *Independent* of 6/10/2017 at http://www.independent.co.uk/news/ world/rohingya-muslim-crisis-burma-children-hunger-malnutrition-latest-a7985506.html and the article of 6/12/2017 by William Worley, 'Hunger gnaws at Rohingya children in Bangladesh's refugee camps' at https://www.reuters.com/article/us-bangladesh-rohingya-hunger/ hunger-gnaws-at-rohingya-children-in-bangladeshs-refugee-camps-idUSKBN1E00JB. On the record high level of food bank use across the UK, see http://www.independent.co.uk/news/uk/home-news/food-bank-use-uk-rise-continue-poverty-family-children-income-benefits-cuts-report-a7703451.html

On the temple cuisine of Buddhist nun Jeong Kwan, see https://www.eater.com/2017/2/18/14653382/jeong-kwan-buddhist-nun-chefs-table

On the decline of families eating together, see the article in the *Daily Mail* of 15/8/2013 at http://www.dailymail.co.uk/femail/article-2392981/Nearly-HALF-British-families-dont-sit-evening-meal-70-NEVER-traditional-Sunday-roast.html.

For Timi Gustafson's article in the Huffington Post of 20/9/2012 entitled 'Eating together as a family has multiple benefits', see https://www.huffingtonpost.com/timi-gustafson/family-dinner_b_1898387.html.

For Will Self's critique of the British obsession with food, see the article of 31/12/2012 at http://www.telegraph.co.uk/foodanddrink/foodanddrinknews/9771648/Britons-must-abandon-their-obsession-with-food-says-Will-Self.html. See also 'The Cult of the Celebrity Chef Goes Global' by Lisa Abend (21/6/2010) at http://content.time.com/time/magazine/article/0,9171,1995844,00.html.

On Michel Roux Jr's dismay at the 'glorification' of celebrity TV chefs and the glut of cookery contests on TV, see John Plunkett's article of 20/10/2015 at https://www.theguardian.com/lifeandstyle/2015/oct/20/michel-roux-jr-hits-out-glorification-of-celebrity-tv-chefs

Roland Barthes' essay 'Reading Brillat-Savarin' is included in his *The Rustle of Language*, trans. Richard Howard, University of California Press, 1986. Mary Fitzgerald's article on Brillat-Savarin's 1825 handbook *Physiologie du Goût* (*The Physiology of Taste*) can be accessed at https://www.theguardian.com/books/2009/nov/22/physiology-of-taste-brillat-savarin. Jonathan P. Eburne's 'The Chef Drive: Cooking Beyond the Pleasure Principle' is from *Contemporary French and Francophone Studies,* Vol. 14, No. 2, March 2010, 169-177.

On the bogus top-rated restaurant, The Shed at Dulwich, see http://www.cbc.ca/radio/asithappens/as-it-happens-thursday-edition-1.4437547/how-this-man-tricked-tripadvisor-into-listing-his-shed-as-london-s-no-1-rated-restaurant-1.4437555

The survey by Lurpak on the national obsession with cookery programmes and 'food media', and Mary Kenny's remarks about the fixation on food culture, were reported by Emma Mills in *The Daily Telegraph* of 22/9/16. Seehttp://www.telegraph.co.uk/food-and-drink/news/we-spend-more-time-watching-food-on-tv-than-we-do-cooking-it/

On the negative impact on health of the food-porn obsession, see Alexander Sehmer's article of 17/10/2015 at http://www.independent.co.uk/life-style/health-and-families/healthy-living/food-porn-obsession-may-be-fuelling-britains-obesity-crisis-scientists-warn-a6697796.html

'Yes, restaurants really do give better seats to attractive diners'. *Telegraph* 4 Jan 2016. See http://www.telegraph.co.uk/food-and-drink/news/yes-restaurants-really-do-give-better-seats-to-attractive-diners/

Joe Pinsker's interview with Eve Turow ('Why Are Millennials So Obsessed With Food?') can be accessed at https://www.theatlantic.com/business/archive/2015/08/millennial-foodies/401105/. Eve Turow's book *A Taste of Generation Yum: How the Millennial Generation's Love for Organic Fare, Celebrity Chefs, and Microbrews Will Make or Break the Future of Food* was independently published in 2015. On the expenditure of cash-strapped millennials on gourmet food, see http://nymag.com/restaurants/features/foodies-2012-4/index1.html

For Chris Hedge's critique of celebrity culture in his essay 'Addicted to Nonsense' (30/11/2009) see https://www.commondreams.org/views/2009/11/30/addicted-nonsense Rowan Williams's comments on British society are from his article 'Is our society broken? Yes, I think it is', *Daily Telegraph*, 17/09/2007.

Wine in Sufi Poetry by Charles Upton

Ibrahim Gamard and A. G. Rawan Farhadi, *The Quatrains of Rumi: Ruba'iyat-é Jalaluddin Muhammad Balkhi-Rumi*, (Sufi-Dari Books, San Rafael, 2008); Javed Nurbakhsh, *Sufi Symbolism* (Farhang e Nurbakhsh), Volume One (Khaniqahi-Nimatullahi Publications, London, 1984); and Charles Upton, *Doorkeeper of the Heart: Versions of Rabi'a*, (Threshold Books, Putney, 1988).

Muslim Veggies by Shanon Shah

The websites for the Vegan Muslim Initiative and the Vegetarian Muslim Society are: https://veganmuslims.com/ and https://en-gb.facebook. com/Vegetarian-Muslim-Society-174872052572033/. There is also 'Animals in Islam', an online resource for Muslim vegans and vegetarians: https://www.animalsinislam.com/. The Climate Stewards website is: https://www.climatestewards.org/ Graham Hill's entertaining and informative TED Talk, 'Why I'm a Weekday Vegetarian', is at: https:// www.ted.com/talks/graham_hill_weekday_vegetarian.

The main academic materials referred to are Kecia Ali. 2015. 'Muslims and Meat-Eating: Vegetarianism, Gender, and Identity.' *Journal of Religious Ethics* 43 (2): 268–88, and Richard Foltz, *Animals in Islamic Tradition and Muslim Cultures* (Oneworld, Oxford, 2006). Also helpful was Ibrahim Abdul-Matin. *Green Deen: What Islam Teaches About Protecting the Planet* (Kube Publishing, Markfield, 2012).

An article demolishing the coconut milk craze can be found at David Derbyshire. 2017. 'Coconut Oil: Are the Health Benefits a Big Fat Lie?' *The Guardian*. July 9, 2017. http://www.theguardian.com/lifeandstyle/2017/ jul/09/coconut-oil-debunked-health-benefits-big-fat -lie-superfood-saturated-fats-lard.

Recent research detailing the carbon footprint of pets is here: Olivia Petter. 2017. 'Pets Have the Same Environmental Impact as 13.6 Million Cars, Study Shows.' *The Independent*. August 5, 2017. http://www. independent.co.uk/life-style/carbon-footprint-animal-dogs-cats-america- study-meat-vegetarian-a7878086.html.

Less straightforward is the debate on almond milk, as demonstrated in these articles: Maria Dolan. 2014. 'Almond Milk Is Not the Problem.' *Slate*, July 23, 2014. http://www.slate.com/articles/life/food/2014/07/ almond_milk_bad_for_environment_tom_philpott_and_mother_jones_ are_wrong.html' Emine Saner. 2015. 'Almond Milk: Quite Good for You –Very Bad for the Planet.' *The Guardian*. October 21, 2015. http://www. theguardian.com/lifeandstyle/shortcuts/2015/oct/21/ almond-milk-quite-good-for-you-very-bad-for-the-planet.

For an argument that debunks the idea that vegetarianism and veganism are more environmentally friendly than diets that include meat, see Wayne Martindale. 'Is a Vegetarian Diet Really More Environmentally Friendly than Eating Meat?' *The Conversation*. 26 Jan 2017. http://theconversation. com/is-a-vegetarian-diet-really-more-environmentally-friendly-than-eating-meat-71596.

Finally, Shell's bloodstained legacy in Nigeria refuses to go away. See Hannah Summers. 2017. 'Amnesty Calls for Criminal Investigation into Shell over Alleged Complicity in Murder and Torture in Nigeria.' *The Guardian*. November 28, 2017. http://www.theguardian.com/global-development/2017/nov/28/amnesty-seeks-criminal-inquiry-into-shell-over-alleged-complicity-in-murder-and-torture-in-nigeria.

Claudia Roden by Boyd Tonkin

Interview with Claudia Roden, London, 29 January 2018. Boyd Tonkin, 'Homage to Catalonia', *The Independent*, 4 May 2012. I have also drawn on material from my interview with Claudia Roden for Borough Market's 'Food Heroes' series, London, 23 August 2016.

Claudia Roden's books include *A Book of Middle Eastern Food* (1968; new edition 2000); *Mediterranean Cookery* (1987); *The Food of Italy*(1990; new edition 2014); *The Book of Jewish Food* (1997; reprinted 2009); *Tamarind and Saffron* (2000); *Picnics, and other outdoor feasts*(2001); *Arabesque: a taste of Morocco, Turkey and Lebanon* (2005); *The Food of Spain* (2011).

See also, Sami Zubaida and Richard Tapper, *A Taste of Thyme: culinary cultures of the Middle East* (2001); Sami Zubaida, *Beyond Islam: a new understanding of the Middle East* (2010); Omar Kholeif, *Michael Rakowitz: backstroke of the West* (2017); Jane Kramer, 'Spice Routes: Claudia Roden's culinary diaspora', *The New Yorker*, 3 September 2007; Louise France, 'Claudia Roden: my life on a plate', *The Times*, 15 March 2014; Yotam Ottolenghi, 'Claudia Roden's *Book of Middle Eastern Food*', *The Guardian* 19 February 2017.

Caucasus Rituals by Gunel Isakova

For more on Azerbaijan food see Feride Buruyan's website azcookbook. com, the quote is from her book, *Pomegranates and Saffron: A Culinary Journey to Azerbaijan*, (A-Z Cookbooks, 2014). A new edition of *Adventures in Caucasia* by Alexandre Dumas is published by Chilton Books, (Philadelphia and New York, 1962). My Azerbaijani food blog can be found at: GunelsKitchen.

Coffee by Tahir Abbas

For more detail, see: William Gervase Clarence-Smith and Steven Topik, editors, *The Global Coffee Economy in Africa, Asia, and Latin America, 1500–1989*, Cambridge University Press, 2003); Ralph S Hattax, *Coffee and Coffeehouses: The Origins of a Social Beverage in the Medieval Near East* (University of Washington Press, 1985); Nabil Matar, *Islam in Britain: 1558-1685* (Cambridge University Press, 1998); Bryant Simon, *Everything but the Coffee*, (University of California Press, Berkeley, 2009); Robert W Thurston, Jonathan Morris, Shawn Steiman, editors, *Coffee: A Comprehensive Guide to the Bean, the Beverage, and the Industry* (Rowman & Littlefield, London, 2017); Catherine M Tucker, *Coffee Culture: Local Experiences, Global Connections* (Routledge, London, 2011); William H Ukers, *All About Coffee*, second edition (The Tea & Coffee Trade Journal Company, New York, 1935); Saime Küçükkömürler and Leyla Özgen, 'Coffee and Turkish Coffee Culture', *Pakistan Journal of Nutrition* 8(10): 1693-1700, 2009.

Halal Fried Chicken by Hussein Kesvani

Susan Bagwell, 'The Role of Independent Fast-Food Outlets in Obesogenic Environments: A Case Study of East London in the UK', *Environment and Planning Journal, 2011*. Other mentions can be found at:

www.standard.co.uk/news/london/furious-backlash-at-goldsmiths-university-freshers-safari-tour-of-london-chicken-shops-a3644696.html

www.thesun.co.uk/news/4558766/goldsmiths-university-freshers -tour-london-chicken-shops/

medium.com/@Sam_Floy/how-to-know-if-where-you-live-is-up-and-coming-fried-chicken-vs-coffee-shops-546080119f98

genius.com/Red-hot-entertainment-junior-spesh-lyrics

genius.com/Stormzy-big-for-your-boots-lyrics

www.dazeddigital.com/music/article/34611/1/fried-chicken-and-flirting -with-the-uks-biggest-grime-mcs

www.telegraph.co.uk/food-and-drink/news-brilliant-videos-londons -takeaway-chicken-shops-youtube-hit/

londonist.com/london/food/what-s-the-vegan-fried-chicken-restaurant-actually-like

blogs.spectator.co.uk/2015/08/sadiq-khan-caught-in-a-flap-over-fried-chicken/

www.buzzfeed.com/husseinkesvani/saidq-khan-vs-chicken?utm_term=.nxPN46NpE#.ceRQRNQ2j

www.foodmanufacture.co.uk/Article/2012/09/19/KFC-halal-chicken -may-not-be-real-halal-Muslim-scholar

www.bbc.co.uk/news/uk-27324224

www.facebook.com/Vegetarian-Muslim-Society-174872052572033/

veganmuslims.com/

tellmamauk.org/more-halal-hysteria-from-the-english-defence-league -by-steve-rose/

www.theguardian.com/world/2017/nov/29/britain-first-anti -islam-group-that-bills-itself-as-a-patriotic-movement

www.independent.co.uk/news/uk/crime/darren-osborne-finsbury-park-attack-who-is-tommy-robinson-muslim-internet-britain-first-a8190316.html

The Haloodies by Imran Kausar

The books consulted for this articles include: Jerry Brotten, *This Orient Isle: Elizabethan England and the Islamic World* (Penguin, 2016), Albert Howard, *An Agricultural Testament* (Oxford University Press, 1940), and 'The State of Food Security and Nutrition in the World' (UN FA), 2017), available from: http://www.fao.org/3/a-I7695E.pdf

On the definition of organic agriculture, see https://www.ifoam.bio/en/ organic-landmarks/definition-organic-agriculture and https://www. grandviewresearch.com/press-release/global-organic-food-beverages -market

On the background to the development of halal, see: nationalhalal.com/ our-story/ and beefandlamb.ahdb.org.uk/wp-content uploads/2016/03 /p_cp_EBLEX_Halal_Meat_FINAL_111110.pdf

http://www.bbc.co.uk/news/uk-england-london-24285693

On the concept and history of *filaha*, and Islamic texts on husbandry, see The Filaha Text Project at: http://www.filaha.org/

Love Stews by Yemisi Aribisala

Pierre Fatumbi Verger's *Ewe: The Use of Plants in Yoruba Society* was originally published in Portuguese in 1995 by the Brazilian company Odebrecht. See also his *Notes sur le culte des Orisa at Vodun a Bahia, la Baie de tours les Saints, au Brasil et a l'ancienne Cote des Esclaves en Afrique* (1957).

CONTRIBUTORS

Tahir Abbas is Visiting Senior Fellow, Department of Government, The London School of Economics and Political Science ● Wasio Ali Khan Abbasi is writer and blogger based in Karachi, Pakistan ● Mohammed Ali 'Aerosol Arabic' is an artist well known for melding street art from the early 1980s with Islamic script and geometrical designs ● Irum Shehreen Ali is a London-based writer and development practitioner ● Yasmin Alibhai-Brown, writer and columnist, is the author of *The Settler's Cookbook: A Memoir of Love, Migration and Food* ● Yemisi Aribisala, a Nigerian essayist, writer and food memoirist, is the author of *Longthroat Memoirs: Soups, Sex, and the Nigerian Taste Buds* ● Timothy Bartel is a former lecturer in philosophy of religion at King's College, London ● Vicky Bishop is a chef from Melbourne, currently living and working in London ● Merryl Wyn Davies is an anthropologist and writer well-known as the co-author of *Why Do People Hate America?* ● Shadab Zeest Hashmi, American Pakistani poet, is the author of *Kohl and Chalk* and *Baker of Tarifa* ● Jeremy Henzell-Thomas is a Research Associate and former Visiting Fellow at the Centre for Islamic Studies, University of Cambridge ● Gunel Isakova is Baku-based food and health activist and blogger ● C Scott Jordan is Assistant Director, Centre for Postnormal Policy and Futures Studies ● Imran Kausar is co-founder of the halal food brand Haloodies ● Hussein Kesvani is a writer and journalist based in London ● Mimi Khalvati is an Iranian-born British poet ● Laych Koh is a Malaysian freelance journalist and writer now based in London ● Misha Monaghan, who works for the Muslim Institute, has launched her own food YouTube channel: 'Made with Misha' ● Samia Rahman is the recently promoted Director of the Muslim Institute ● Shanon Shah is Deputy Editor of *Critical Muslim* ● Boyd Tonkin is a writer and journalist ● Becky Trow is an anthropology graduate who currently lives in New Zealand ● Colin Tudge, biologist and writer, is co-founder of the College for Real Farming and Food Culture ● Charles Upton, writer and poet, is the author of *Day and Night on the Sufi Path*, *What Poets Used to Know*, and other books ● Sami Zubaida is Emeritus Professor of Politics and Sociology at Birkbeck, University of London.